Synthesis Lectures on Technology and Health

The series publishes state-of-the-art short books on transformative technologies for health, wellness, and independent living. Our scope of publishing in the expanding health tech field includes:

- Technology in support of active and healthy living and aging
- Digital technologies for health- and social-care improvement
- Diagnostic, screening, and tracking tools
- Assistive and rehabilitative technologies

The series includes a subseries of books published in partnership with Canada's AGE-WELL NCE that specifically addresses their 8 AgeTech Challenge Areas.

Each lecture introduces the context in which the technology is used—wellness, health, medicine, special needs, or other contexts. Authors present and explain the technology and review promising applications and opportunities as well as limitations and challenges. They include material on their own work while surveying the broader landscape of related research, development, and impact.

Gregg Vanderheiden · Jonathan Lazar ·
Amanda Lazar · Hernisa Kacorri ·
J. Bern Jordan

Technology and Disability

50 Years of Trace R&D Center Contributions and Lessons Learned

Springer

Gregg Vanderheiden
University of Maryland iSchool
College Park, MD, USA

Jonathan Lazar
University of Maryland iSchool
College Park, MD, USA

Amanda Lazar
University of Maryland iSchool
College Park, MD, USA

Hernisa Kacorri
University of Maryland iSchool
College Park, MD, USA

J. Bern Jordan
University of Maryland iSchool
College Park, MD, USA

ISSN 2771-7054 ISSN 2771-7070 (electronic)
Synthesis Lectures on Technology and Health
ISBN 978-3-031-09213-8 ISBN 978-3-031-09214-5 (eBook)
https://doi.org/10.1007/978-3-031-09214-5

This Springer imprint is published by the registered company Springer Nature Switzerland AG
The registered company address is: Gewerbestrasse 11, 6330 Cham, Switzerland

Forewords

The computer and its software represent possibly the most versatile technology ever invented. And yet, like the telephone, it is often out of reach for people with disabilities, despite the fact that the device can be made to accommodate user interface needs with sufficient thought and creativity. The Trace Center and its founder, Gregg Vanderheiden, are the concrete manifestations of that aspiration. For half a century, the Center has been animated by the dedication and infectious spirit of its founder and the enthusiasm and determination of all who have worked with or for it. There remains a great deal still to accomplish, and this historical retrospect points the way into a future where computer-based systems have the flexibility to adapt to user needs in a seamless and seemingly effortless way. You cannot read this book without feeling optimism for the future and gratitude for the past.

Vint Cerf, Internet Pioneer

What a joy to read about the "trick" at the origin of Dr. Vanderheiden's work and the founding of the Trace Center, and then to trace the evolution of accessible and inclusive design over time and across so many technologies. It is a gift to the community of engineers, advocates, and policymakers to have this chronicle available to learn from. It's a valuable resource as we face an ever-expanding array of emerging technologies, each of which might present new barriers in the lives of people with disabilities, but all of which can provide new opportunities for technology-enabled equitable participation in society, when these new technologies are designed thoughtfully and informed by the lessons in this book.

Judy Brewer,
Director of the Web Accessibility Initiative
at the World Wide Web Consortium

The Trace Center has been an international leader in technology and disability for 50 years. The book insightfully covers the evolution and societal impact of the Center's work, most of which has been adopted and can be found in a majority of the current available mainstream information and communication technologies.

Gavriel Salvendy,
President, Academy of Science, Engineering
and Medicine of Florida

There is only one way to describe the Trace Center: a tour de force that has been amazingly successful in its 50-year struggle to ensure that people with disabilities have access to the technologies that are so important to our everyday lives. Navigating obstacles and overcoming challenges, the Trace Center's endless stream of accessible products, software, standards, prototypes, tools, and guidelines have paved the way for policymakers to craft laws essential to safeguarding disability access, and for IT companies to incorporate accessibility solutions that are critically important to the productivity, independence, and integration of people with disabilities everywhere.

Karen Peltz Strauss,
National Disability Advocate and Former Deputy Chief of the FCC's Consumer &
Governmental Affairs Bureau under Presidents Clinton and Obama

For more than a half-century, the Trace Center, together with its many capable staff and collaborators, has been the indispensable engine propelling accessibility forward for people with disabilities. From its start as a student project developing a communication aid for an individual boy with cerebral palsy, the Trace Center grew into a steady, persistent, unwavering force operating at the nexus of science, technology, policy, standards, and industry to drive a vision of inclusion and equity that is nothing short of revolutionary. It is no exaggeration that virtually every accessibility feature, in virtually every computer, phone, tablet, kiosk, and voice assistant, is a direct descendent of the Trace Center's own work, and the work of the people they have so effectively influenced.

This book speaks to both the past and the future of the accessibility field. It tells the story of the Trace Center's 50-year history, going into fascinating detail of many of their most significant accomplishments. But even more valuable than a history of the accessibility field, this book is filled with key insights, deep wisdom, and concrete guidance for the next generations to use in future decades of accessibility work.

Peter Korn,
Director of Accessibility, Amazon Lab126

It's clear that the Trace Center has been at the forefront of accessibility and inclusive design before many people or companies had ever heard of it. Even the inception of the Center started with a project that exemplified a fundamental principle of inclusive design to solve for one and scale to many. In addition to leading by example, the Trace Center helped make the path to making accessible experiences easier by doing the extremely hard work of developing standards that have become a critical tool for companies and governments to ensure more equitable product experiences. As someone dedicated to the field of accessible and inclusive design, I am grateful for the path the Trace Center has paved and am excited for the work they continue to do.

Jen (Kozenski) Devins,
Head of UX, Accessibility and Disability Inclusion, Google

The Trace Center has been unique in that not only has it performed groundbreaking research on how to help people with a wide range of disabilities, but it has also been a leader in establishing policies, standards, and specifications so that companies and governments can provide solutions that work for everyone across a wide range of abilities. Even more impressive, they have succeeded with the technology transfer to bring these innovations directly to the people who need them, providing solutions that not only help the individuals, but also light the way forward for others. As with other research in this area, the solutions not only help the targeted people with the disabilities, but they also help the public at large, in the grand tradition of Universal Design. So it is safe to say that everyone who uses technology is grateful to the Trace Center for its research, innovations, advocacy, products, and services. This book provides a wonderful overview and summary of all the impressive work that they have done.

Brad A. Myers, Ph.D.,
Professor, Human-Computer Interaction Institute,
School of Computer Science, Carnegie Mellon University

The Trace Center was a catalyst for a global movement. Trace asked questions that had not been asked before and gave voice to a community that had been ignored or denigrated. Emerging at a time when new technology and digital networks had only unexplored potential, the Trace Center laid claim to the potential for bridging barriers. It can be said that the Trace Center was the seed or the necessary energy source for many of the global efforts that followed, including augmentative and alternative communication, assistive technology, web accessibility, and inclusive resource networks. Trace earned and demanded the respect of decision makers in power, opening doors, and demanding respectful consideration for the field and the community members.

Jutta Treviranus, Ph.D.,
Professor and Director, Inclusive Design Resource Center (IDRC),
OCAD University, Toronto Canada

This impressive historical review reports on how the Trace Center's staff and many partners produced global benefits for users with disabilities, which also were helpful to every user of modern electronic technologies. Their work on hardware, software, and user interfaces for early computers, laptops, websites, kiosks, e-commerce applications, and widely used consumer devices had a profound impact on these technologies and their users, while inspiring several generations of students, researchers, practitioners, and policymakers to find creative solutions that improved accessibility and universal usability.

This review presents compelling stories of how Trace Center teams came to understand the ways users with diverse disabilities could benefit from improved designs. Then Trace Center teams worked closely with industry to understand how solutions could be implemented. Next, they validated the solutions in testing with many users, making refinements as needed. The close industrial partnerships meant that the solutions were implemented by leading corporations in major operating systems, commercial products, web services, and beyond. The features added to products were important, but then the lessons learned were integrated into national policies and international standards, which ensured their continuing and widespread impact.

The Trace Center story shows how a clear understanding of the problems, technical knowledge to develop realistic solutions, devotion to industrial and international partnerships, and commitment to do the hard work of shaping standards were necessary for success. However, one more attribute was needed—persistence in the face of failed solutions, changing technology, and skepticism. This half-century project shows that positive contributions are possible while remaining an inspiration for the next half-century.

Ben A. Shneiderman,
Founding Director of the Human-Computer Interaction Lab
at the University of Maryland and a member of the National Academy of Engineering

This book describes the history, current position, and further plans for the Trace Center, an incredibly successful group focused on developing technology for a wide range of disadvantaged people. They have worked with many international researchers, users, developers, and commercial companies; they have always been at the leading edge of rapidly changing technology. The group worked both on web and product accessibility and universal design, e.g., the book includes an excellent set of seven universal design principles, and the concept of "Digital Affinity" is a very useful addition to this field.

There is something for everyone in this book including much useful insights and wisdom for people working in this, and other fields, all illustrated by illuminating examples.

The narrative style is an interesting approach, which is easy to read and works well. It starts by describing why and how the researchers started in this field in the early 1970s—some of the very earliest days of this field, and how their work led to a wide range of commercial products and clinics as well as standards. Chapter 1 describes this amazing tour de force. Subsequent chapters include some very useful and interesting observations and details, which are well worth reading. Chapters 11–13, in particular, contain some really useful philosophies and strategies. The book concludes with some really good and sound ideas for future work in this field.

This is an extremely interesting book from a number of perspectives, including:

a. historical—of a new, not universally popular, but rapidly growing technological field;
b. strategic—how to work in, and have a real impact on such a field;
c. strategies for working with companies, and how best to make important achievements in technology transfer;
d. examples of what can stand in the way of progress and suggestions on how to combat this;
e. the importance of how one can respond to essentially lucky situations; and
f. for younger researchers, a view of working in a technological world that has completely changed.

This indeed could be considered as containing two or three books, for various audiences: interesting, informative, and insightful. Highly recommended.

Emeritus Professor Alan F. Newell, Ph.D. MBE, FRSE, FBCS, FACM;
formerly of School of Computing, University of Dundee, Scotland

For 50 years, the Trace Center has presented a forward-looking vision. They worked on the conceptual underpinnings of current issues, filled in the practical gaps that were needed, and painted a picture of the future. Over 20 years ago, Gregg came into a meeting with a piece of cardboard, unfolded it, and said this will be the next communication device—it will be a computer, a camera, and a telephone and will fit into your pocket—it seemed impossible then—but today we'd be lost without our smart phones. He was already thinking about how to make it accessible.

There's always going to be a need for organizations like the Trace Center that can bring together engineering and disability perspectives. One of the things that makes the Trace Center so unique is its capability to see a need, help fill that need, and then develop tools that others can use to solve problems. As the Access Board was developing the first set of accessibility standards for Section 508, it became apparent that there were some policy holes in the standards. There was no tangible way to test the flicker of a web page or whether something flashed too fast and posed a problem for people with photosensitive epilepsy. So Trace created a tool for analyzing content for potential seizure-inducing material and put that tool into public use. Another hole in the standards was a lack of a way to measure color contrast. And so the Center stepped in and developed an open-source color contrast analyzer tool. They saw a need, helped fill that need, and then got tools out to others so people interested in promoting accessibility had the tools they needed.

The Center has positioned itself to be a valuable asset for accessibility information for upcoming technologies that aren't well regulated as well. One such technology is self-service transaction machines. Currently, the only ADA requirement for self-service transaction machines, like a kiosk or a point-of-sale machine, is that it be at a height where a person in a wheelchair can get to it. The Trace Center has done research for the Access Board about how to enhance accessibility of self-service transaction machines for more than wheelchair access. Another issue is autonomous vehicles. The Trace Center has helped the Access Board and others understand the issues for people with sensory and cognitive disabilities in accessing autonomous vehicles to help move this issue along.

During the development of the updated Section 508 standards and the development of new European accessibility standards, a new form of technology called real-time text became available, but not a lot of people knew about it. The Access Board turned to the Trace Center to learn more about what real-time text is and its benefits for people who are deaf or hard of hearing or who can't speak. Trace would demonstrate what real-time text is and show us the value of it, and that really helped us in the development of the updated 508 standards, and also helped to ensure that the European standard addressed real-time text.

Without accessibility information from an organization like the Trace Center, federal agencies can be left to their own devices when addressing public policy issues, and sometimes that's not a good thing. So, it's essential that there are organizations like the Trace Center to bring together engineering and disability perspectives and present a forward-looking vision of what the future holds.

David Capozzi,
Executive Director of the U.S. Access Board from 2008–2020

Acknowledgments

Any success of the Trace Center or impact of its work is the result of efforts by many people. Over 400 students, faculty, and staff have worked at the Trace Center over its 50 years to accomplish these results. Others did not work at Trace, but Trace could not have survived its infancy without their taking time out of their careers or in some cases stepping far outside of normal expectations for their positions to allow an undergraduate group of students to evolve into the Trace Center. The Center was also helped in many ways by others at our university, colleagues, and partners in our field, companies, and other organizations providing support or expertise, people with disabilities and the professionals, family, and friends who shared their insights and experience, and the government agencies and others who provided funding. This section lists just some of them and their contributions.

Persons Key to the Early Survival of the Student Group That Became Trace

Some of the people responsible for Trace's surviving the first fragile and unlikely stage of its development are listed below:

- **Professor Richard Marleau**: who, quite remarkably, gave up his personal analog computer lab/classroom, moving all of his analog computers to the back of a large storage room where he then proceeded to teach his classes, in order to provide a place for the students to meet and work on the project.
- **Professor C. Daniel Geisler**: who took on advising this diverse group, even though it and its complications slowed his own personal and quite different area of research in neurophysiology.
- **UW Electrical Engineering Department and its chair, Professor Vincent Rideout**: who provided departmental funds to pay for the military surplus parts used in the first AutoCom prototypes.
- **UW Chancellor Edwin Young**: who contributed money from his office furniture fund when the group had no other funds.
- **Dr. Max Ward, of the National Science Foundation's Student Originated Studies Program**: who was responsible for Dr. Phillips (Head of the Office of Experimental Projects and Programs of the NSF Education Directorate) seeing the work of the students which led to the awarding the first key NSF grant to the student group.
- **Dr. Lyle Phillips, of the National Science Foundation**: who funded this student group, working on a disability-oriented project, even though there was no program for the topic or for supporting a student group with a regular NSF grant.
- **UW College of Engineering Dean Robert Marshall, Chancellor Edwin Young, and Professor Dan Geisler**: who sought and secured special permission for a Master's student to act as a principal investigator for a federal grant, enabling the student group to apply for the full NSF grant, and subsequent grants, that allowed the work to continue.
- **UW Professor David Yoder**: who provided the non-engineering oversight of the program, mentored its students in communication and language development, proposed the creation of the Communication Clinic (CASC) to UW Hospitals, invited Deberah Harris and Gregg Vanderheiden to the Gulf Shores conference, and much more. Also,

at a time when Augmentative Communication was young and somewhat controversial at the American Speech and Hearing Association (ASHA), Professor Yoder, together with Professor Jon Miller and others, helped to get Augmentative Communication recognized and accepted as a legitimate facet of the profession.

- **The UW College of Engineering and Dean Marshall**: who trusted in a student group's ability to design, build, and deliver 40 AutoComs—enough to guarantee the funds (equivalent to $800,000 in today's dollars) to allow the group to proceed.
- **UW Professor Leo Jedynak**: who acted as the student group's advisor during much of this period and helped to convince the College to trust the group and both go into debt (see above) and free up and assign an additional 2,000 ft^2 in an old temporary building (in addition to the 1,800 ft^2 occupied by the student R&D group), to allow the group to create a production facility for the 40 AutoComs.
- Many different individual contributors who helped support the students during the early years. The Trace Center had about 30 students and 2 full-time staff, operating from an average of 8–10 different small funding sources at any time, with the full team never funded more than 6 months in advance.
- The following early industry supporters provided funding or in-kind support that enabled a student group with very little money to design and build multiple AutoComs for different users:
  - **Hamlin Corporation** (donated reed switches for all the early AutoComs, then developed custom modifications at no cost).
  - **Intel Corporation** (contributed expensive memory components for early AutoComs).
  - **Digital Equipment Corporation** (worked with the Trace team to figure out how to make the DECtalk serve as an output device for the AutoCom, including modifications needed to meet additional user needs).

Partner Organizations

The following organizations have been long-time partners and collaborators with the Trace Center:

- **Gallaudet University's Technology Access Program**: first led by Judy Harkins, then succeeded by Christian Vogler; partnered on four Telecommunication RERC grants, including significant joint efforts related to policy, standards, and real-time text.
- **Inclusive Design Research Centre (IDRC)**: at OCAD University (formerly the Adaptive Technology Research Centre, University of Toronto) led by Jutta Treviranus and Colin Clark were key partners on a range of projects including those related to the Global Public Inclusive Infrastructure.

- **Raising the Floor—US (Washington DC) and Raising the Floor—International (Geneva)**: The Trace Center has partnered closely for the last two decades with these nonprofit organizations focused entirely on development and support of digital equity for people facing barriers due to disability, literacy, digital affinity, or aging.
- **Web Accessibility Initiative (WAI) of the W3C**: led by Judy Brewer has been a key partner on all things dealing with Web accessibility, from guidelines to needs analysis to research.

Key External Contributors to the Trace Center's Work

- **Alan Brightman**: who founded and led Apple's accessibility efforts and tied Trace directly into Apple's development teams, and that led to Apple being the first company to incorporate accessibility features directly into its mainstream products, all before there was any mandate or regulations requiring it.
- **Randy Battat and John Sculley**: who went out on a limb and committed to building accessibility directly into Apple's mainstream products at a time when there were no accessibility mandates or regulations—thus adding people with disabilities into Apple's "mainstream customer base."
- **Greg Lowney**: The Windows Manager from Microsoft who ended up leading the accessibility efforts within Microsoft and without whose support Trace would not have been able to create the robust accessibility features it did, nor get them built into Windows 95 onward. After his retirement from Microsoft, he became one of the most active members of Trace's team for HFES 200 and an on-call expert on industry practicality for almost all of Trace's standards work.
- **Gunnar Hellström (Omnitor)**: who was the key technical contributor to all of Trace's work on real-time text and also author of Total Conversation—and the cross-disability telecommunication work of Trace.
- **Jim Tobias (Inclusive Technologies)**: who was a key partner on all of Trace's stakeholder work as well as the primary interviewer for the study on industry motivations for universal/inclusive design and a core member of the team who worked on the Global Public Inclusive Infrastructure (GPII).
- **Steve Jacobs (Ideal Group)**: who partnered on numerous projects over the years developing prototypes and testing out new ideas—as well as helping to advocate for accessibility with industry.
- **Karen Peltz Strauss, author of "A New Civil Right"**: who for many years acted as the accessibility policy expert for the joint Trace-Gallaudet Telecommunication Access

RERCs, helped us learn how to draft clear and effective comments, and contributed in so many ways to the field of accessibility (CVAA, etc.).[1]

Key Contributors to the Trace Center

There is no room to list the hundreds of students and professionals who worked at Trace over the last 50 years. Here are just some of the many Trace team members who made particularly significant contributions to the Center's work and impact.

- **Candace Hill Vegter**: whose amazing research skills and ability to find both published and fugitive literature provided the knowledge base for most of the Center's early work and also laid the groundwork for the Center later acting as a source of summative information for the field in the pre-Google world.
- **Andy Volk**: the first technical director for Trace, who was responsible for all of the technical engineering and fabrication of the early Trace prototypes.
- **David Kelso**: was Technical Director for Trace for 40 years, who did most of the research and engineering for the Contrast and Epilepsy provisions—and spearheaded the engineering of the Trace Center's free Photosensitive Epilepsy Analysis Tool (PEAT). He also did all of the Kiosk test prototype implementations in support of the Kiosk accessibility and standards research teams.
- **Deberah (Mackenzie) Harris**: led the Trace Center's language and communication development research and training efforts including the National Workshop Series.
- **Donna Depape**: created the first Communication Aids and Systems Clinic from scratch with no similar model to work from.
- **Joni Nygard**: took the clinic through its adolescence cementing it as a leading Augmentative Communication and Interface Clinic.
- **Julie Gamradt**: took both the Clinic- and the County-based Communication Development Program through the toughest funding times so successfully that other county programs that were competing with her programs for decreasing county funding were recommending the funding of the Trace program.
- **Charles Lee**: inspired by an article on abbreviation expansion techniques, created the first 1-finger program that then evolved into StickyKeys. He also led the technical development of the original MouseKeys, BounceKeys, SlowKeys, and along with David Kelso did the engineering of the T-TAM.
- **Mark Novak**: took over from Charles and led the team that expanded on these, creating the Access Packs and AccessDOS (which was used directly as an IBM product—a

[1] CVAA—Twenty-First Century Communications and Video Accessibility Act (CVAA) updated federal communications law to increase the access of persons with disabilities to modern communications. https://www.fcc.gov/consumers/guides/21st-century-communications-and-video-accessibility-act-cvaa.

singular accomplishment). He also led the implementations in Windows, Linux, OS/2, and the X Window System.

- **Joe Schauer**: was with the Trace Center for three decades, helped to create all of the access utilities and tools of Trace.
- **Barry Rogers**: for his work on the KEI and GIDEI standards and introduced the COATTAILS approach to accessibility.
- **Jon Gunderson**: once again proved that if you don't tell a student that no one has figured out how to do something—the student can often succeed where much more senior researchers have failed.
- **Wendy Chisholm**: (Trace, then W3C, now Microsoft) spearheaded the work on the Java Accessibility report and Unified Web Accessibility Guidelines, who worked extensively to make the WCAG Techniques document a reality, and then served as Staff for the WCAG working group while at the W3C.
- **Ben Caldwell**: was one of the Editors of WCAG but also worked essentially full time in supporting the work of the entire WCAG working group with implementations and tools and was a solid advocate for both consumers and for practicality in the Guidelines.
- **Drs. Robert Radwin and Justin Williams**: and grad student Elizabeth Felton for leading the work on moving brain-controlled interfaces from scientific experimentation toward practical use through the first known application of human factors to optimize BCI for human use rather than scientific variation.
- **Gottfried Zimmermann**: came to Trace as a post-doc but within 6 months was promoted to a permanent team lead position. He led the efforts on ISO/IEC-24752 series of standards and the supercomputing grid accessibility work among other things and also works on the Global Public Inclusive Infrastructure (GPII).
- **Maureen Kaine-Krolak**: helped craft the Center's strategies around digital accessibility and co-authored the National Council on Disabilities' 1996 report on access to emerging information technologies for people with disabilities. She was also a major contributor to the development and pilot testing of Morphic.
- **Rachael Bower**: led the outreach program for Trace in the 1990s, creating the first Trace web presence, spearheaded "Taste of the Web" to help educate others in this emerging new technology, and then returned in 2016–2020 as a special consultant on outreach for the Morphic development program.
- **Neal Ewers**: started as advisor to Trace and then Trace team expert on screen reading and blind access starting with the Apple IIe.
- **Jane Berliss**: led the information program, created the guidelines and checklist for library accessibility, and, on the side, was the best quality assurance tester. She continues to work closely with the center in all these capacities years later.
- **Yao Ding's**: extensive cross-standard analysis and review of the many drafts of Section 508, 255, EN 301 5490 and other accessibility standards contributed so much to the shaping of comments for improvement of them.

- **Roger O. Smith**: Associate Director of Trace, did so much to help Trace as its programs and team expanded, developed OT FACT evaluation tool, and founded the Occupational Therapy's Technology Specialization (Tech Spec) program until his graduation when he moved to the University of Wisconsin-Milwaukee where he founded the Rehabilitation Research Design and Disability (R2D2) Center.
- **Kate Vanderheiden**: came to the Trace Center temporarily in 1993 to help out with administration when the Associate Director was lost to UW-Milwaukee but never escaped and went on to become program manager, outreach manager, and to lead strategic planning for the center until her retirement in 2021.
- **Christine Thompson**: served as assistant to the director for decades including typing almost all of the Center's proposals and editing newsletters for Trace, the Human Factors SIG and TG.
- **Corrine Bahr, Sharon Esser, and Liz Loy**: each in turn provided the oversight of all of the support for the Trace Teams over the years.
- As one would expect, the creation of summative information across the fields of communication, control, and computer access, especially pre-Internet, required the work of many, many people. However, some stand out, in particular, for their leadership roles in this area over the years including: **Candace Hill Vegter, Mary Jo Luster, Warren P. Brown, Craig Holt, David Buelow, Jana Fothergil, Dale Bengston, Peter Borden, Sara Brandenburg, Mary Brady, Barry Rogers, Cynthia Cress, and Kelly Ford**.
- Finally, to all the people in Trace and outside who contributed to all that Trace accomplished—but who did not necessarily get individual recognition or were not the lead on a team. Many or most of the ideas and innovations attributed to leaders of Trace originated were inspired or were shaped by the unsung members of the teams.

Funding Acknowledgments

The work presented here was funded by a wide range of funding agencies and organizations over the years. A partial list of them includes The National Science Foundation, U.S. Department of Education's Bureau for the Education of the Handicapped, Office of Special Education Programs, National Institute on Handicapped Research, National Institute for Disability and Rehabilitation Research, Rehabilitation Services Administration, U.S. Access Board, Institute of Medicine, National Academy of Sciences, Computer Science and Telecommunications Board, National Research Council, National Library Service (Library of Congress), U.S. Department of Labor, U.S. Department of Justice, National Institute on Standards and Practice, U.S. Dept of Commerce, European Union 7th Framework and Horizon Programmes, Information Technology Foundation, Consumer Electronics Foundation, Adobe Foundation, Microsoft, Apple, IBM, Unisys, Google, Amazon, Facebook, Sun Microsystems, Ameritech, ARINC, AT&T, Battelle, Compaq, DEC, ECCS, Hewlett Packard, Honeywell, Motorola, Telesensory Systems,

Unisys, Verizon, Polhemus Navigation, Basic Telecommunications, AccessComputing, ACM, Computing Research Associates, Technology-Related Assistance Act Program, Disability and Business Technology Assistance Centers, American Occupational Therapy Association, Rehabilitation Engineering and Assistive Technology Society of North America (RESNA), University of Wisconsin-Madison, University of Maryland, College Park, Computers to Help People Inc., and Dane County Services.

No endorsement by any of the funders of any of the work documented here should be inferred.

Contents

About the Authors

Dr. Gregg Vanderheiden is the Founder and Director Emeritus of the Trace R&D Center and Professor in the iSchool at the University of Maryland. He has been active in the field of technology and disability for 50 years and was a pioneer in the field of Augmentative Communication (a term originating from his writings), assistive technology, and computer access. Access features developed by him and the Trace Center team can be found in every computer and mobile device internationally (Windows, MacOS, iOS, and Linux,...) as well as kiosks, ticket machines, and more. He has also been a long-time leader in the area of web accessibility, creating the first set of Web Accessibility guidelines in 1995 and serving as co-editor and co-chairing the WCAG 1.0 and 2.0 Working Group. At the *6th World Wide Web Conference*, he was the third annual recipient of the Yuri Rubinsky Memorial World Wide Web Award. His most recent work has focused on development of Morphic and proposing a completely different way to approach accessibility for next-next-generation ICT. He is a past President and Fellow of RESNA, a Founding Fellow of the American Institute of Medical and Biological Engineering (AIMBE), and Fellow in the Human Factors and Ergonomics Society.

Jonathan Lazar Ph.D., LLM is a Professor in the College of Information Studies (iSchool) at the University of Maryland. He has authored or edited 14 books, including *Accessible Technology and the Developing World* (co-edited with Michael Stein); *Research Methods in Human-Computer Interaction* (2nd edition, co-authored with Heidi Feng and Harry Hochheiser); *Ensuring Digital Accessibility Through Process and Policy* (co-authored with Dan Goldstein and Anne Taylor), *Disability, Human Rights, and Information Technology* (co-edited with Michael Stein); Universal Usability: *Designing Computer Interfaces for Diverse User Populations, and Web Usability: A User-Centered Design Approach.* He has published over 150 refereed articles in journals, conference proceedings, and edited books, frequently serves as an adviser to U.S. government agencies, regularly provides testimony at the federal and state levels, and multiple U.S. federal regulations cite his research. At the University of Maryland iSchool, he teaches courses on human–computer interaction, user-centered design, accessibility, and legal research methods. He is the recipient of the 2021 ACM SIGCHI Academy Award, the 2020 ACM SIGACCESS Award for Outstanding Contributions to Computing and Accessibility, the 2017 University System of Maryland Board of Regents Faculty Award for Excellence in Research, and the 2016 ACM SIGCHI Social Impact Award. He recently served as the General Chair of the ACM ASSETS 2021 conference. At the University of Maryland, he is a faculty member in the Human–Computer Interaction Lab (HCIL) and was recently appointed as the Director of the Trace Research and Development Center, the nation's oldest research center on technology and disability.

Amanda Lazar is an Assistant Professor in the College of Information Studies with an affiliate appointment in the Department of Computer Science at the University of Maryland, College Park. She received her Ph.D. in Biomedical and Health Informatics. Her research in human–computer interaction examines the design of technology for older adults as well as individuals with dementia to support social interaction and engagement in life. In parallel, she examines the ways that technologies shape (and are shaped by) attitudes toward these populations. Her research draws on the health sciences as well as critical frameworks. She regularly publishes her research with her students at conferences such as the *ACM CHI Conference on Human Factors in Computing Systems (CHI)* and *Computer Supported Cooperative Work and Social Computing* (CSCW). Her research group has received multiple Best Paper and Honorable Mention awards. Her work is supported by a CAREER grant from the National Science Foundation (NSF), as well as other grants from the NSF and the National Institute on Disability, Independent Living, and Rehabilitation Research (NIDILRR).

Hernisa Kacorri is an Assistant Professor in the College of Information Studies. She holds an affiliate appointment in the Department of Computer Science and the Human–Computer Interaction Lab at the University of Maryland, College Park and serves as a core faculty at the Trace R&D Center. She received her Ph.D. in Computer Science from The Graduate Center at City University of New York and has conducted research at the University of Athens, IBM Research-Tokyo, Lawrence Berkeley National Lab, and Carnegie Mellon University. Her research focuses on accessibility and human-centered artificial intelligence, with an emphasis on rigorous, user-based experimental methodologies for assessing impact. Her most recent work on teachable machines does not see end-users as passive consumers but as active directors of AI-infused technology. She is recipient of a Mina Rees Dissertation Fellowship in the Sciences and was recognized by the Rising Stars in EECS program of CMU/MIT. Her collaborations with students, colleagues, and advisors have received honorable mention and best paper awards at ACM ASSETS, ACM CHI, IEEE WACV, and IEEE VL/HCC. Her work is funded by NSF and NIDILRR.

J. Bern Jordan Ph.D. is an Assistant Research Scientist at the Trace R&D Center in the College of Information Studies (iSchool) at the University of Maryland. He received his Ph.D. in Biomedical Engineering from the University of Wisconsin–Madison. Interested in accessibility and its practical applications, he works to improve both the technology side and the standards and practice around accessibility. His work has included the development of techniques for cross-disability access to kiosks and public ICT, analysis and contributions to accessibility standards and regulations, the development of hands-on accessibility training workshops, and research into automatic user interface generation and adaptation. He has been appointed to the Disability Advisory Committee of the U.S. Federal Communications Commission (FCC). He has 10 patents related to access for kiosks and touchscreens and has worked with over a dozen companies large and small on making their products and services more accessible.

1 Trace Center Origin and Evolution

1.1 Tricked!

Interestingly, the Trace Center owes its inception to a benevolent deception. In October 1971, Gregg Vanderheiden, an undergraduate Electrical Engineering student, was working as a technician in the Behavioral Cybernetics Lab at the University of Wisconsin–Madison when he was approached by David Lamers—a fellow EE student. David was looking for Pat, a researcher at the lab who had done early eye-tracking research. David thought that eye-tracking might be a technique that could be used by a boy at a local school who had cerebral palsy and could not communicate except with a wooden communication board. David's biomedical engineering professor (whose wife worked as a psychologist at the boy's school) made an announcement in his class at his wife's request, asking if any students would like to go out to the school and see if they could find a better solution for the boy. Pat (the eye-tracking researcher) whom David sought was not there, but as David left, he ran into Gregg again and Gregg expressed doubts that eye-tracking would be a practical solution, since (at that time) it required a bite-block, a completely dark room, and 15 min to adjust the diodes on glasses each time the user puts them on.

When David returned the next day, Pat was in and demonstrated the eye-tracking setup, letting David try it himself. David came to the same conclusion as Gregg—that it would not work outside of the lab, much less in a classroom for exactly the reasons Gregg had cited. However, David again ran into Gregg on the way out. Gregg nodded as David explained, but then Gregg proposed three different solutions he had thought of that might work. David said he didn't understand, even after repeated descriptions, and suggested that Gregg accompany him to the school "just for a bit, to show me what you mean." Gregg explained that he couldn't just walk out of work in the middle of the day, but David insisted he didn't understand. So eventually, David talked Gregg into leaving work and accompanied him to the school.

G. Vanderheiden et al., *Technology and Disability*, Synthesis Lectures on Technology and Health, https://doi.org/10.1007/978-3-031-09214-5_1

Fig. 1.1 Lydell pointing to a letter on his wooden communication board with the alphabet and a few words woodburned into it

There Gregg met Lydell, a bright 12-year-old boy with severe cerebral palsy. Lydell could not speak, and his only means of communication, or doing anything at school, was pointing to letters and a few words that were woodburned into a board (Fig. 1.1). Even this was very slow. Lydell could only point to the letters at a rate of about one letter every 2–4 s. This was about 3–4 words per minute, which was 40 times slower than the average rate of speech for other children in the class. More importantly, he could only communicate if someone was completely focused on watching Lydell's hand on the communication board for the entire time he was communicating. Looking up was the same as muting him. And since there was no one available at the school to provide this continuous support for him, and the teacher could not stop class for the 5 min it would take to even get a sentence or two from him, Lydell had no means of participating in the class or doing any "written" work there.

Gregg had not intended to be involved beyond the visit to explain his ideas. But he was taken with Lydell, whose bright but irreverent communication style and dry humor combined with his painfully slow and laborious means of communicating convinced him that a better way was needed for this child.

Of the three solutions proposed, Gregg threw out the first one (using a head pointer) as soon as he met Lydell. The second, a keyguard, was eliminated when Lydell tried it. The third (what is now called scanning) worked, and had the potential to give Lydell an independent means of communication and writing, but was even slower than his current way of communicating. Convinced that some way to allow Lydell to use his pointing could be found, Gregg quit his job the next day and joined with David Lamers to work on a solution for Lydell. (It was later that Gregg realized that David, a senior in Electrical Engineering, could not possibly have "not understood" Gregg's three ideas—and that David had feigned an inability to understand in order to get Gregg to accompany him out to the school. He had correctly assumed that if he could just get Gregg out to the school to meet Lydell—he would have a colleague in his quest.)

Fig. 1.2 Lydell using the first prototype AutoCom with his speech therapist, Mrs. Sprague. The "auto-monitoring communication board," made of sheets of aluminum sandwiching a matrix of reed switches, is on the table in front of Lydell. He is pointing out letters with a custom-molded slider handpiece with a magnet on it. The controller, made of army surplus parts, is exposed on the table next to a commercial power supply. The Friden Flexowriter is on the table to the left

The pair felt they needed help, so they began recruiting fellow undergraduate students, first from engineering and then from other disciplines. The first was Andrew Volk, Gregg's friend and fellow tinkerer, who became the first technical director for the group. Other early members of the team were Jim Pazaris (Electrical Engineering), Candace Hill-Vegter (Communicative Disorders), Kathleen M. Muehlbauer (Occupational Therapy), Richard D. Thompsen (Electrical Engineering), Christina M. McNelis, and Marcia Meizel. The group grew over the next 2 years to include students from eight departments in four different schools at the University of Wisconsin–Madison, representing the fields of communicative disorders, electrical engineering, biomedical engineering, special education, educational psychology, occupational therapy, physical therapy, and journalism.

Within 6 months, working with funds provided by Gregg, David's car, $500 from an Institute of Electrical and Electronics Engineers (IEEE) Vincent Bendix award, and a parts donation from the UW Department of Electrical Engineering, the group had created a solution. It was built out of army surplus parts, including an 85-lb Friden Flexowriter, relays, a hand-built diode array, an 80-V power supply (to drive the Flexowriter solenoids), and a few TTL logic chips (Fig. 1.2).

How auto-monitoring worked and why a new method was needed

Because of Lydell's mixed spastic-athetotic cerebral palsy, his movements were very choretic, causing his hand and arm to move about erratically whenever he tried to use them. He also could only slide reliably to the left once his hand was on the board. Moving to the right usually required that he raise his hand up and back above his shoulder, and then ballistically aim for a new spot on the communication board. Once his hand landed, he would press down hard on the board for control, trying to inch his hand and fingers to the next letter with his fingers constantly moving. Using a headpointer (the first approach) did not work since he did not have stable head movement. Using a keyguard on a computer (Gregg's second idea) did not work, as Lydell's hand just kept "flailing" back and forth across the keyboard hitting random keys, even with a keyguard. The third idea (scanning) where the items are presented in sequence and he would hit a switch to stop it, worked, but it took him between 1 and 3 seconds to successfully hit a switch once the choice had been reached. Since scanning requires each choice to be presented long enough for the person to react, and each choice is usually five or more presentations and two switch actions to select it, this would give Lydell an independent means of communication and writing, but it would be 5–10 times slower than his current already slow communication board.

The solution in the end turned out to be a combination of (1) a handpiece that Lydell could use to slide around on the smooth surface (allowing him to press down for the control he needed but not have the friction that prevented him from moving around once his hand was on the surface); (2) an array of magnetic sensors underneath the surface that could be used to track the position of a magnet on the handpiece that he would use to point; and (3) circuitry that would ignore all of the letters that he pointed to as he moved erratically around the board until he finally centered his movements around the letter he wanted. Even then he would move on and off of the letter he wanted, pointing to other surrounding letters since he could rarely hold his hand still. So, the trick was to use a combination of hysteresis and delayed acceptance to determine which of the many letters, which he was activating with the pointer (magnet), was at the center of his continual movements.

Using the above-described technique, the AutoCom was able to correctly determine what he was pointing to better than most humans who were watching his pointing, unless they were experienced at interpreting his athetotic pointing motions.

1.2 The Challenge Grows

In the spring of 1972, the undergraduate group was asked if they would appear on a United Cerebral Palsy telethon to help raise funding for the local UCPA chapter. The group agreed and appeared with Lydell on the telethon which was broadcast statewide and to neighboring states (Fig. 1.3).

Immediately after the telethon, the student group started receiving letters from parents who had similar children in grade school and high school who were unable to communicate or write due to severe cerebral palsy, asking if a system like that shown on the telethon could be created for their child.

Fig. 1.3 Standing from the left, the UCPA Telethon Host, Gregg Vanderheiden, David Lamers, C. Daniel Geisler (Advisor), and (seated) Lydell

The group therefore decided to see if they could make something that was not only more durable and sustainable for Lydell but also could be replicated for the others who had contacted them.

A few months later, David Lamers graduated and went off to work for GD Searle in order to support his young family. Gregg Vanderheiden and many of the students who were continuing their education stayed on, continuing, and expanding the work.

1.3 The Group and Scope Expand

Over the summer of 1972 and into the next year, the group continued the work. Funding was pulled together from a variety of sources, including bake sales carried out by the parents or schools of the children, small donations, and some funds from the University Chancellor's furniture and honorarium fund that he contributed when he heard of the students' efforts. During this time, the group worked to create a more replicable design, replacing the 85-lb Flexowriter with a TTY (Teletypewriter), and learning more about the other students with cerebral palsy. They also wrote and submitted their first grant application for $16,000 to the National Science Foundation's Student-Originated Studies

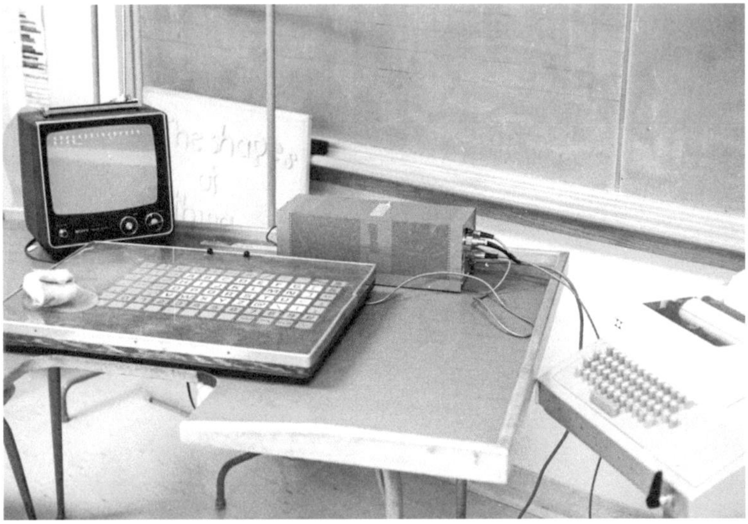

Fig. 1.4 Second-Generation AutoCom with Ann Arbor Terminal and Teletypewriter as the printer

(SOS) Program run by Dr. Max Ward. The purpose of the NSF SOS program was to fund groups of students over a summer to carry out a research project of their own devising.

The NSF SOS grant application was successful, and the group received its first formal funding in the summer of 1973. This allowed them to put together a team that included not only the engineering but also the communication, language, and disability studies students needed to create an effective, portable, replicable, and reliable communication and writing system that would work for the different students with cerebral palsy from Wisconsin and Illinois that had written to the group for help. The result was an all-digital version of the AutoCom. This new version used donated video display controllers from Ann Arbor Terminals that allowed the users to display their output on a TV monitor so that they could correct their mistakes and do math (something not possible when going straight to a printer). The TTY was continued as the most affordable available printer option (Fig. 1.4).

1.4 The Student Group Evolves

As a part of their work over the summer of 1973, the student group collected as much information as they could about other research and clinical efforts related to developing communication systems for individuals with severe disabilities. Two projects in particular stood out: the BlissSymbol program in Canada at the Ontario Crippled Children's Center

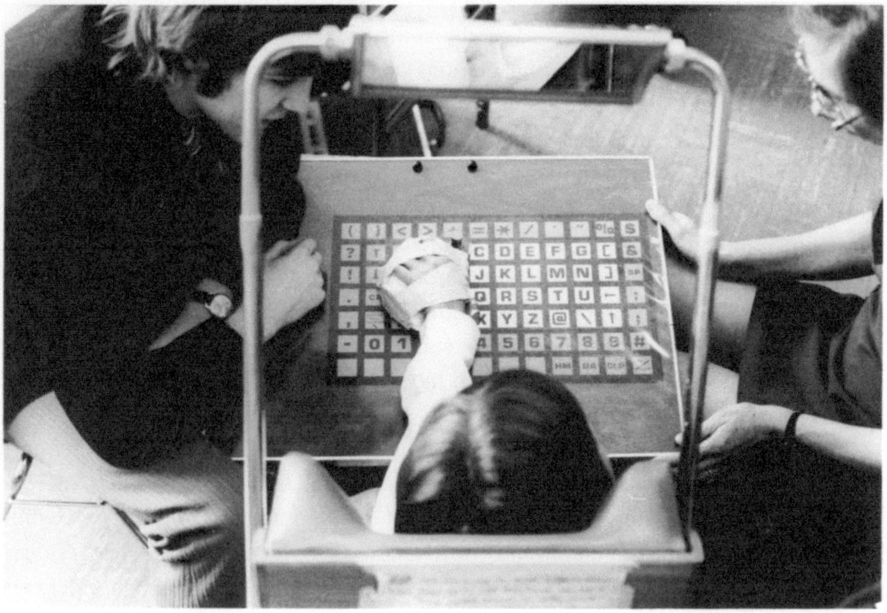

Fig. 1.5 Gregg Vanderheiden demonstrating the AutoCom with children at the OCCC in Toronto

(OCCC)[1] and the research work on communication boards[2] that was being done by Drs. Eugene McDonald and Adeline Schultz at the Home of the Merciful Savior for Crippled Children[3] in Pennsylvania. In September, Gregg Vanderheiden visited these two programs and also stopped by the National Science Foundation in Washington, D.C., to express thanks for its support and to present the results of its funding to Dr. Ward.

The trip to Toronto introduced the group to the use of symbols and symbol sets and led to future work and collaboration on BlissSymbols (see Chap. 2) (Fig. 1.5).

The trip to Pennsylvania provided a wealth of information about communication boards and language development in non-vocal individuals and led to a partnership with Dr. McDonald on both the national workshop series the Trace Center did later and a chapter in Dr. McDonald's book on intervention with children with cerebral palsy.[4]

The trip to the National Science Foundation went even better than expected and resulted in a watershed event for the group. When shown the results of the summer project,

---

[1] Now The Hugh MacMillan Rehabilitation Centre.

[2] McDonald, E. T. and Schultz, A. R. (1973). Communication boards for cerebral-palsied children. *Journal of Speech and Hearing Disorders*, 38, 1 (pp. 73–88). https://doi.org/10.1044/jshd.3801.73.

[3] Now the Home of the Merciful Savior - HMS School for Children with Cerebral Palsy.

[4] Vanderheiden, G. (1987). Advanced technology aids for communication, education, and employment. In E. T. McDonald (Ed.), *Cerebral Palsy: Nature, Pathogenesis, and Management*. Baltimore: University Park Press.

Dr. Ward set up a conference room and invited others from the division to come by and see it. He was particularly impressed by the ability of the AutoCom prototype to be able to interpret erratic, athetotic pointing motions and correctly identify which letters were being pointed at even when most humans could not. The Director of the Education Directorate of NSF came by and after viewing it casually commented, "This work should not stop." When Dr. Ward was told of this, he urged Gregg to ask the director what he meant by that. The Director responded, "Just what I said." When then asked if he would fund a proposal to continue the work (the NSF Directorate had no program related to disability at the time), the director thought for a moment and then said that he would have such a proposal reviewed if and only if it came from the student group, and not from a professor.

Gregg shared the results of these visits with the team and with the faculty advisor for the group, Dr. C. Daniel Geisler—and then the team went back to work, employing what Gregg had learned on the trip.

A week or two later Dr. Geisler informed the group that special permission from the Chancellor had been given for Gregg to act as principal investigator on the NSF grant, even though Gregg was only a master's student at the time. He was told that, even though there was a state statute stipulating that only tenure-track faculty should act as principal investigators on grants, the statute contained a clause allowing for exceptions under certain circumstances. The chancellor stretched this clause to grant Gregg, as the director of the student group, the ability to act as a principal investigator at the university, despite being only a master's student.

A grant proposal was prepared and, with a special cover letter from the chancellor to allow its processing by the University of Wisconsin, it was submitted. After review, it was funded by NSF,[5] thus setting a precedent within the university for the group to submit its own grants—and laying the groundwork for the next chapter of the group's evolution from a student volunteer project to today's multidisciplinary research center.

1.5 The Improbable Path and Support that Allowed the Trace Center to Come Into Existence

In looking back, it is interesting to note that there would be no Trace Center today if any one of a number of different people had not gone above and beyond what would be expected of them and done something extraordinary to help the small group of students.

- If Professor Richard Marleau had not donated his analog computer lab/classroom to the group (moving all of his analog computers to the back of a large storage room where he then proceeded to teach his class) so that the group would have a place to gather, form, and work on the project ...

[5] NSF Press Release, October 15, 1973 "Nsf Awards University of Wisconsin Grant for Student Project to Help Physically Handicapped to Communicate" https://go.umd.edu/1973nsf-award.

- If Professor C. Daniel Geisler had not devoted the time to advising this diverse group, even though it and its complications slowed his own personal and quite a different area of research in neurophysiology …
- If Dr. Max Ward of the National Science Foundation had not pushed Gregg Vanderheiden to ask—and if the Director of the Education Division of NSF had not gone outside of his funding programs and normal procedures to accept and award a disability-related grant to a master's student as Principal Investigator …
- If Dean Robert Marshall and Chancellor Edwin Young had not stretched university policy quite considerably to provide special permission for a master's student to act as a principal investigator on the second NSF grant and on subsequent grants …

… the student project would not have gotten off the ground or would have had to wind down like all other student projects after a semester or two. Its continuation and development into the Trace Center was not just the dedication of the students but also the encouragement and support (sometimes extraordinary support) that individual faculty, deans, and the chancellor at the University of Wisconsin provided.

And this support did not end here. The university also allowed the student group to produce and distribute 40 AutoComs (at cost) to meet requests from the field, including amassing a debt of approximately $881,772 in 2021 dollars in order to design and build the 40 AutoComs before they could be shipped, and costs recovered (see Chap. 2).

1.6 Evolution of the Center Over the Decades

From these beginnings, the Trace Center's program has evolved over the decades both by expanding to cover all disabilities and by expanding to encompass new and evolving technologies.

The student group started out working on a communication and writing solution for just one individual. This grew into solving a problem for a group of similar individuals, and from there into different individuals with different needs. Along the way, it also evolved into a source for all manner of information on assistive technologies (AT), its development, study, and practice that was available from any source. This led to the Trace Center becoming a primary resource to the field for summative information (information that brought together comprehensive summaries of all information from all sources on a topic) in the era before the Internet and electronically searchable information. The Center published annual "ResourceBooks" and created a "Reprint Service" that produced other summative information on demand for a variety of other topics related to augmentative communication and later computer access. An introduction and update for researchers and practitioners on communication techniques and aids for people with severe communication disabilities were provided via a series of national and international workshops. In 1974, 3 years after the students first came together to work on a solution for Lydell, the group changed its name formally to the Trace Research and Development Center when it submitted a major multidimensional proposal to fund the expanding scope of its work.

With the advent of personal computers in the 1980s, the Trace Center expanded its focus from communication and control to include access to the newly emerging personal computers. It also was successful in getting the National Institute on Handicapped Research to fund a Rehabilitation Engineering Research Center (RERC) in a new area: "Access to Computers and Electronic Equipment." This work again included both summative work and guidelines as well as the development of new approaches and technologies to allow full access to computers and software. In 1984, the Center shifted from a student-run group when Gregg, its director, received his interdisciplinary Ph.D. in "Technology in Communication, Rehabilitation, and Child Development" and in 1986 was offered a faculty position in the Human Factors group of the Industrial Engineering Department at the University of Wisconsin–Madison.

In the 1990s, the Center was at the forefront of accessibility of the Web, creating the first guidelines and working on new techniques and tools for Web access. Trace also joined up with Gallaudet University to address the issues of accessibility of telecommunications, jointly creating the first RERC on Telecommunication Access, which operated in parallel with the Computer Access RERC.

In the 2000s, the Center expanded its work on Web access to include the new Web technologies, creating new tools and measures to extend what could be included in Web accessibility. It also expanded its work into kiosks and other information and transaction machines (ITMs), creating the EZ Access techniques and hardware which was deployed in kiosks, ticket machines, and postal stations across the country to make these self-service public systems more accessible for people with vision, hearing, physical, and cognitive/language/learning disabilities.

In the 2010s, the Center began working on creating global infrastructures to support and allow more inclusive information systems worldwide. The Trace Center collaborated with more than 50 groups and companies across the United States, Canada, and Europe to develop a Unified Listing of all ICT access tools, a DeveloperSpace to facilitate the development of new solutions, and the auto-personalization technology that enables people who depend on assistive technologies and interface adaptations to move between devices and have their accessibility follow them. In 2016, the Trace Center moved from the University of Wisconsin to the University of Maryland, College Park, and expanded its work in Artificial Intelligence (AI) and Dementia/Aging (Table 1.1).

Table 1.1 Provides a rough overview of the Trace Center's evolution and focus over the decades

Period	Focus
1970s	• Initially focused on augmentative communication with individuals having physical disabilities • Expanded to meet the needs of those with language and learning disabilities • Adopted "Trace" as its name (1974) • Captured and disseminated information about all types of communication and control devices, interfaces, and techniques • Coined the term "Augmentative Communication" (1979) • Broadened into all types of control and interface, toward the end of the decade • Beginning in the late 1970s, with the advent of the personal computer, the Trace Center shifted its primary focus to computer access
1980s	• Expanded its cataloging to include all types of communication, interface, and computer access technologies • Focused on "transparent access" where individuals with disabilities could access computers in a fashion that the computers "thought" the user was using the standard keyboard and mouse. In this way, people with disabilities would have access to all computer programs • Created the first computer and software accessibility guidelines (1985) • Shifted from being a student-led group when its director completed his Ph.D. (1984) and accepted a faculty position (1986) in Industrial Engineering—Human Factors group
1990s	• Expanded into Web, telecommunication, and kiosk access • Created the first Telecommunication RERC in partnership with Gallaudet University, which Trace operated in parallel to its Information Technology RERC • Created the first Web accessibility guidelines in 1995 and (in 1996) the Unified Guidelines that were used by the W3C as the basis for WCAG 1.0 in 1999 • Created the first cross-disability kiosk access program in 1999—which was deployed at the Mall of America • Created the first cross-disability voting machine prototypes in 1999
2000s	• Expanded access to all types of digital technologies • Expanded work on public kiosks and ITMs with deployments of an advanced form of EZ Access in Automated Postal Stations, Amtrak Ticket Machines, WWII memorial, Homeland Security Kiosks, and Smithsonian • Began exploring cloud-based accessibility solutions

(continued)

Table 1.1 (continued)

Period	Focus
2010s	• Began work on creating global infrastructures to support and allow more inclusive information systems worldwide • Participated as a leader in two large-scale projects in Europe, bringing together more than 50 groups and companies across the United States, Canada, and Europe • Led development of the **Unified Listing** (of all ICT assistive technologies) and the **DeveloperSpace** (to facilitate development of new access solutions) • Developed Morphic, a technology that simplifies computer use and provides new capabilities to assistive technology users, including the ability to have their AT and interface adaptations follow them to any device they encounter and need to use • With a move from the University of Wisconsin to the University of Maryland in 2016, expanded its research on dementia, aging, artificial intelligence, teachable interfaces, and policy

The Trace Center's program also evolved over time in terms of the type of accessibility work:

- from purpose-built assistive technologies (starting with communication and then moving to computer-based assistive technologies) …
- to adaptive assistive technologies (i.e., assistive technologies that provide access to mainstream technologies) …
- to universal/inclusive design …
- to accessibility infrastructures.

And it evolved in its information and resource areas as well:

- from cataloging and serving as a central reference point (pre-internet) …
- to accessibility guidelines …
- to standards …
- to accessibility frameworks.

Over the course of its development, the Center also grew from being internally focused on a goal to having a focus more on the field as a whole. It developed the characteristics it has become known for such as:

- acting as an information and research resource for consumers, industry, and government agencies;
- providing support for the field in general and to other programs, especially younger ones;
- trying to forecast where the field and technology in general are going, where the gaps will occur, and trying to fill the gaps before or as they occur;

- supporting the development of practical, harmonized, accessibility standards and creating tools to make them easier to apply;

…and, in all its work, focusing on impact and transfer of (Trace's and other's) ideas from research into the hands of consumers and others where they will directly impact the lives of people with disabilities.

The following chapters provide a more detailed description of each of these phases of the Center's evolution along with the specific activities, products, contributions, and lessons from each. The chapters are organized by topic area. These are roughly in chronological order but there is overlap in that work continued on past areas as new topics were added. The topics are:

Chapter 2. Augmentative Communication
Chapter 3. Pre-Internet/Pre-Web Information Resources
Chapter 4. Computer Access
Chapter 5. Electronic Consumer Product and General Accessibility
Chapter 6. Web Access
Chapter 7. Telecommunication Access
Chapter 8. Voting, Kiosk, and ITM Access
Chapter 9. Accessibility Infrastructures

These chapters are followed by:

Chapter 10. … covering the move from the University of Wisconsin–Madison to University of Maryland, College Park;
Chapter 11. … summarizing the unique characteristics that have defined the Trace Center over the years;
Chapter 12. … providing lessons learned over the first 50 years; and
Chapter 13. … looking forward and providing a brief summary of the current and future directions of the Trace Center.

Augmentative Communication (1971–)

2

2.1 The AutoCom

As noted in the origin story, the Trace Center started out working on a communication aid for a single individual, Lydell, a young boy whose only means of communication was a wooden communication board. This device developed with him became the Auto-Monitoring Communication Board or AutoCom.[1]

The first version of the AutoCom was built with spare parts, spare change, what could be found in military surplus, along with donated reed switches from Hamlin Corporation. It used a hand-built diode array as a custom "reed-relay-array-keyboard-to-Flexowriter codec," relays, a few TTL gates, a monostable, and a World War II Friden Flexowriter that used 80 V signals to control it.

After the telethon, the work expanded to developing systems for more than just Lydell. Using funding assembled from a number of different sources, the original components were repackaged to create a safer version for use in a school. However, the Flexowriter was not replicable, so it was replaced by a TTY.

---

[1] Vanderheiden, G., Lamers, D., Volk, A., and Geisler C. (1973) Communications Device for Severely Handicapped, Abstract, Archives of Physical Medicine. https://doi.org/10.1145/800192.805743.

Vanderheiden, G. C., Lamers, D. F., Volk, A. M., and Geisler, C. D. (1973). *Proceedings of the Annual Meeting of the Biomedical Engineering Society*, 4,153.

Vanderheiden, G. C., Volk, A. M., and Geisler, C. D. (1973, September). The auto-monitoring communication board (Autocom), A new communication aid for the severely handicapped. *Proceedings of the Carnahan Conference on Electronic Prosthetics*. Lexington, Kentucky.

Vanderheiden, G. C., Volk, A. M., and Geisler, C. D. (1973). A new communication aid for severely handicapped people. (Abstract) *Proceedings of the Association for Computing Machine Conference*. https://doi.org/10.1145/800192.805743.

G. Vanderheiden et al., *Technology and Disability*, Synthesis Lectures on Technology and Health, https://doi.org/10.1007/978-3-031-09214-5_2

In its next stage of evolution, carried out under the NSF Student Originated Studies summer program, the AutoCom was rebuilt from scratch into a pure digital logic version that used a video controller donated from Ann Arbor Terminals to provide the users with an easier-to-read display. The use of the television display also allowed the students, for the first time, to be able to correct their output and to write, and to solve math problems, onscreen. A TTY was used as the output printer to allow permanent copy, homework, etc. This version was replicated and distributed to the five users in Wisconsin and Illinois[2]: Lydell Swenson, Diana Creer, Timothy Hartwig, Craig Coates, and Mary Ann Merchen.

The next version was developed with funding from the second NSF grant to the student group. This round saw the development of the first portable communication aid and, using the vocabulary research done under the SOS grant and continued in this grant, included the first custom vocabularies to accelerate the speed of communication.[3] For portability, this unit used a strip printer taken from a calculator as its output form.

The strip printer was later replaced with a wide portable adding machine printer that was modified to provide mini pages of output (and turned sideways was used for the Bliss-Symbol printing version of the AutoCom). This was then replaced with a digital, correctable, display mounted directly on the portable aid.

At each step, the students incorporated the latest technologies available at the time. For example, when the first CMOS microprocessors were announced in 1974, the team led by David Kelso designed a version of the AutoCom that incorporated the two-chip version of the COSMAC microprocessor even before it was sampled. Going only from the specification sheets, the entire circuit board was created, and preliminary software was written. By the time the first samples of the microprocessor were released, the AutoCom circuit boards were all finished and sitting, waiting for the parts to arrive. The chipset arrived, and David plugged them into the circuit board. It didn't work. After an hour of troubleshooting, it was determined that one of the pinouts of the microprocessor was the inverse of what the spec sheet had specified. Using a flywire to the only unused inverter on the board and back, the AutoCom sprang to life. It worked—though the software needed additional development before it was ready for users.

---

[2] Vanderheiden, G. C., Volk, A M., and Geisler, C. D. (1974). An alternate interface to computers for the physically handicapped. *Proceedings of the National Computer Conference*. https://doi.org/10.1145/1500175.1500196.

[3] Vanderheiden, G. C. and Kelso, D. P. (1977). Development of teacher-modifiable communication aids for NVSPH individuals. *Proceedings of the 4th Annual Conference on Systems and Devices for the Disabled*. Seattle, WA.

Along the way, the student group created a number of firsts, including the first portable user-programmable communication aid, and the first portable aid with correctable display. It also arguably created the first portable speech output communication aid when it mounted a specially modified 16-lb DECtalk speech synthesizer[4] to the back of a wheelchair and used it as an output device for an AutoCom for a child. Since the DECtalk drew 3 amps when it was running, the team designed it to turn on just long enough to speak and then shut back down again, each time the user used it to talk. In order to do this, the Trace Center had to get Digital Equipment Corporation to add a special routine to the boot-up ROM and add jumper pins to the master circuit board of their commercial product. Adding a jumper across the pins caused the DECtalk to alter its boot sequence to omit announcing its name, models, and status every time it was turned on (so that the student's "on-speak-off" power saving technique could be used) (Figs. 2.1 and 2.2).

2.2 Creating Its Own Production Design and Product Run

During this time, requests continued to come in from across the country from families and clinicians who had heard about the AutoCom and were interested in getting one for their children and students. In late 1975–76, the student group therefore proposed building 40 copies of a new and improved design of the communication aid to handle the continued requests. This meant that the university would have to take it on faith that the student group would be able to complete such a design, successfully build and ship them, and that the 40 families or schools would pay for the devices when completed. With help from their student advisor Dr. Leo Jedynak, they were able to convince the University to advance them the funds to design and build 40 portable AutoComs. Looking back, it is not clear how the university had such confidence in the group, as this would require the university to commit $160,000 ($881,772 in 2021 dollars) on the promise that the students could deliver them and get reimbursed (the cost of each of the 40 portable AutoComs was $4,000). Within 2 months, all 40 AutoComs were spoken for.

By 1977, the group had successfully designed, built, shipped, and ultimately recouped the costs from the AutoCom recipients.[5] In order to do this, the group had to design a commercial-quality version of the AutoCom that could be produced in medium quantity (40) and that could be robust enough to withstand the stress that it could experience when used as a lap tray (ramming open doors) and operated by (some very strong) users with cerebral palsy. (One was a weightlifter with cerebral palsy who accidentally flung his arm to the side one day, hitting the director, who was seated next to him, in the chest and flinging him up into the air to land on his back on the floor, breathless, several feet away.)

[4] https://en.wikipedia.org/wiki/DECtalk.

[5] October 4–27, 1977, *Computers and the Learning Society—Report from the Hearings before a subcommittee of the Committee on Science and Technology*, U.S. House of Representatives No. 47, P474.

Fig. 2.1 The evolution of the AutoCom. Shown are: (1) the first version made primarily of spare and military surplus parts; (2) the version repackaged for schools with a TTY for printer; (3) the first all-digital version with correctable TV display; (4) the first portable version with strip printer; and (5) the production version with correctable display that was provided to 40 individuals around the country (Photo courtesy of Wisconsin Newspaper Association.)

As part of the early testing of the designs, therefore, the team subjected the AutoCom to some fairly severe tests, such as sending it end-over-end down a 35-foot concrete stairway and running over it with a car. (It survived both tests and was fully operational.)

When showing the AutoCom to the Subcommittee on Science and Technology of the U.S. House of Representatives, the Trace Director also demonstrated the durability of the aid by throwing the AutoCom across the front of the hearing room and then retrieving it

Fig. 2.2 The original DECtalk voice synthesizer

Fig. 2.3 Pictures of 2 of the 40 AutoCom recipients taken from articles in their local papers. Photos courtesy of (L-R) Wisconsin Newspaper Association and Republican-Herald archives

and continuing the demonstration. (The inspiration for this came from the fact that two entire table-sized copies of another technology being demonstrated in the same hearing had been brought in—in case one of them failed to survive the trip to Capitol Hill. To emphasize that communication aids for children with cerebral palsy had to be rugged enough to withstand whatever happened to them, Gregg took the aid off the wheelchair and spontaneously tossed it across the room to land 10 feet away—demonstrating its durability—and also demonstrating his youth and lack of decorum.) (Figs. 2.3 and 2.4).

Fig. 2.4 Gregg Vanderheiden presenting to the U.S. Congressional Subcommittee on Science and Technology in 1978 (demonstrating a copy of 1 of the "40" AutoComs)

2.3 First Commercial Transfer

After successfully building and placing the 40 AutoComs around the country, the student group did not want to meet continuing requests for the AutoCom. The Trace Center therefore held an open competition for companies who wanted to produce it commercially to bid on taking it over. The two top contenders were Everest and Jennings and Telesensory Systems Incorporated. In 1978, Telesensory Systems Inc. was chosen and awarded a royalty-free license to build the AutoCom, along with support from the student group. This was the first in what was to be a long series of commercial transfers from the group over the years.[6] It was also the first time that an augmentative communication aid had been developed by a research group in this way and successfully transferred to a completely independent company.

[6] https://trace.umd.edu/history/.

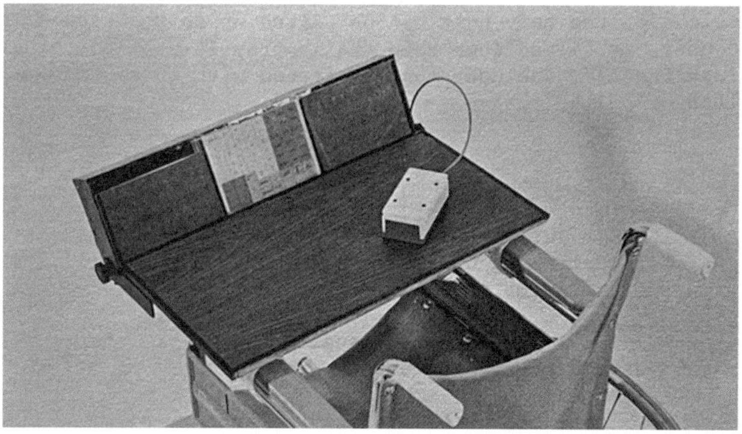

Fig. 2.5 The VersiCom was a scanning, direct selection, and encoding version of the AutoCom

2.4 Special Versions

In addition to the standard versions of the AutoCom, the team also created some special versions.[7] These included a version that could support a wide variety of communication strategies including direct selection, scanning, directed scanning, encoding, and more. To reflect its versatile nature, the aid was called the VersiCom (Fig. 2.5).

The Trace Center also created a special version of the AutoCom for a student, which included speech output via the specially modified version of the DECtalk as described above.

2.5 BlissApple and BlissCom

At the request of the BlissSymbol organization in Canada, the Trace Center had developed BlissApple, a BlissSymbol displaying and printing communication software for an Apple IIe (Fig. 2.6). Building on the expertise it had developed in creating the BlissApple, the group developed a special version of the AutoCom called the BlissCom.[8] To create this, the group took a tape-printer version of the AutoCom and mounted the tape printer sideways. This allowed the user to print out complete BlissSymbol communication

[7] Vanderheiden, G. C. and Kelso, D. P. (1977). Factors in the design of communication aids through the use of common control systems. *Proceedings of the Workshop on Communication Aids for the Non-Verbal Physically Handicapped*. Ottawa, Canada.

[8] Vanderheiden, G. C., Silverman, H., and Kelso, D. P. (1977, June). The Bliss-Com: A portable symbol printing communication aids. *Proceedings of the 4th Annual Conference on Systems and Devices for the Disabled*. Seattle, WA.

Fig. 2.6 The first BlissSymbol communicator/printer developed by Trace for an Apple IIe

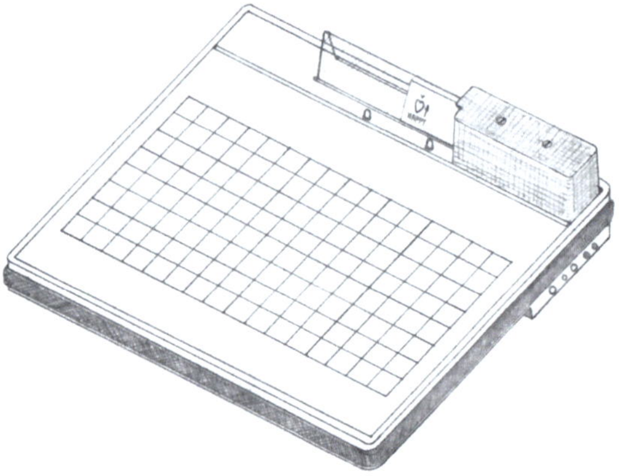

Fig. 2.7 BlissCom adaptation of AutoCom

sentences on the portable aid with the sentences parading across the front of the aid for the user and others to see. It also gave these children their first portable ability to write letters, homework, jokes, etc., using BlissSymbols that could be preserved, sent, or turned in (Fig. 2.7).

2.6 Other Augmentative Communication and Interaction Aids

During the 1970s, in parallel with and subsequent to the development of the AutoCom, VersiCom, and BlissCom, the Trace Center worked on a number of other augmentative communication techniques and aids to address the needs of an ever-expanding range of disabilities, including among others, cerebral palsy, spinal cord injury, ALS, locked-in-syndrome, Guillain Barre Syndrome, head injury, and cognitive, language, and learning disabilities.

Fig. 2.8 Trine, shown with optional keyboard. It could also be used with an LED display for scanning or head pointing, as well as by itself for keyboard operation or encoding (Morse and other methods)

In support of the development activities, the Center carried out research on language development in individuals using augmentative communication aids, as well as vocabulary studies to identify more efficient communication board, and communication aid, strategies. These were used in the different designs and features of the AutoCom. They also formed the basis for QuicKeys and other acceleration techniques, some of which were used in the design of the communication aid used by Dr. Stephen Hawking.

The final communication aid developed by the Trace Center was actually the world's first communication, writing, and computer access aid. This portable aid, called the Trine, was based on the HX-20 portable computer with custom hardware modules (a voice synthesizer module, custom switch interfaces, and an LED array panel that supported scanning, directed scanning, and head pointing). This allowed the Trine to address individuals with a wide range of disabilities, including those who could use a standard keyboard (with or without a guard), those who use headsticks or "lightbeam" head pointers, and individuals who were paralyzed or otherwise could only operate a single switch (of any type including an eye gaze switch). Along with allowing users to customize the vocabulary of their devices, the Trine provided individuals with the ability to communicate in speech or writing as well as control other standard computers. This compact, light, and portable aid allowed users to communicate, write, do homework, and control mainstream computers, including the ability to use all of the standard software on the computers using any of the above techniques and their custom vocabularies to reduce effort and increase speed. This was an important bridge for individuals who not only needed to use special adaptive input techniques to communicate but also needed to be able to access the standard computers which were beginning to show up in classrooms and workplaces. The Trine was transferred (again royalty-free) to two different assistive technology manufacturers (ACS and Words+) who then took over manufacture and distribution of the aids (Fig. 2.8).

2.7 Toy Modification

Early in its work, the Trace team discovered the value of children being able to control things in their environment as a means of cognitive, language, and motor development. It also noted a number of battery-operated toys on the market that seemed to play with themselves. (The child simply turned them on, and they entertained the child.) While this didn't seem to be the best kind of toy in general, it looked like a great way to teach cause and effect to children with severe cerebral palsy who could do little with regular toys. It could also give them an experience of physical control over their environment and the ability to have something done successfully, which lack of control of their limbs did not often afford them. Finally, it allowed the development of motor control and switch operation.

The Trace Center therefore developed a simple toy modification kit made from a piece of circuit board, some wire, and a jack into which any momentary or push-on/push-off switch could be plugged. Trace even found and adapted some toggle treadle switches that were indestructible. Trace created instructions for people to do it for themselves—including a design for a "pillow switch" that could be made at home and used safely with very young children, even if they had very strong choretic movements. These were released both as do-it-yourself instructions and as an inexpensive kit. Trace continued to make these available until toy adapters and adapted toys became common in the marketplace.

In addition to the pillow switch and tread switch, the Center also worked on head switches, eyebrow switches, blink switches, button switches, EMG switches, etc., for both control and communication aids.

2.8 Interface Interaction Standards—The First Standards Work of the Trace Center

While working on the AutoCom, sibling communication aids (BlissCom, VersiCom, RotoCom, etc.), and the special switch interfaces to control them, the Trace Center searched for a standard connector to use for the single- and multi-switch interfaces on its designs. However, it quickly discovered that there were no standards for these interfaces. At that time, there were 15 different companies making switches or multi-switch controls that plugged into their communication or control devices—switches that Trace would like to be able to use as interface options for its devices. Ironically, even though the companies were all creating similar types of switches and switch arrays, none of the 15 companies even accidentally used the same connector and pin assignments. With funding from the National Science Foundation, the Trace Center set out to develop a standard for the interfaces for communication and control aids.

This was more difficult than it would seem, as there were varied demands. Connectors had to be available in all countries, easy to insert, and durable. They also needed to be easy to remove but must not fall out accidentally. Any standard would also need to be acceptable to all of the different manufacturers. This last point was particularly sticky as it meant that, if/when a company switched to a new standard, all of its existing products would not work with the new switches (without adapters) and vice versa.

The Trace work resulted in two standards. The first was a simple electronic transducer standard (SET standard) that settled on a 3.5-mm audio jack (similar to those used on all headphones today). Both mono and stereo versions were specified to allow one- and two-switch configurations. The second standard used a D-connector and had pinout configuration specifications that allowed it to support a very wide range of different types and combinations of simple and smart switches.

Thanks in large part to the leadership of the Prentke Romich Company, who were the first to agree to change all of their interfaces to the new SET standard, all of the manufacturers eventually changed to the new pinout formats. Today, this Trace-developed standard is used ubiquitously worldwide for communication and control aids and also for games and almost any other device that uses single or double switches. It has become so ingrained in the field for so long that only early pioneers remember that there ever was a problem or that everyone did not originally use this connector.

The second multi-switch standard was made into an ISO standard and has been used widely for decades in power wheelchairs and controls that are used for control of both wheelchairs and other devices.

2.9 Origin of the Term "Augmentative Communication"

Deberah Harris and Gregg Vanderheiden, both from the Trace Center, were invited to participate in a special workshop/retreat to present their research on both the devices and language development research at the Trace Center, and the information they had collected on research elsewhere. The workshop/retreat was held at Gulf Shores, Florida, and organized by Richard Schiefelbusch in preparation for his new book on nonspeech communication. It was in connection with the presentation at this conference (captured in Dr. Schiefelbusch's subsequent book[9]) that Gregg Vanderheiden coined the term "augmentative communication,"[10,11,12] a term later used for the name of the field.

At this time speech pathologists were being fired for giving children communication boards because, it was said, they were practicing outside of their profession of speech therapy. Even though children had no understandable utterances, it was felt that the use of any other technique was not to be permitted by a speech therapist, and any such activities violated the medical rule of not practicing outside of their professional training or certification as a speech therapist.

The term "augmentative communication" was used in the workshop presentation and subsequent chapter to make the point that these techniques did not replace speech, but rather augmented it. This was based on clinical reports that it was rare that individuals given communication boards would decrease attempts to speak. Rather, it was reported that the more common result was that individuals using communication boards would actually increase their utterances. Being able to successfully communicate for the first time was a powerful motivator to learn to communicate better. Speech (when it worked—and with whom it would work) was so much faster than the slow pointing on the communication board. They would therefore try speech first and fall back on the board when speech did not work—or with people who could not understand them. It was also reported that their speech was often more intelligible when they had a communication board to fall back on, as they were under less pressure to succeed the first time they tried to speak (knowing they could fall back on the communication board if they failed). Especially for people with cerebral palsy, *trying hard* to speak clearly (or *trying hard* to do any motor task) usually led to increased interference and loss of control compared with trying the same task when more relaxed.

[9] Schiefelbusch, R. L. (Ed.) (1980). *Nonspeech Language and Communication. Analysis and Intervention.* Baltimore: University Park Press, 1980.

[10] Harris-Vanderheiden, D. and Vanderheiden, G. (1980). Augmentative communication techniques. In R. Schiefelbusch (Ed.), *NonSpeech Language and Communication: Analysis and Intervention* (pp. 259–301). Baltimore: University Park Press.

[11] Vanderheiden, G. (1980). Augmentative modes of communication for the severely speech and motor impaired. In M. Urist (Ed.), *Congenital Malformation—Its Clinical Management; Clinical, Orthopedic, and Related Research* (Number 148). https://doi.org/10.1097/00003086-198005000-00011.

[12] Vanderheiden, G. (1980). Augmentative modes of communication for the severely speech- and motor-impaired. *Clinical Orthopedics and Related Research*, 148, 70–86. https://doi.org/10.1097/00003086-198005000-00011.

2.10 The Communication Aids and Systems Clinic and the Communication Access Program

In addition to its research and development work, the Trace Center established one of the first clinics on augmentative communication and, later, computer access. While still a student group, the Trace Center along with Dr. David Yoder, a professor in Communicative Disorders at the University of Wisconsin–Madison, was able to convince the University of Wisconsin Hospital administrator to create a Communication Aids and Systems Clinic (CASC). Housed at the Trace Center (across the street from the hospital), but funded as a hospital clinic, CASC combined interface, seating, and speech and language specialists to provide an interdisciplinary approach.

Originally, the Trace Center would design special aids for CASC clients when commercial aids did not exist that would meet their needs. However, the Center soon found several problems with this approach.

> First, the Center wanted CASC to be a model for other clinics—and there were no other clinics that had a research center like Trace to support them. A clinic that had an R&D center to create custom solutions for it was not replicable.
>
> Second, when creating a custom device, the Center was solving a problem for one client—but not anyone else in the world who had the same problem.
>
> Third, the client now had nowhere to go for maintenance of their aid—or to replace it at the end of its life.

The Trace Center and CASC therefore abandoned this mode of operation. Trace no longer created any special products for CASC clients. If an aid did not exist on the market that clinic patients/clients needed, the Center would develop such an aid, then transfer it to an assistive technology company. CASC would then (and only then) recommend the solution be purchased for the client, using standard procedures, from the AT manufacturers' stock. It was painful and slow, but motivating, and in the long run a much better and more equitable expenditure of research funding.

2.11 Other Early Contributions to Augmentative and Alternative Communication

The Trace Center also supported the efforts of others in this young and developing field. It provided logistical (typing and mailing) and financial support, including carrying out a special workshop to raise funding to cover a large, unexpected expense for Communication Outlook, an important early newsletter in the field edited by Dr. John Eulenberg at Michigan State University. Trace also collaborated in the founding of the International

Society for Augmentative and Alternative Communication (ISAAC). The Center contributed two of the first three chapters to the American Speech and Hearing Association's (ASHA's) field-defining book, *Augmentative Communication*,[13] in 1986.

Finally, the Trace Center served the field for many years as an information resource, compiling and distributing information on everything from research to organizations to products that were available in the field.

[13] Blackstone S. W. (1986) *Augmentative Communication: An Introduction*, Rockville MD: American Speech and Hearing Association.

Pre-internet/Pre-web Summative Information (1970s–1990s)

3

For the first 25 years of the Trace Center's life, there was no "Internet" or Web as it exists today. It is increasingly hard to imagine what that was like. Think about trying to find information about assistive technologies, or the nearest clinical program, or who is working on augmentative communication or any related topic **without** using the Internet/Web in any way. How would you do this? You could go to the library, but there were no books listing which assistive technologies were available or who was working in the field. Some researchers may have published in journals you knew of, and those journals might have been available in your library. Most of the information on augmentative communication and control systems, however, was "fugitive literature" (not published in a way that it would appear in a library or searchable resource) or information that was not documented at all. In short, there was very little published in the early days, and historical information was sparse and very hard to find.

3.1 The Trace Center as an Information Resource

As part of its efforts in developing the AutoCom, the VersiCom, the RotoCom, and other communication aids, the Trace Center wanted to build on what was already known and either implement or extend that knowledge. Toward this end, the team gathered information on all the different techniques, strategies, and aids that were either available on the market or being researched at that time. This inventory included even one-off aids that were designed to meet the needs of a particular individual.

Almost none of this information was available in peer-reviewed publications but instead had to be tracked down from clinical, commercial, and other sources. Special credit goes to Candace Hill-Vegter, a member of the Trace team who initiated and led this effort.

G. Vanderheiden et al., *Technology and Disability*, Synthesis Lectures on Technology and Health, https://doi.org/10.1007/978-3-031-09214-5_3

This was so much work that the team at Trace decided to make the information gathered available to others. The goal was twofold. First, to ensure that people who needed assistive technologies could find them all and choose the best for the individual. Second, to ensure that people developing assistive technology were aware of what already existed so they would be able to develop better assistive technologies and built-in accessibility features.

Beginning in the first years of the student group's work, collection of information on what anyone and everyone else was doing was a high priority. This included not just research but also clinical work (not usually published), development (notoriously not published), and commercial (only published in product literature—and only about their product). Trace then turned around and made this information available. This dissemination work took a number of forms.

3.2 1974 CEC Conference

The first widespread dissemination of the gathered information was a presentation at the Council for Exceptional Children (CEC) conference in 1974, where the Trace Center presented an overview of all of the work it had discovered. The response to Trace's presentation made it clear how much this information was sought after (standing room only, with people climbing up into the windowsills and spilling out the door and into the hall).

The response encouraged the Trace to develop the ResourceBooks, the National Workshop Series, and the Trace Publication Service—all summarizing and distributing summative information on all aspects of communication and control that were not covered by the journals.

3.3 National Workshop Series

In an effort to get more information to both researchers and clinicians in a form best suited to them, the Trace Center launched a national workshop series on non-vocal communication techniques and aids. To do this, the Center brought together Dr. Eugene McDonald, Shirley McNaughton, Deberah Harris, and Gregg Vanderheiden in order to include the full spectrum of language and child development through symbol systems, communication development, and communication techniques and aids. Workshops were conducted in Boston, Chicago, and Los Angeles. To keep the number of participants to a manageable size, prospective attendees were asked to apply and went through a selection process.

The content from the original three workshops was later expanded to incorporate additional information discovered by participants of the first workshop series. Another 30 workshops with between 30 and 75 people each were conducted across the United States and England. The updated workshops now included the extensive work of Beverly Vicker from the University of Iowa Hospital School, and all attendees were given a copy of her book, *Nonoral Communication System Project*[1] as part of the workshop materials. The workshop also included demonstrations on how to easily build communication boards, including constructing a wheelchair-mounted lap tray communication board in less than 5 min using a Velcro mounting system with materials available in any home workshop.

The Trace National Workshop Series on Technology and Augmentative Communication trained approximately 1,000 researchers, clinicians, and educators on augmentative communication techniques. Many leaders in the field later mentioned that the workshop series was their first introduction to the field.

Later, with the introduction of personal computers, the Trace Center developed and carried out a second national workshop series, this time on accessibility and personal computers. The purpose of this second series of workshops was twofold. The first objective was to introduce clinicians and teachers to personal computers, overcome their fear and awe of the machines, and help them understand their potential usefulness both as assistive technologies and as general classroom tools that could help level the playing field for people with disabilities. The second objective was to introduce them to strategies for providing full access to computers for individuals with disabilities. The workshops served not only as the first introduction to accessibility strategies but, for many, it was their first introduction to personal computers as well.

3.4 Nonvocal Communication Techniques and Aids for the Severely Physically Handicapped

The next effort was the publication of the first summative book on this topic. The reception of Trace's presentation at the CEC Conference and its national workshops was noted by Lyle Lloyd, Chair of the Communicative Disorders Department at Purdue University and Communication Series Editor for University Park Press who attended that presentation. At Dr. Lloyd's invitation, the Trace team took the information from the workshop series and combined it with other summative information to create *Nonvocal Communication Techniques and Aids for the Severely Physically Handicapped* (1976).[2] This book covered communication boards, symbol systems, communication development, and the different techniques and aids for communication. It traced the roots of communication aids back to the 1950s in Europe and provided a catalog and description of their evolution up through the state of the art at that time. This book also laid out for the first time most of the basic terminology used today in augmentative communication. To further enhance the

[1] Vicker, B. (Ed.). (1974). *Nonoral Communication System Project: 1964–1973.* University Hospital School, University of Iowa.

[2] Vanderheiden, G. C. and Grilley, K. (1976). *Non-Vocal Communication Techniques and Aids for the Severely Physically Handicapped.* Baltimore: University Park Press.

dissemination of the information on these topics, the Trace Center (with the reluctant agreement of the publisher) published the book without a formal copyright statement (which then allowed anyone to use the content of the book in any way they wished without seeking permission from the authors or publisher). The book went on for eight reprintings over the next decade until the Trace Center finally refused permission to reprint due to the age of the book. Instead, the Trace Center co-authored two summative chapters (1 and 3) in the American Speech and Hearing Association's book, *Augmentative Communication* which came out in 1986 and served as the new reference text for the field. The Center then referred everyone to this book or, for information on currently available products, Trace's *ResourceBooks*.

3.5 ResourceBooks

This work of aggregating information continued and was expanded with the Trace Center *ResourceBooks*. This series of books cataloged all of the communication, computer access, and general interface controls that were available, as well as cataloging all of the written documents and "fugitive literature" the Center's team had been able to find. The *ResourceBooks* were published annually. Each one was about 2-inch thick, with 900 pages cataloging more than 1,500 different devices and including 250 pages of cross-indexes by product name, manufacturer, product type, input/output technique, input/output switch type, and type of computer. There were also 21 pages of references to other resources.

The first *ResourceBook* was funded by United Cerebral Palsy (UCP) Research and Education Foundation and published by University Park Press in 1978. It was, in fact, the first grant from the UCP Foundation for anything other than the prevention of cerebral palsy, and its first non-medical research grant. A side effect of this "ice-breaking" grant was the expansion of the UCP Research Foundation's grant-giving to a broad range of other efforts to assist individuals who already had cerebral palsy rather than focusing only on its prevention (Fig. 3.1).

Trace then issued "update pages" (to replace those in the original binder) until 1987. In 1987, the *ResourceBook* was picked up by College Hill Press and published as a three-volume set covering Communication Aids, Switches and Controls, and Computer Hardware and Software (Fig. 3.2).

The publisher was unable to support continual updating and republishing of the *ResourceBooks* each year, which the Center felt was necessary. Thus, after a couple of years, the Trace Center began to self-publish the *ResourceBooks* with a new comprehensive *ResourceBook* published approximately every year. The three-volume *ResourceBooks* were consolidated into one 2-inch-thick book described previously.[3] During this period

[3] 1991–92 Edition—*Trace ResourceBook*, Trace Center Resource and Publication Service.

Fig. 3.1 Original *ResourceBook* in 3-ring binder—funded by United Cerebral Palsy Research and Education Foundation and published by University Park Press (1978)[4]

Fig. 3.2 Trace *ResourceBooks* from College Hill Press (1987)

before the World Wide Web, the *ResourceBooks* became the "Bible" for the field, as there was no other way for consumers, clinicians, or researchers to keep up with what was available.

3.6 Hyper-ABLEDATA and Co-Net

With the advent of personal computers (but still pre-World Wide Web), the Trace Center moved the *ResourceBooks* into electronic form and created electronic, easy-to-use databases that Trace distributed on CDs (in parallel with the print editions of the *Resource-Books*, since personal computers were still not ubiquitous). The first versions were in HyperCard and ran only on the Mac. The PC version required the development of a special search program (HyperCard had one built-in) and was created later.

[4] Vanderheiden, G. (Ed.) (1978). *Non-Vocal Communication Resource Book*. Baltimore: University Park Press.

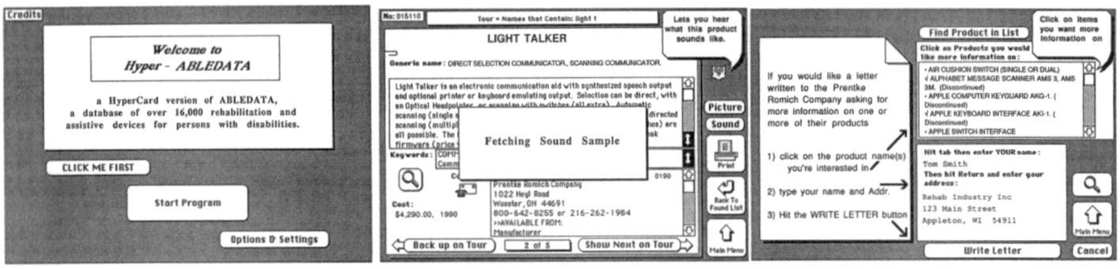

Fig. 3.3 Hyper-ABLEDATA moved the ABLEDATA database into the hands of clinicians for the first time. Previously, one had to call in to get information and was unable to search or explore the database oneself. It also provided features like the ability to see pictures or hear sound samples of products—as well as a feature that would help you write for more information, at a time when this was one's only option for getting detailed information on products. (Full set of screenshots at Trace Archive https://go.umd.edu/trace-archive.)

To create Hyper-ABLEDATA, Trace teamed up with Marian Hall, who had created the ABLEDATA database. (ABLEDATA cataloged all types of assistive technologies, whereas the Trace Center was focused on communication, control, interface, and computer access aids.) ABLEDATA had started off years earlier as a "Rolodex-like" system of cards, each describing a different assistive technology. Users would phone in to ask what types of AT were available to meet their needs. Later it was converted into a computer database, with people continuing to phone in. When Trace teamed up with ABLEDATA, the Trace-collected information was moved into ABLEDATA and both HyperCard and a DOS version of ABLEDATA were created to run on personal computers. These databases (called "Hyper-ABLEDATA" and "DOS ABLEDATA"), along with a service delivery directory and other resources, were combined into a series of Cooperative Network CDs (called "Co-Net" CDs). For 10 years before the Web became widely available, these CDs provided a wealth of easily searchable information for which there was no parallel. To get an idea of the value of this resource, during the period when the information was only available via Hyper-ABLEDATA on the Mac, clinics were known to buy Macintosh computers (costing $2,600, approx. $6,979 in 2021 dollars) just to run the Co-Net CD databases. All versions were distributed at cost from the Trace Center's Reprint Service (Figs. 3.3 and 3.4).

3.7 Moving to the Web

As soon as the World Wide Web came into being, the Trace Center moved all of this information, including all of ABLEDATA, onto the Web where it was made freely available. For a while, however, many clinical settings and other locations did not have access to the Internet and did not know much about the Web. The Trace Center therefore continued the Co-Net CDs until 1998.

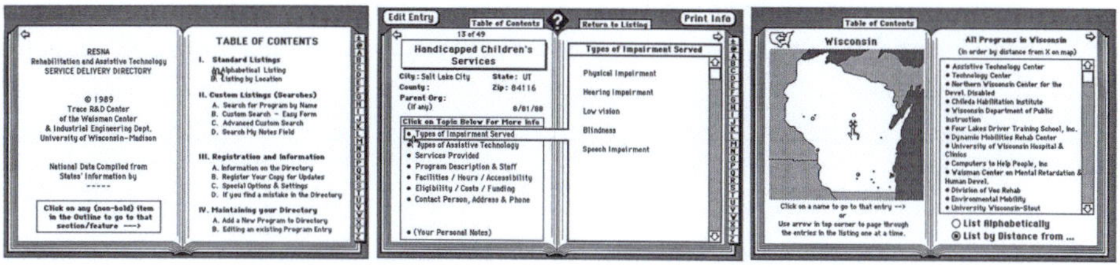

Fig. 3.4 The Trace Service Delivery Directory database provided an easy-to-use interface with unique features like "List programs by distance from." An innovation in these very early days of graphical user interfaces. (Full set of screenshots at Trace Archive https://go.umd.edu/trace-archive.)

To help people who did not have Internet connections learn about the Internet and its benefits, Trace added an extra CD ("A Taste of the Web") to the Co-Net CD case. The "Taste of the Web" CD provided a sampling of all the different types of information available on the Web in a form that could be run from the CD on a computer that was not connected to the Internet—but would give them an experience that was identical to the experience they would have if they were connected (Fig. 3.5).

Fig. 3.5 Co-Net CDs 1989–1998 along with the two bonus "Taste of the Web" CDs included with the last two issues of Co-Net

Today, the Trace Center continues to disseminate information through efforts such as the Unified Listing,[5] the DeveloperSpace,[6] and a new effort to create a global AT resource.

3.8 Tools

In addition to information resources, the Trace Center also worked to create tools for clinicians, consumers, and industry. The Co-Net CDs were one example of information tools for clinicians and users. Another example from the 1980s was OT FACT.

In 1979, AOTA formally recognized the need for a profession-wide document which would help delineate the diverse and numerous functional areas in which occupational therapists evaluate and treat their clients. OT FACT was developed to address this. Working from the AOTA Uniform Terminology document and the Comprehensive Evaluation Checklist, Roger Smith, Associate Director of Trace, developed an OT Evaluation interview and report tool that used trichotomous scales and a hierarchical design to create a simple step-by-step tool that automatically expanded its questions where needed and allowed quick progression where they were not. It then automatically created complete detailed summary reports of the results. In 1991, it was computerized by Trace and released.

In addition to the print and e-document resources, the Trace Center has also released numerous online tools to help researchers, clinicians, industry, and students to understand the full spectrum of disability needs and strategies for addressing them. The first was the Trace Center Ideas Browser. This online design tool was designed to assist product designers in making mass market products across disability accessible. The free online tool provided access to techniques and strategies that are compiled from over 1,000 individual guidelines. This was followed by the Accessibility MasterList and Unified ICT Accessibility Standards Comparison Tool (described later).

[5] Unified Listing https://ul.gpii.net.

[6] DeveloperSpace https://ds.gpii.net.

4 Computer Access (1980–)

With the advent of the personal computer, the Trace Center's primary focus shifted from communication to computer access. At that time, the focus of many working with people with disabilities as an early focus of the field was on creating special programs for personal computers to meet the user's needs, essentially using the computer to create new types of assistive technology. Although using personal computers to create new types of AT was a great idea, the Trace Center team was concerned that not enough attention was being paid to ensuring that people with disabilities would be able to use the standard software being created for personal computers, which they believed would soon be central to education and employment. If people with disabilities could only use special software designed for them but were unable to use the standard software on the computers, they would be at a significant disadvantage as computers were integrated into education, employment, and daily living.

Since most software would be created without people with disabilities in mind, some method for providing "transparent access" was needed. That is, methods were needed where a person could use alternate interfaces (e.g., scanning, encoding, head pointing, special keyboards, etc.) but it would look to the computer and its software like the person was using the standard computer keyboard (and later, mouse). The alternate interfaces would be transparent, or invisible, and all software would work with the alternate interface techniques and aids the people might need to use.

The Trace Center therefore set out to create both "transparent access" hardware, software, and adapters along with the standards needed to allow people to access and control computers "transparently" from their assistive technologies.

G. Vanderheiden et al., *Technology and Disability*, Synthesis Lectures on Technology and Health, https://doi.org/10.1007/978-3-031-09214-5_4

4.1 Transparent Access Software

The Trace Center developed a number of computer access software packages. All of these were released free of charge to the field and/or transferred to and incorporated into assistive technology products from AT vendors or mainstream computer companies.

The first program developed was called Ten Branch[1,2] and was a simple acceleration routine for computers and communication aids. The software used branching techniques to significantly decrease the number of motor actions needed to complete words, sentences, and more. The goal here was not just to provide access to computers, but to ensure that people who had disabilities that would slow their input would have acceleration techniques that would allow them to better compete with their fellow students or employees. Ten Branch was commercially transferred and used in AT company products in the 1980s and beyond.

The second input acceleration program developed around the same time was a program called QuickKeys,[3] and later called SpeedKey.[4] It was an abbreviation expansion algorithm based on Trace's vocabulary studies and computer simulations. This software helped to decrease the gap in performance between users with disabilities and their peers without disabilities while using computers. QuickKeys/SpeedKey was transferred commercially in 1984 and was found (when a user contacted Trace about it) to still be in use 30 years later.

The long-range optical pointer (LROP)[5,6] was a small device about the size of a lipstick that could be worn on the head and used to point out items on a computer screen. Using the computer's CRT retrace, it was possible to control a 3/8th-in diameter spot on the screen that behaved exactly as if it was being projected from the pointer on the person's head to the screen (even though it was being generated on the screen in reaction to signals received from the long-range pointer). With the LROP, the individual could use the spot

---

[1] Kelso, D. P. and Vanderheiden, G. C. (1982). Ten branch abbreviation expansion for the greater efficiency in augmentative communication systems. *Proceedings of the 5th Annual Conference on Rehabilitation Engineering*, 3.

[2] Smith, R. O., Christiaansen, R., Borden, B., Lindberg, D., Gunderson, J., and Vanderheiden, G. (1989). Effectiveness of a writing system using a computerized long-range optical pointer and 10-branch abbreviation expansion. *Journal of Rehabilitation Research and Development*, 26(1), 51–62.

[3] Lee, C. C., Gunderson, J., Vanderheiden, G. C., and Croker, K. (1986) *QuicKey User's Manual.* Trace Research and Development Center Reprint Service, August 1986.

[4] Vanderheiden, G. C. (1984, June). A high-efficiency flexible keyboard input acceleration technique: Speedkey. *Proceedings of the 2nd International Conference on Rehabilitation Engineering*, pp. 353–354.

[5] Vanderheiden, G. C. and Gunderson, J. R. (1983). Direct optical headpointing input to standard computers using a TV screen based keyboard. *Proceedings from Discovery 83: Computers for the Disabled Annual Conference*, pp. 87–91.

[6] Vanderheiden, G. C. (1982). Hybrid optical headpointing techniques. *Proceedings of the 5th Annual Conference on Rehabilitation Engineering*, p. 24.

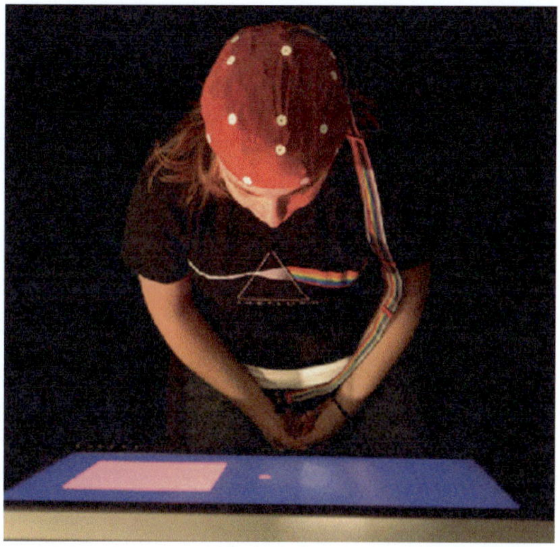

Fig. 4.1 Early BCI research at Trace focusing on human actors and functional use of BCI

on the screen to point to keys or items on the screen with high accuracy and stability. In effect, it gave the person a head-controlled mouse that was rock-solid stable and accurate. The development of the LROP led to the first patent for Jon Gunderson while he was still an undergraduate student.[7]

"One Screen"[8] was a "terminate-and-stay-resident" program that provided an on-screen keyboard combined with transparent access. This program was developed to take full advantage of the long-range optical head pointer. One screen allowed people using head pointing to use the same screen for both input and output rather than needing two separate computers or a computer and an assistive technology, as required with previous systems. This program was also successfully transferred to an AT vendor.

The Trace Center also carried out the first brain control interface (BCI) research that focused on functional use and on human factors of BCI as an interface.[9] The first Tweet done with BCI was sent from the Trace Center BCI Lab by a student to his professor, Dr. Justin Williams, who was having supper at home at the time (Fig. 4.1).

---

[7] Gunderson, J., Kelso, D. P., and Vanderheiden, G. "Long range optical pointing for video screens," U.S. Patent No. 4,591,841 (issued May 27, 1986).

[8] Gunderson, J. and Vanderheiden, G. (1988, June). One screen multiplexed keyboard for transparent access to standard IBM PC software. *Proceedings of the International Conference of the Association for the Advancement of Rehabilitation Technology (ICAART)*. Canada: Montreal.

[9] Felton, E. A., Williams, J. C., Vanderheiden, G., and Radwin, R. G. (2012). Mental workload during brain-computer interface training. *Ergonomics* 55(5), 526–537. https://doi.org/10.1080/00140139.2012.662526.

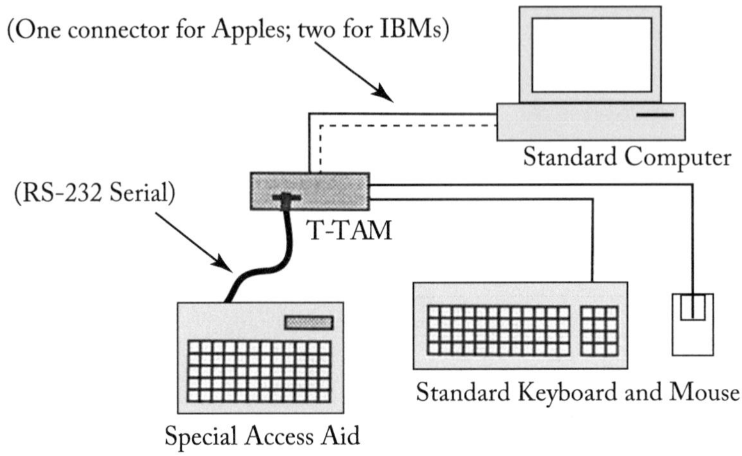

Fig. 4.2 The T-TAM went between the keyboard/mouse and the computer. With an assistive technology plugged into it, the computer could be controlled by the keyboard/mouse or the assistive technology. Both would look identical to the computer

4.2 Keyboard and Mouse Emulating Interfaces

In order to allow individuals to use their communication aids to control computers, the Trace Center developed a keyboard emulator interface (KEI) module. The KEI could be inserted between the keyboard and the computer, allowing communication, control, or other assistive technology to emulate input and control the computer in a way that looked identical to standard keyboard use. With the advent of the mouse, the Trace Center created the Trace Transparent Access Module (T-TAM). The T-TAM could be inserted between the keyboard/mouse and the computer and emulate both (Fig. 4.2). Once developed and proven, both the KEI and T-TAM modules were transferred to multiple assistive technology companies (royalty-free) that manufactured them and made them available.

4.3 Supporting Standards Development

To support this new focus on computer access in a way that could be mass adopted, the Trace Center had to enter into a new series of standards efforts. Although the existing SET and multi-switch standards were sufficient for products such as the adaptive firmware card and special-purpose assistive technologies built out of microcomputers, the Trace Center also needed a number of other interface standards.

The first of these was a standard to support keyboard emulating interfaces. A KEI standard was developed that would allow any assistive technology, communication aid, or even another computer, to be able to use simple serial input commands to emulate every type of input that

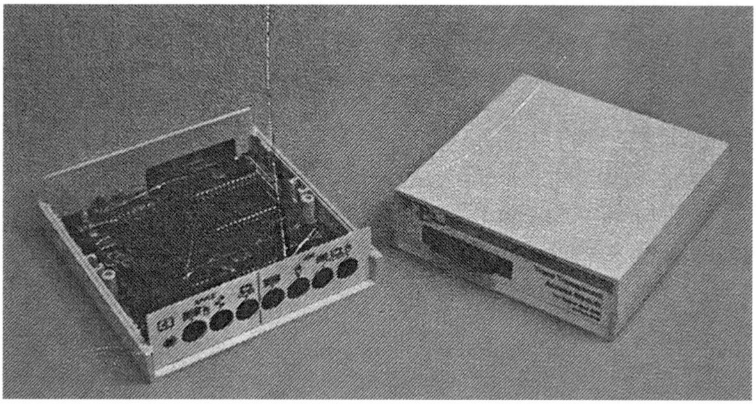

Fig. 4.3 The T-TAM as designed by the Trace Center and directly manufactured by two assistive technology companies—Prentke Romich and Words+

a standard keyboard could, including every key and key combination a regular keyboard user could create. The goal was to ensure that people with disabilities could access and use all of the **standard** software on the computer—just like everyone else. Once created, this standard was used to create the keyboard emulating interfaces described above.

With the advent of the mouse, this interface standard was expanded into a General Input Device Emulating Interface (GIDEI) standard. The GIDEI standard would allow not only complete emulation of all keyboard actions but also all mouse as well as all mouse-and-keyboard combined actions. Again, it had to create all of the commands and protocols to allow all of this control through a standard serial input using ASCII commands. Once developed, the GIDEI standard was used to create the T-TAM described above and shown in Fig. 4.3.

4.4 Software-Based Emulating Interfaces

The advent of Windows and its keyboard interface architecture made possible the creation of a full software implementation of a GIDEI. Trace therefore created a software equivalent for the T-TAM for Windows and called it SerialKeys. SerialKeys took input from the serial port on the computer and then seamlessly fed it into the operating system and its keyboard and mouse architecture in a manner that, to the software running on the computer, it looked exactly the same as if the person were using their standard keyboard and mouse. Trace also created a DOS version that was included in the Trace Center's "AccessDOS" package that was distributed both by Microsoft and IBM. SerialKeys (using the GIDEI standard) was built directly into Windows starting with Windows 95. When the USB replaced the serial port, SerialKeys was retired, as it then became possible to simulate both keyboard and mouse through the USB port.

The Trine system mentioned previously in the chapter on Augmentative Communication used these standards to allow individuals to control any standard personal computer (and any terminals using a standard personal computer keyboard and mouse).

As a result of the KEI and GIDEI standards and the modules implementing them, people who relied on assistive technologies were, for the first time, able to directly control mainstream computers (PC and Mac) and all of their software programs with their AT allowing AT users to employ the special interfaces and acceleration techniques of their AT when using computers.

4.5 Building Access Directly into Mainstream Computers

4.5.1 White House Meetings on Computer Accessibility

Starting in the 1980s, the Trace Center began working with Apple, IBM, Microsoft, Ameritech, Unisys, and other IT companies to build accessibility directly into their mainstream products. These efforts included both developing guidelines for use within each of these different companies and working directly with their teams to build accessibility features into their hardware and software.

The work with mainstream companies on building accessibility into their products began after the White House meetings on computer accessibility. In 1983, Gregg Vanderheiden from Trace and Dr. Frank Bowe, a deaf author, advocate, and Communication and Barriers Specialist with the US Access Board, met with Dr. Larry Scadden who was blind and newly appointed Associate Director for the National Institute on Handicapped Research.[10] They met to discuss developments in computer access—and in particular the move to graphic user interfaces. With the support of Madeleine Will, the new Assistant Secretary for the Office of Special Education and Rehabilitation Services (and wife of political commentator George Will), the group was successful in getting the Reagan White House to invite computer hardware and software companies to a meeting to be held in the Old Executive Office Building of the White House. The premise was that most people (and companies) find it difficult to ignore an invitation to attend an event at the White House, and this was the most likely way to get the computer companies to show up for a meeting on this topic.[11]

[10] The National Institute on Handicapped Research (NIHR) was renamed the National Institute on Disability and Rehabilitation Research (NIDRR) in 1986 and then renamed in 2014 as the National Institute on Disability, Independent Living, and Rehabilitation Research (NIDILRR) when it was moved from the U.S. Dept. of Education to the Administration for Community Living (ACL) in the U.S. Dept. of Health and Human Services.

[11] Scadden, L. (2008). *Surpassing Expectations, My Life without Sight*, Xlibris Corporation, U.S. Available in hardcover, softcover, ebook and Kindle. This autobiography is of interest both for its insights into blindess and as an account from another leader in disability of the events of the time around technology and disability.

THE WHITE HOUSE

WASHINGTON

Meeting
[redacted] on Computers and Handicapped Persons

February 24, 1984
The Indian Treaty Room, Old Executive Office Building

A G E N D A

10:00a - Welcome and Meeting Objectives:

* Mr. James K. Coyne, Special Assistant to the President for Private Sector Initiatives, The White House

* Mrs. Madeleine Will, Assistant Secretary, Office of Special Education and Rehabilitation Services, Department of Education

* Dr. Douglas Fenderson, Director, National Institute of Handicapped Research, OSERS, Department of Education

10:30a - Presentations and Topical Discussion:

* Moderator: Dr. James B. Reswick, Director, Veterans Administration RR&D Evaluation Unit, Washington, D.C.

* "Reasonable Accommodations" by Dr. Frank Bowe, Communication and Barriers Specialist (after March 4th) Architectural and Transportation Compliance Board, Washington.

* "Handicapped People in the Computer Age--Irony or Equality?" by Dr. Lawrence A. Scadden, Program Director for Science and Technology to Aid the Handicapped, National Science Foundation

* "Low and No Cost Modifications to Standard Hard and Soft Ware to Facilitate Use by Handicapped--and Normal--Users" by Dr. Gregg C. Vanderheiden, Director, Trace Center, Madison, Wisc.

12:00n - Luncheon Will Be Served in The Indian Treaty Room.

1:30p - General Discussion and Next Step Actions:

* Feasible Cost/Effective Strategies

* Persons and Places to Implement Strategies

* Follow-on Workshop for Implementors, Facilitators, and Users

3:30p - Adjournment

Fig. 4.4 Agenda of the meeting at the White House OEOB in February 1984. Gregg Vanderheiden was listed as Dr. Vanderheiden even though he did not complete his Ph.D. until later that year[12]

On February 24, 1984, the meeting was held in the Indian Treaty Room in the Old Executive Office Building located immediately to the west of the White House's West Wing. Only five companies sent senior officials: Apple, AT&T, Hewlett-Packard, IBM, and Tandy Radio Shack. Several other people attended the meeting, including some key individuals from the disability advocacy community and, for a time that afternoon, James Coyne, a senior advisor to President Reagan (Fig. 4.4).

[12] https://go.umd.edu/1984white-house-agenda.

Dr. Larry Scadden detailed the needs of individuals who are blind; Dr. Frank Bowe spoke on the needs of individuals who are deaf; and Gregg Vanderheiden spoke on the needs of people across disabilities and described strategies for making computers accessible without increasing manufacturing costs.

Although only five companies attended, they were key companies—and the presenters were successful in making their case. Company officials expressed genuine surprise at the information presented, saying they had not realized how important computer usage was for people with disabilities, nor that there were affordable things they could do to help. They asked for more information about disabilities, existing barriers, and the types, scope, and nature of the solution strategies being presented. A working task force was called for that would develop a white paper addressing these issues and describing practical strategies for addressing them. At the conclusion of the meeting, the companies committed to a second meeting asking for more specific and detailed information on what they could do to make their products more accessible.

The second meeting, formally called "Technical Meeting of the NIHR-White House Committee for Equal Access to Standard Computers and Computer Systems," was held on October 25, 1985, in the Rayburn House Office Building on Capitol Hill. In preparation for this meeting, the Trace Center spearheaded the creation of what was to be the first set of computer accessibility guidelines.[13] These guidelines were used in the meeting and formed the basis for the development of a string of later accessibility guidelines for computers and software. After the meeting, development work commenced at the Trace Center—and later at Apple, Microsoft, and IBM—on different extensions or modifications to PC operating systems to make PCs more accessible.

4.5.2 Trace Developed Modifications for DOS, Windows, and Mac Operating Systems

Previously, Trace had created a program called *1-finger* that allowed individuals using DOS computers to type with a single finger or head stick. Once it was activated by pressing the shift key five times in a row, the *1-finger* program (later called StickyKeys), would cause all of the modifier keys (e.g., Shift, Alt, Control; keys that only function in combination with other keys) to become "sticky." If a modifier key was pressed, it would stay pressed (logically) until the next key was pressed. Pressing any modifier key twice would lock the key so that multiple modified keys could be typed. The modifier key would stay down until another tap released it. A good example of the usage of StickyKeys is one-handed typing of @ in an email address by first pressing the shift key (a modifier

[13] Vanderheiden, G. C., Lee, C. C., and Scadden, L. A. (1987) Features to increase the accessibility of computers by persons with disabilities: Report from the Industry/Government Task Force. *Proceedings of the 10th Annual Conference on Rehabilitation Technology*, San Jose, California, June 1987.

key) and then the "2" key, which produces the @ symbol. The shift key automatically disengages once the "2" key is pressed.

With the advent of the Macintosh computer and the mouse, the Trace Center began work on a feature called MouseKeys. This feature allowed individuals who could only use a keyboard, but not a mouse, to be able to control a "virtual mouse" pointer and buttons using only the keys on the keyboard. Individuals with tremors or those with physical disabilities who typed with a headstick or mouthstick, for example, benefitted from MouseKeys. (As it turned out, it was also very useful to graphic artists or others who wanted the greater single-pixel precision of movement that MouseKeys provided.)

With the advent of Microsoft Windows, Trace created implementations of StickyKeys and MouseKeys for Windows, as well as other access features, and collected them into an **Access Pack for Windows**. While the exact order of the development of the different features and the exact release dates for each feature are lost to time, the features in the final Access Pack (and Access DOS, when it was later released) are summarized in Table 4.1. The incorporation of the features into different mainstream computer operating systems[14,15,16,17] is outlined in Table 4.2.

4.5.3 Progress Within the Computer Companies

As noted above, at the October 25, 1985, "Technical Meeting of the NIHR-White House Committee for Equal Access to Standard Computers and Computer Systems," the guidelines were presented, and commitment was made by the companies in attendance to work on accessibility in their companies. (N.B. At this time, there were no laws or regulations specific to computers and software—so all of the commitments and actions at this time were voluntary.)

[14] Lee, C. C. and Vanderheiden, G. C. (1988, June). Accessibility of OS/2 for individuals with movement impairments: Strategies for the implementation of 1-Finger, Mousekeys, and Software Keyboard Emulating Interfaces using device drivers and monitors. *Proceedings of the International Conference of the Association for the Advancement of Rehabilitation Technology (ICAART)*. Canada: Montreal.

[15] Lee, C. C. and Vanderheiden, G. C. (1988) Accessibility of OS/2 for individuals with movement impairments: Strategies for the implementation of 1-finger, mousekeys, and software keyboard emulating interfaces using device drivers and monitors. *Proceedings of the International Conference of the Association for the Advancement of Rehabilitation Technology*, Montreal, Canada, June 1988.

[16] Accessibility and operating systems: https://cs.stanford.edu/people/eroberts/courses/soco/projects/2005-06/accessibility/oscompare.html.

[17] https://opensource.com/life/15/8/accessibility-linux-blind-disabled.

Table 4.1 Operating system access features developed by the Trace Center

Feature	Description
StickyKeys	Allows individuals who have one hand, or use a head stick or hand brace, to press modifier keys sequentially with themselves and other keys rather than needing to be pressed simultaneously
MouseKeys	Allows the "mouse cursor" on screen to be controlled from the keyboard for individuals who cannot physically operate a mouse
SlowKeys	Allows keyboards to be used by individuals with choretic or other movements that cause them to strike unwanted keys on their way to the desired key
BounceKeys	Allows individuals with tremor to be able to use keyboards without getting double key strikes when pressing or releasing a key
RepeatKeys	Extends the key repeat rate and delay by 2–3 times normal
ToggleKeys	Provides an auditory cue as to the status of the locking keys on a keyboard for individuals who cannot easily see the visual indicators on the keyboard (the only way to determine locking key status until recently)
SoundSentry	Monitored the "speaker" bit in early hardware systems and provides a visual indication of sounds
ShowSounds	Created a flag to be read by the OS and apps to indicate that a visual equivalent of information presented via sounds and speech should be provided
SerialKeys	Allows alternate devices to be connected to a computer's serial port and yet appear to be the standard keyboard and mouse. Individuals who cannot operate the standard keyboard and mouse can then use special communication and interface aids to create "keystrokes" and "mouse movements" that are treated as standard input by application programs

After the meeting, Microsoft increased its collaborations with the Trace Center to create new features for the Access Pack, coordinated by and through Windows product manager Greg Lowney (who later became head of accessibility for Microsoft). Microsoft continued to include the Trace Access Pack as part of its "supplemental software drivers" discs and later distributed the Trace-developed Software and Hardware Accessibility Guidelines to all of their Windows developers inside and outside the company. Microsoft also commissioned the Trace Center to create content to go into the Intel-Microsoft computer design book, which was the bible for creating Windows-compatible computers in those days.

However, it was Apple that made the first move to build accessibility directly into its operating system. Alan Brightman, Ph.D., who became head of the special-education office at Apple after 18 years of teaching students with disabilities, attended the October 1985 White House technical meeting. Upon his return to Cupertino, he set up a workshop at Apple, inviting a variety of people who had been working on accessibility around the country, including Gregg Vanderheiden, the Director of the Trace Center.

Table 4.2 Computers and Operating systems that incorporated Trace Access Features. "/" indicates a similar feature or capability

Feature	Apple IIe (1987)	Apple IIgs (1986)	macOS (1987 onward)	Trace Access Packs for Windows	Trace AccessDOS (developed for IBM)	Windows 95 (1995 onward)	OS/2	X-Windows	Linux (Gnome)
StickyKeys	X	X	X	X	X	X	X	X	X
MouseKeys		X	X	X	X	X	X	X	X
SlowKeys			X	X	X	X	X	X	X
BounceKeys				X	X	X	X	X	X
RepeatKeys			/	X	X	X	X	X	X
ToggleKeys				X	X	X	X	X	X
SoundSentry			/	X	/	X	/		
ShowSounds				X	X	X	X		
SerialKeys				X	X	X			

An account by the Trace Center Director of that visit and events leading to Apple's efforts to build accessibility into their computers is included in the following.

"Apple CEO John Sculley and the head of product development Randy Battat were both invited to attend the luncheon at a full day workshop at Apple in April 1986 arranged by Dr. Alan Brightman. I was asked to do an impromptu presentation at the lunch summarizing the issues and providing examples of strategies that could be easily implemented in Apple's hardware and software to make them more accessible. A series of excellent posters, produced by Alan and highlighting people with disabilities, encircled the room. The posters provided a perfect backdrop to the presentation, and I was able to refer to the images as I spoke, making the concepts real and addressing issues of real people. At the end of the lunch Randy Battat and John Sculley consulted briefly. John Sculley thanked me on his way out of the room, and Randy Battat asked that I come back in three weeks and meet with him and his team over a three-day period.

"When I returned three weeks later, I was invited by Mr. Battat to come back every three months to spend a week with the Apple engineers, advising them on how to make Apple's products accessible. When asked how I would go about making Apple's products accessible, his response was, "That's what I'm hiring you for." I was provided with a top-secret document listing all of the products under development, their features, market position, costs, risks, and so forth. I was not to disclose the existence of the report that I was given, since its existence was also controlled within the company. I was told I had permission to go anywhere and speak to anyone at Apple about any product. The only place that was off-limits was a special building where work was being done on a Cray computer.

"On that first trip, Mr. Battat had arranged meetings for me with every product group's design team, and Randy or his designee showed up to assure each team that I did in fact have blanket permission to learn everything about their products. At one point Randy joked, "Gregg has permission to know things that I don't!" (Not true but it made the point) (Fig. 4.5).

"I was also given 40 KB worth of space on the system disk to put any modifications or extensions to the operating system that might be developed. Ironically, this disk space was more impressive and did more to establish my credibility with the engineers than my carte blanche access did.

"As I visited each team, I made a point of complimenting them on anything they had accidentally done correctly (both to give them credit and to make sure that those design features didn't disappear because their accessibility aspect was not understood). As I reviewed each product, I also made small suggestions, especially around physical design, to make their products more accessible. Interestingly, in this visit and every visit that I paid to a mainstream company in the decades that followed, I was always asked about other user interface problems for their mainstream users and was able to make suggestions or to solve problems they had been having. Often the ideas occurred to me because I was thinking about how to make the product more accessible and, when posed with the problem faced by mainstream users, it was the same or a derivative of the same idea I was pondering for a person with a disability.

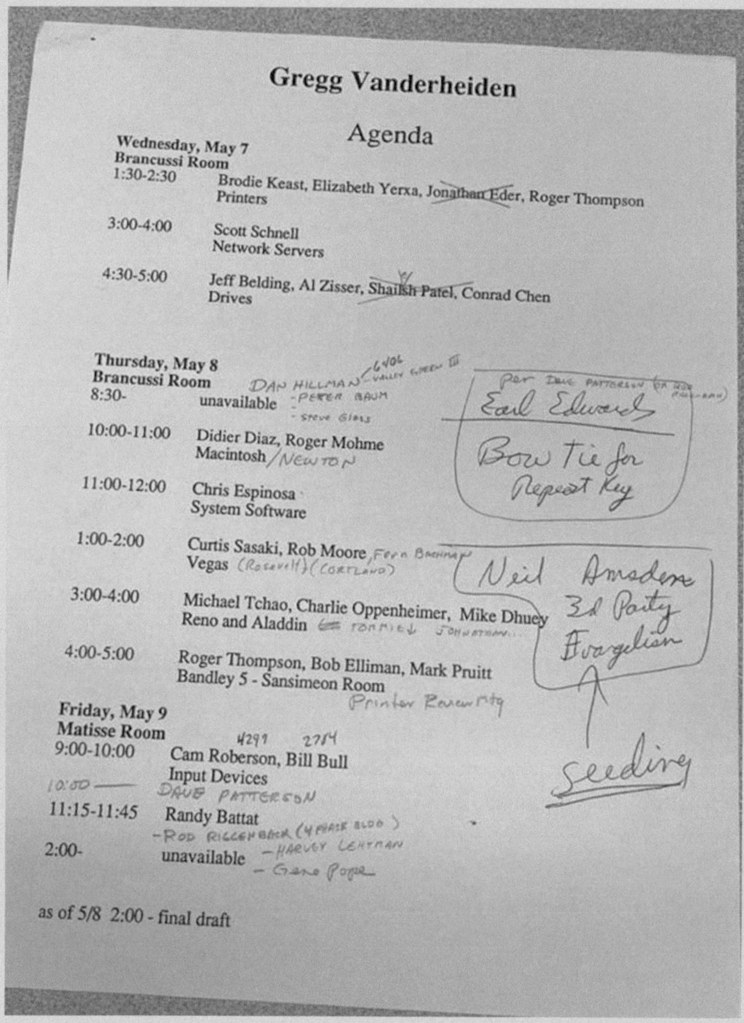

Gregg Vanderheiden

Agenda

Wednesday, May 7
Brancussi Room

1:30-2:30	Brodie Keast, Elizabeth Yerxa, Jonathan Eder, Roger Thompson Printers
3:00-4:00	Scott Schnell Network Servers
4:30-5:00	Jeff Belding, Al Zisser, Shailsh Patel, Conrad Chen Drives

Thursday, May 8
Brancussi Room

8:30-	unavailable
10:00-11:00	Didier Diaz, Roger Mohme Macintosh
11:00-12:00	Chris Espinosa System Software
1:00-2:00	Curtis Sasaki, Rob Moore Vegas
3:00-4:00	Michael Tchao, Charlie Oppenheimer, Mike Dhuey Reno and Aladdin
4:00-5:00	Roger Thompson, Bob Elliman, Mark Pruitt Bandley 5 - Sansimeon Room

Friday, May 9
Matisse Room

9:00-10:00	Cam Roberson, Bill Bull Input Devices
11:15-11:45	Randy Battat
2:00-	unavailable

as of 5/8 2:00 - final draft

Earl Edwards
Bow Tie for Repeat Key
Neil Amsden 3d Party Evangelism
Printer Review mtg
Seeding

Fig. 4.5 Picture of the agenda for Gregg on the first visit to Apple, May 7–9, 1986

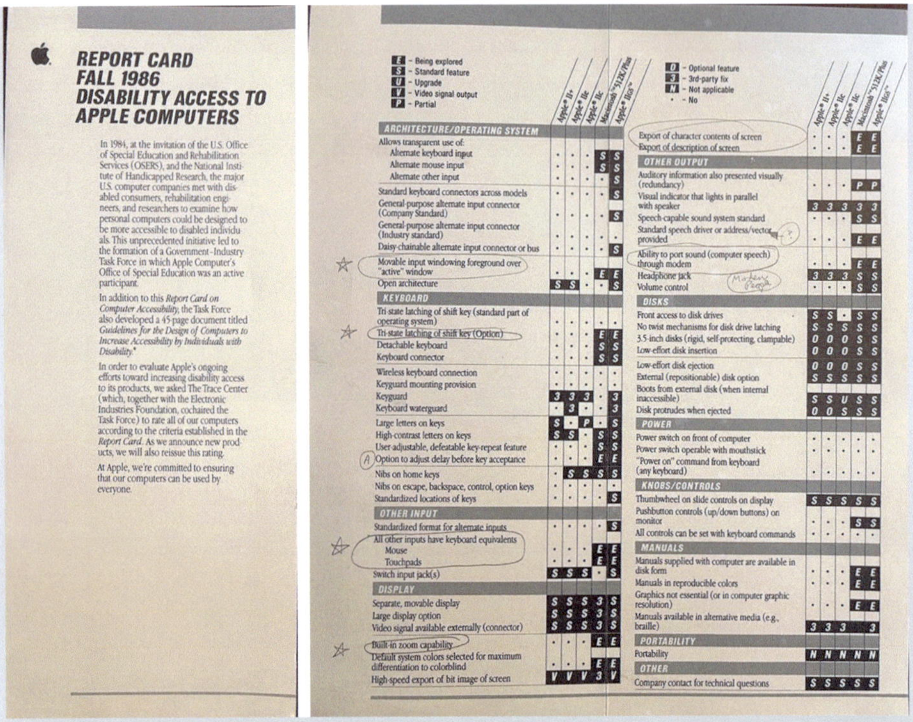

REPORT CARD
FALL 1986
DISABILITY ACCESS TO APPLE COMPUTERS

In 1984, at the invitation of the U.S. Office of Special Education and Rehabilitation Services (OSERS), and the National Institute of Handicapped Research, the major U.S. computer companies met with disabled consumers, rehabilitation engineers, and researchers to examine how personal computers could be designed to be more accessible to disabled individuals. This unprecedented initiative led to the formation of a Government-Industry Task Force in which Apple Computer's Office of Special Education was an active participant.

In addition to this *Report Card on Computer Accessibility*, the Task Force also developed a 45-page document titled *Guidelines for the Design of Computers to Increase Accessibility by Individuals with Disability*.*

In order to evaluate Apple's ongoing efforts toward increasing disability access to its products, we asked The Trace Center (which, together with the Electronic Industries Foundation, cochaired the Task Force) to rate all of our computers according to the criteria established in the *Report Card*. As we announce new products, we will also reissue this rating.

At Apple, we're committed to ensuring that our computers can be used by everyone.

E - Being explored
S - Standard feature
U - Upgrade
V - Video signal output
P - Partial
O - Optional feature
3 - 3rd-party fix
N - Not applicable
· - No

	Apple® II+	Apple® IIe	Apple® IIc	Macintosh™ 512K/Plus	Apple® IIGS™
ARCHITECTURE/OPERATING SYSTEM					
Allows transparent use of:					
Alternate keyboard input	·	·	·	S	S
Alternate mouse input	·	·	·	S	S
Alternate other input	·	·	·	·	S
Standard keyboard connectors across models	·	·	·	·	S
General-purpose alternate input connector (Company Standard)	·	·	·	·	S
General-purpose alternate input connector (Industry standard)	·	·	·	·	·
Daisy-chainable alternate input connector or bus	·	·	·	·	S
Movable input windowing foreground over "active" window	·	·	·	E	E
Open architecture	S	S	·	·	S
KEYBOARD					
Tri-state latching of shift key (standard part of operating system)	·	·	·	·	·
Tri-state latching of shift key (Option)	·	·	·	E	E
Detachable keyboard	·	·	·	S	S
Keyboard connector	·	·	·	S	S
Wireless keyboard connection	·	·	·	·	·
Keyguard mounting provision	·	·	·	·	·
Keyguard	3	3	3	·	3
Keyboard waterguard	·	3	·	·	3
Large letters on keys	S	·	P	·	S
High-contrast letters on keys	S	S	·	S	S
User-adjustable, defeatable key-repeat feature	·	·	·	S	S
Option to adjust delay before key acceptance	·	·	·	E	E
Nibs on home keys	·	S	S	S	S
Nibs on escape, backspace, control, option keys	·	·	·	·	·
Standardized locations of keys	·	·	·	·	S
OTHER INPUT					
Standardized format for alternate inputs	·	·	·	·	S
All other inputs have keyboard equivalents					
Mouse	·	·	·	E	E
Touchpads	·	·	·	E	E
Switch input jack(s)	S	S	S	·	S
DISPLAY					
Separate, movable display	S	S	S	3	S
Large display option	S	S	S	3	S
Video signal available externally (connector)	S	S	S	3	S
Built-in zoom capability	·	·	·	E	E
Default system colors selected for maximum differentiation to colorblind	·	·	·	E	E
High-speed export of bit image of screen	V	V	V	3	V

	Apple® II+	Apple® IIe	Apple® IIc	Macintosh™ 512K/Plus	Apple® IIGS™
Export of character contents of screen	·	·	·	E	E
Export of description of screen	·	·	·	E	E
OTHER OUTPUT					
Auditory information also presented visually (redundancy)	·	·	·	P	P
Visual indicator that lights in parallel with speaker	3	3	3	3	3
Speech-capable sound system standard	·	·	·	S	S
Standard speech driver or address/vector provided	·	·	·	E	E
Ability to port sound (computer speech) through modem	·	·	·	E	E
Headphone jack	3	3	3	S	S
Volume control	·	·	·	S	S
DISKS					
Front access to disk drives	S	S	·	S	S
No twist mechanisms for disk drive latching	S	S	S	S	S
3.5-inch disks (rigid, self-protecting, clampable)	O	O	O	S	S
Low-effort disk insertion	O	O	O	S	S
Low-effort disk ejection	O	O	O	S	S
External (repositionable) disk option	S	S	S	S	S
Boots from external disk (when internal inaccessible)	S	S	U	S	S
Disk protrudes when ejected	O	O	S	S	S
POWER					
Power switch on front of computer	·	·	·	·	·
Power switch operable with mouthstick	·	·	·	·	·
"Power on" command from keyboard (any keyboard)	·	·	·	·	·
KNOBS/CONTROLS					
Thumbwheel on slide controls on display	S	S	S	S	S
Pushbutton controls (up/down buttons) on monitor	·	·	·	S	S
All controls can be set with keyboard commands	·	·	·	·	·
MANUALS					
Manuals supplied with computer are available in disk form	·	·	·	E	E
Manuals in reproducible colors	·	·	·	E	E
Graphics not essential (or in computer graphic resolution)	·	·	·	E	E
Manuals available in alternative media (e.g., braille)	3	3	3		3
PORTABILITY					
Portability	N	N	N	N	N
OTHER					
Company contact for technical questions	S	S	S	S	S

Fig. 4.6 Apple Accessibility Report Card progressed and became a point of pride—and was published for the public (on released products only)

"On subsequent visits, I was left on my own to set up appointments with the different product groups. Each time I returned I would be given a fresh copy of the confidential report (which was numbered and had to be destroyed when I was finished with it). My work with Apple was somewhat complicated by the fact that each time I arrived all of the products had different codenames, and often products disappeared, mutated, or were combined, meaning that each visit required somewhat of a reboot.

"Early in the process I created a report card that listed items that had been done and others that were recommended. In the beginning the report card had about half a dozen items on it, three of which were checked (because they had already been done accidentally before I arrived). Over time the number of items that were checked off increased each time—as did the number of unchecked items. The result was always a scorecard with an increasing record of success and new challenges. After a while—it became a point of pride and they published it (Fig. 4.6).

Space does not allow for the many stories that came from these visits, but a few are instructive.

"On one trip, I was pulled aside by Ed Tecot who was working on the keyboard drivers for the Macintosh. He had implemented the StickyKeys feature one Saturday afternoon, but was afraid to tell anyone for fear that he would be fired, dropped from the team, or something similar. When I asked him why, he said it was because it was number seven on the priority list and they were under strict orders to never work on anything that was below their top three priorities. Noting that he said it was done on a Saturday afternoon I asked if he was required to work on Saturdays. He said no, but if you do work on Saturdays you must work on the top priority items on your list. Between that visit and the next I worked out a strategy for breaking it to the administration, but he informed me on my arrival that that was not necessary. The topic had come up at a meeting about a month after he had done the work, and he admitted he had already done it. Probably because it was a month after the fact (so immediate implications were lost to time) he said it went unremarked on other than a look, and the feature was now on its way into the build for the next release.

"I was at work one day at Trace when I received a phone call. The caller identified himself as Chris Espinosa, the VP of software at Apple. I had met Chris on my original visit and in passing later, but did not otherwise interface much with him, so I was surprised at the phone call. He asked me how to turn on that feature where you could operate the computer with one hand. I told him "Just look in the instruction book. It is easy to find because it is in large print."

"He replied, "This is software engineering. We don't have instruction books." I advised him to tap on the Shift key five times and look for the icon. He tried it, it worked, and he proceeded to thank me. But before he hung up, I asked why he was so interested. He told me that the previous week he had fallen while traveling in Paris and smashed his elbow. One arm was completely out of commission and he was unable to get his work done. Ironically—or just good karma, this incident occurred just about one month after the StickyKeys feature debuted for the first time in the latest Macintosh OS release.

"On another visit, I was told that the person working on the Apple IIe wanted to meet with me. When we met up, he excitedly told me about a visit he had made to a Macintosh users group. With great excitement he told me that one of the members of the group was an individual with disabilities who was a programmer. I mentioned that that was quite common. He replied, "But you don't understand. He wasn't a user, he was a programmer." To which I responded, "Yes…" He went on, "The other programmers come to him for advice on how to program." And I said, "Yes, there are people with disabilities in leadership roles in IT in different companies. There is a blind individual in charge of an entire programming group at IBM."

"He remarked that this encounter had really changed his whole perception of people with disabilities and computers. On a subsequent visit, he announced that he had incorporated StickyKeys into the Apple IIe. I told him that such a change wouldn't work because the software at the time would read the keyboard keystrokes directly from the hardware keyboard encoder on the Apple IIe. He said he knew, and then just stared at me with a smile. He had actually had the keyboard encoder redesigned so that it was possible to inject keystrokes into the keyboard encoder that would then come back out of the keyboard encoder as if they had been typed on the physical keyboard. Such was the impact of his discovery that people with disabilities were colleagues and not just people to help. He was always a strong supporter in the company for accessibility, but that discovery led him to actually change the silicon in the computer to make it more accessible."

Apple was the first company to build accessibility directly into its operating system and distribute it to all of its customers. Further, it did so across all of its computers from the Apple IIe through the Macintosh. These features have continued and been expanded on over the years beyond anyone's hopes or imagination. During a change in leadership, there was a period where the accessibility features regressed briefly, but they then came back and are now legendary in their scope and implementation both in the Mac and now in iOS.

In parallel with this work, the Trace Center also worked with Microsoft, IBM, and other companies. As noted above, the work at Microsoft was led by Greg Lowney. Greg began working with Trace on accessibility features while he was still a Windows manager. He was enormously enthusiastic and helpful to Trace at every stage of the process. Lowney soon became known at Microsoft as the person with the disability access answers, and the Trace Center collaborated by providing any answers or information requested of him by Microsoft.

Lowney arranged that each of the Trace-developed access features, and the Access Pack when it became available, were included on the Windows Supplemental Drivers Disk. Lowney also distributed Trace's accessibility guidelines to all of the Windows developers and included the Trace Center's contact information in the back of the Microsoft software manuals. Unfortunately (for those who answered Trace's phones), the Trace Center's contact information was initially presented more prominently in Microsoft's manuals than Microsoft's own contact numbers. As a result, Trace received an inordinate number of technical support calls intended for Microsoft on non-disability-related issues until this was resolved with the next year's manual.

Based on his knowledge and work in the area, Greg Lowney was later named the first director of accessibility at Microsoft. In that position, he oversaw the development of Windows-specific accessibility guidelines and also contributed extensively and productively to the accessibility guidelines of the Trace Center, the Access Board, the Human Factors and Ergonomics Society, the ISO standards, the Web standards, and more. In 1995, he brokered the incorporation of the Access Pack features directly into Windows 95. Nine of the first ten accessibility features in Windows were licensed royalty-free from the Trace Center for incorporation into Windows 95.

Trace worked with IBM starting in 1984, just after the White House meetings. Trace worked on both their hardware and software designs. Specific hardware design changes that resulted from these consultations included disk drive eject designs, power switches, and function key arrangements on laptops to increase their tactile discernability by individuals who are blind. In 1987, Trace also worked with them on their internal accessibility guidelines for hardware and software products.

4.5.4 AccessDOS

In 1990, IBM approached the Trace Center about creating a package of access features for its IBM DOS operating system. At first, there was a problem because Trace had a policy of not designing accessibility features for any one company in a way that precluded their free release to other companies. On the other hand, IBM had a rule, after its experience of losing control of MS-DOS to Microsoft, that it would never commission the development of software without complete ownership and distribution control. Eventually, an arrangement was worked out whereby IBM would license, in advance, the use of a product the Trace Center would develop and call AccessDOS. Trace would use the advance royalty payment to develop the software which IBM would then be free to use and sell. The result was AccessDOS, which included all of the features in the current Access Pack for Windows plus some additions (that were then migrated back to the Access Pack as well). The product was completed, tested by IBM, and released as an IBM product in its product catalog in 1991. It is notable that, other than a code review and a few minor tweaks to better integrate with DOS, the AccessDOS code written by the Trace Center was shipped directly as the IBM product. Trace was told that this was the only IBM product that was ever shipped using the code written outside of the group and not rewritten inside the organization (Fig. 4.7).

Interestingly, a problem arose in that, although AccessDOS was free to consumers, the IBM purchasing system required the entry of a credit card number before one could complete the "purchase." Trace staff spent many hours with consumers explaining to them that it was safe and that they would not be charged despite the necessity of providing a credit card in order to get a copy of AccessDOS. For consumers that did not have a credit card, however, this was not sufficient and proved a difficult problem to solve.

4.5.5 Work With Other Computer Companies

The Trace Center also worked with other companies on the development of their products and the training of their employees. One of the most effective strategies when doing a workshop for a company (or even just a consultation visit) was to begin by listing all of the concerns that they might have about allocating staff time to design accessibility into

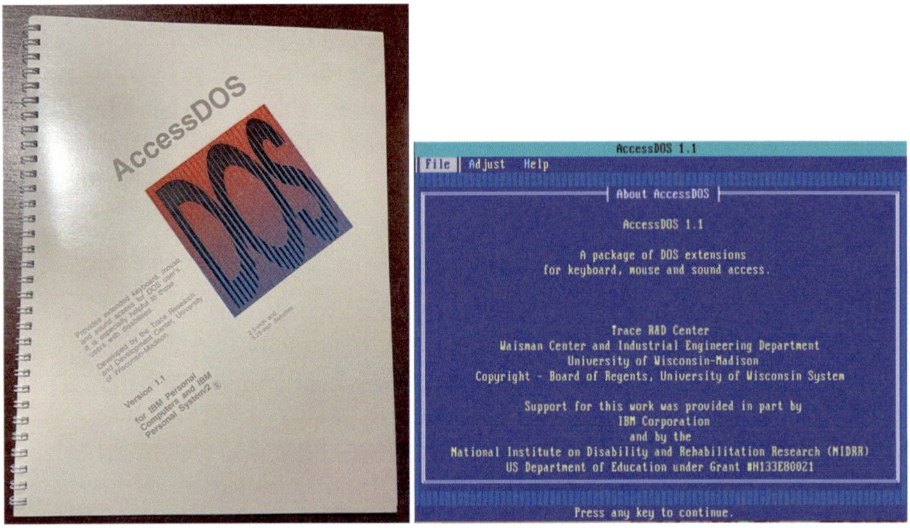

Fig. 4.7 AccessDOS package of accessibility features as released by IBM as an IBM product

their products—everything from delaying product launch to constraining design options to increasing technical support calls. These issues were not presented as excuses made by industry for inaction, but rather as real and genuine problems and constraints faced by industry that we recognized. Enough detail about each issue was included in order to demonstrate Trace's understanding. The workshop or visit could then move on to present ways to increase accessibility while still addressing these valid concerns. In addition, the presentations would include all the benefits of incorporating accessibility—not only for people with disabilities but also for mainstream users.

After one such workshop, Trace was told that the design team was taken completely by surprise and that the introduction showing that Trace knew, understood, and respected the constraints they faced had likely eliminated a full morning that they thought they would have to spend "educating" us on the realities in their company and why they wouldn't be able to do what we would be suggesting they do. While everyone didn't necessarily agree that creating accessible products was easy, the design team lead said the team was much more open to listening, since it was clear that Trace had been listening to industry.

Another instructive encounter happened in a visit that several Trace team members had with a major IT company executive. According to Trace Center Director Gregg Vanderheiden:

> One of the most striking conversations from this period was an interview we had with an executive of a major IT corporation. During a meeting in his office, we explained the importance of accessibility, that people with disabilities needed to use their products like everyone else, and described some of the problems they faced. We also laid out some realistic strategies for

making their company's products more accessible. At the end of the presentation, as we were about to leave, he asked "Why don't you just pass a law that says we have to make our products accessible?" We sat there somewhat stunned for a while, not expecting this from an IT company executive. When we expressed our surprise and asked him why he would say that, he replied:

When you first set up this appointment, I didn't see a way to get out of it. I thought that I would listen politely and then, after the meeting, I would drop whatever you gave me in my circular file as I went back to my desk. But you've changed my mind completely. First of all, I never thought about the fact that people with disabilities would use our products. Second, it never occurred to me that somebody who was blind would have problems that were different than somebody who is deaf. It's not because that's not immediately logical and obvious, it's because I never thought about people with disabilities at all. But you've convinced me, and when I get back to my office I'm not going to 'file your materials circular'. I'm going to put them on the corner of my desk. However, they will be on my desk alongside a number of other piles, some of which are smoking and some of which are on fire. I will put out the ones that are on fire, and then try to see how many of the smoking ones I can extinguish. In the midst of this, my secretary will walk in and give me several more stacks, at least one of which will be smoking and probably one of which will be on fire. In three months, I will be still putting out fires and attacking smoking stacks. Yours will still be on the corner of my desk sitting there. If you passed a law that said that our company had to make its products accessible, that stack would begin to smoke.

4.5.6 Spreading the Word

In addition to developing software, strategies, and guidelines for accessibility, and working with companies as requested to incorporate them, the Trace Center also spent a considerable amount of time just trying to spread the word, within the accessibility field, to industry, and to the general public (Fig. 4.8).

In September 1982, the Trace Center authored an article in a special issue of Byte magazine summarizing the approaches to computer accessibility and making the case for it.[18] The Center also worked with Paul Schwejda to document his amazing adaptive firmware card that to this day is one of the most amazing feats of software and hardware engineering around accessibility.[19] Trace documented it both to help spread information about the existence of the card from a little two-person organization—and to document the strategies used so that others would be inspired to create accessibility solutions. The adaptive firmware card, once inserted into an Apple IIe, was able to allow transparent access to mainstream software and games running on the computer, adapt games' speed

[18] Vanderheiden, G. (1982). Computers can play a dual role for disabled individuals. *Byte*, 7(9), 136–62. http://archive.org/stream/byte-magazine-1982-09-rescan/1982_09_BYTE_07-09_Computers_and_the_Disabled#page/n137/mode/2up.

[19] Schwejda, P. and Vanderheiden, G. (1982). Adaptive-firmware card for the Apple II [input for physically disabled]. *Byte*, 7(9), 276–314. http://archive.org/stream/byte-magazine-1982-09-rescan/1982_09_BYTE_07-09_Computers_and_the_Disabled#page/n277/mode/2up.

Fig. 4.8 Special issue of *Byte* magazine in 1982 dedicated to "Computers and the Disabled". (Byte Vol 7 Issue 9)

and input modes, provide multiple adaptive input techniques from keyboard through scanning in Morse code, and more. This was all done by a physics major who was driving a cab and had to teach himself both programming and digital design in order to create it. He worked on the development of the card and programs with Judy McDonald, a speech therapist he met at a coffee shop who inspired his efforts.

A second major effort to spread the word was the **Trace Center National Workshop Series on Computer Access**. Based on the success of the national workshop series on augmentative communication, which was able to pay for itself, the Trace Center launched the first national series of workshops on access to computers on a self-funding, cost-recovery basis. This series provided clinicians, special educators, researchers, and others across the United States with their first training in computers and disabilities. More than half of the people attending the workshops had never used a computer before and/or had no idea how computers worked or how to program. The series was a success, covered its costs, and provided a first introduction for many people to computer accessibility (and for many their first introduction to computers as well).

Over the course of this work the Trace Center originated a number of the key concepts and terms used in computer access today, including *transparent access* and *keyboard emulation*,[20,21] and even terms to advance the broader ideas such as "*computer curbcuts*" and "*electronic curbcuts*."[22]

4.6 Computer Accessibility Guidelines

In addition to working on specific changes to products, Trace worked with most of the major computer companies to help create guidelines for their products and technologies, as well as for their third-party developers.

The first set of guidelines was created at the request of the computer industry participants at the first White House meeting and presented at the second meeting.

The work at Apple described above included the development of the Apple Accessibility Report Cards.

In 1987, IBM approached the Trace Center asking for assistance in developing a set of internal accessibility guidelines that were tuned to IBM's products and could be used within the corporation. These guidelines covered both software and hardware design and were incorporated into the internal-use-only IBM document "Increasing Handicapped Accessibility of IBM Workstation Products," published in 1988 and disseminated to designers, developers, and engineers within IBM (Fig. 4.9).

This company-specific guidelines work was followed by the development of a set of guidelines for hardware and software commissioned by the Information Technology Foundation (ITF). Trace created an updated set of hardware and software accessibility guidelines for ITF that summarized all of the information, techniques, and advice Trace had been providing to various companies. Microsoft Corporation asked for permission to distribute these guidelines to all of their software developers inside and outside of the company. Later, Microsoft asked for and was given permission to freely borrow from these guidelines in the development of their own set of guidelines that would be tuned specifically to Microsoft products, in particular to Windows products.

At the request of and with funding from Sun Microsystems, the Trace Center authored the "Java Accessibility Report." According to comments from Sun Microsystems, this report drove much of the work on built-in accessibility to the Java technologies that followed.

Trace continues to provide consultation and guidelines for information and communication technology companies of all types today.

---

[20] Vanderheiden, G. C. and Kelso, D. P. (1982, August). Dual and nested computer approach to vocational and educational computer systems. *Proceedings of the 5th Annual Conference on Rehabilitation Engineering*, p. 46.

[21] Vanderheiden, G. C. and Enders, A. (1984, June). Rapid transparent access to the Apple II computer for high spinal cord injured individuals. *Rehabilitation Technology Review*.

[22] Vanderheiden, G. C. (1983) "Curbcuts and Computers: Providing Access to Computers and Information Systems for Disabled Individuals," Keynote Speech at the Indiana Governor's Conference on the Handicapped.

Fig. 4.9 IBM internal guidelines, "Increasing Handicapped Accessibility of IBM Workstation Products"

4.7 Standards Work

The Trace Center has provided information to, research for, participation in, and support for almost every accessibility standard working group over the last three decades. Trace served as an expert participant in the working groups of ISO on its ISO 9241–171 "Ergonomics of human-system interaction—Guidance on software accessibility" and ISO 9241–151 "Ergonomics of human-system interaction—Part 151: Guidance on World Wide Web" user interfaces and CEN/CENELEC (the European Committee for Standardization) on its accessibility standard EN 301 549 "Accessibility requirements suitable for public procurement of ICT products and services in Europe."

Trace Center personnel served on all three of the U.S. Access Board's accessibility advisory committees: the Telecommunication Access Advisory Committee—TAAC; the Electronic and Information Technology Access Advisory Committee—EITAAC; and the Telecommunications and Electronic and Information Technology Advisory Committee—TEITAC. These efforts led to the development of both versions of the Section 508 Information and Electronic Technology Accessibility Standards adopted by the Access Board and both versions of the Section 255 Accessibility Standards for Telecommunication adopted by the Federal Communications Commission (FCC). The Trace Center also provided the technical expertise for the European Disability Forum's participation in the European working group for the EN 301 549[23] accessibility standard for Europe.

[23] EN 301 549 Accessibility requirements for ICT products and services https://www.etsi.org/deliver/etsi_en/301500_301599/301549/03.01.01_60/en_301549v030101p.pdf.

The Trace Center also chaired and worked extensively on Part 2 of the Human Factors and Ergonomics Society HFES 200 Ergonomics Standard that dealt with accessibility. This work included harmonizing HFES 200—Part 2[24] with ISO 9241 172,[25] which at one time was harmonized but had diverged considerably over the years. This work was complicated by the fact that both sets of standards were anchored in larger standards environments that had predefined some usability terms differently. In the end, after many person-months of effort, all 86 provisions of the two standards were completely harmonized.

In addition to working on these existing standards projects, the Trace Center also launched a new effort in collaboration with the National Institute on Standards and Technology (NIST) to standardize an interface for virtual remote access to information communication and control technologies. The objective of the standard was to create a standard "virtual socket" that could be used to allow any third-party device such as a phone, tablet, computer, or assistive technology, to be able to plug into the socket and control the mainstream product using an interface that was different optimized to the abilities of the user rather than the products standard interface. The approach was called the Universal Remote Console and it was eventually adopted as ISO/IEC 24,752 Information technology—User interfaces—Universal remote console (multi-part standard).[26]

Trace played a major role in development of Web Accessibility standards as described in Chap. 6 on Web Access, and also contributed to the development of the IEEE standards on voting accessibility, the Canadian accessibility standards, and many other accessibility standards, and accessibility provisions in other mainstream standards.

Key in most all of these was the role the Trace Center played in tackling the outstanding problems, identifying or filling gaps, carrying out needed background research, developing consensus language, or creating needed tools that were required, handling editing, or doing whatever else was needed to overcome problems or stumbling blocks to progressing the standards, or important provisions so they could be included in the standards. Trace would act as unpaid staff to the working groups. It was not always alone in doing things like this on a standard, but it was usually just an individual that operated in similar ways—not a center or team. Trace viewed it as part of its duty or role to provide this type of support to those working on standards, who were mostly volunteers who were working without staff or the support generally available to those working on technical (vs. accessibility) standards.

[24] ANSI/HFES 200–2008 Human Factors Engineering of Software User Interfaces https://webstore.ansi.org/SDO/HFES.

[25] ISO 9241–171:2008(en) Ergonomics of human-system interaction—Part 171: Guidance on software accessibility https://www.iso.org/obp/ui/#iso:std:iso:9241:-171:ed-1:v1:en.

[26] ISO/IEC 24,752–1:2014 Information technology — User interfaces — Universal remote console — Part 1: General framework https://www.iso.org/standard/60821.html.

Fig. 4.10 The Trace Center Director, presenting the closing keynote for the Association of Computing Machines (ACM) Conference on Human Factors in Computing Systems, or CHI, in 2001

4.8 Shifting Computer Accessibility Efforts in Response to Maturing of the Field

As efforts expanded at AT manufacturers, and as mainstream companies moved forward building accessibility directly into their products, it was no longer necessary for the Trace Center to develop and promote basic accessibility techniques, or to actually design computer access hardware for AT manufacturers, as it was in the 1980s and early 1990s. Both AT manufacturers and mainstream computer companies are now carrying on their own R&D and pushing the field forward.

In response to this, the Trace Center shifted its focus, first toward making accessibility more mainstream, moving the message from accessibility specialists to mainstream designers, and making the case for accessibility as a path to better mainstream design—as with the closing keynote address at the CHI 2001 Conference held in Seattle.

As companies embraced built-in accessibility even more, Trace shifted its effort toward making it easier to coordinate between built-in and third-party accessibility products. This included providing ways for users to have their accessibility move between computers that they have to use—and to move between platforms. Both of these are areas that the computer companies have not pursued due to their complexity and the cross-platform, cross-company coordination they required (Fig. 4.10).

4.8.1 Digital Affinity

As part of its most recent work Trace unexpectedly discovered the depth to which "digital affinity" (the natural talent for understanding and use of digital technologies), or rather the lack of digital affinity, impacts the lives of people with all types of disability and even those who would previously not have been considered to have a disability. Trace has therefore added a focus on trying to make computers simpler and easier for that portion of the population who find them too complicated to use, or who can no longer deal with the complexity of computers and therefore lose access.

Both of these last two efforts (coordination of built-in and third-party assistive technologies, and low or very low digital affinity) have been brought together to create a free open-source tool called Morphic, released in 2021 by the Trace Center through the non-profit Raising the Floor.[27]

4.8.2 Importance of Flexibility and Pivoting to Meet Emerging Needs

The need to continually evolve one's efforts and approaches in response to changes in the field has been a hallmark of the Trace Center in all areas but is nowhere more clearly needed than in the computer access area. If one is to fill gaps, especially newly emerging gaps, one by definition will be continually launching new efforts. As fields mature and the commercial (AT and mainstream) players cover those areas (or even if another program covers the area), the practice of the Trace Center was to pass that on to the other players and move to the next gap that was not being addressed. In the case of computer access, the field is not only evolving with regard to inclusion of accessibility in its products but also evolving from computers to information, communication, and interaction technologies writ large.

In talking about the Trace Center's work and ability to pivot to address an ever-changing field and needs, credit needs to be paid to the Rehabilitation Engineering Research Center program of the National Institute on Disability, Independent Living, and Rehabilitation Research (NIDILRR), now at the Administration for Community Living (ACL), HHS which has provided both the ability for the long-term (competitive renewal) funding needed to carry out this work but also the ability to evolve the program to meet shifting needs.

[27] Morphic https://morphic.org.

Electronic Consumer Products and General Accessibility (1990–) 5

5.1 Consumer Product Guidelines

In 1992, the Trace Center drew from its work around computer and software access, its work with consumer product companies, its work with students in its accessible design courses, and with discussions with colleagues to create *Accessible Design of Consumer Products: Guidelines for the Design of Consumer Products to Increase Their Accessibility to People with Disabilities or Who Are Aging.*[1] This was the first known set of consumer product accessibility guidelines of its type. It is also the first accessibility guideline that introduced protection for individuals who have photosensitive epilepsy. These guidelines were introduced into the *Handbook of Human Factors and Ergonomics*[2] in 1997 and have been a part of this mainstream handbook ever since.

5.2 Principles of Universal Design

In the late 1990s and extending into 2000, the Trace Center worked with the Center for Universal Design on the development of Principles of Universal Design. The goal of the principles was to provide a concise and easily remembered set of **statements of the key concepts** embodied in the principle; a **definition of the principle** (a brief description of

[1] Vanderheiden G. C. and Vanderheiden K. R., (1991, 1992) *Accessible Design of Consumer Products: Guidelines for the Design of Consumer Products to Increase Their Accessibility to People with Disabilities or Who Are Aging Version* 1.7 at https://go.umd.edu/ConsumerProductsGuidelines.

[2] Vanderheiden, G. (1997). Design for people with functional limitations due to disability, aging, or circumstances. In G. Salvendy (Ed.), *Handbook of Human Factors and Ergonomics* (pp. 2010–2052). New York: John Wiley & Sons.

G. Vanderheiden et al., *Technology and Disability*, Synthesis Lectures on Technology and Health, https://doi.org/10.1007/978-3-031-09214-5_5

the principle's primary directive for design); and **guidelines** (a list of the key elements that should be present in a design which adheres to the principle).

The Trace Center's contribution was primarily focused on extending the guidelines that were originally focused on products and the built environment to also include coverage of information, communication, and consumer product physical and digital interfaces.[3]

The final seven principles, with their definitions and guidelines, are as follows:

1. **Equitable Use**: The design is useful and marketable to people with diverse abilities.
   a. Provide the same means of use for all users: identical whenever possible; equivalent when not.
   b. Avoid segregating or stigmatizing any users.
   c. Provisions for privacy, security, and safety should be equally available to all users.
   d. Make the design appealing to all users.
2. **Flexibility in Use**: The design accommodates a wide range of individual preferences and abilities.
   a. Provide choice in methods of use.
   b. Accommodate right- or left-handed access and use.
   c. Facilitate the user's accuracy and precision.
   d. Provide adaptability to the user's pace.
3. **Simple and Intuitive Use**: Use of the design is easy to understand, regardless of the user's experience, knowledge, language skills, or current concentration level.
   a. Eliminate unnecessary complexity.
   b. Be consistent with user expectations and intuition.
   c. Accommodate a wide range of literacy and language skills.
   d. Arrange information consistent with its importance.
   e. Provide effective prompting and feedback during and after task completion.
4. **Perceptible Information**: The design communicates necessary information effectively to the user, regardless of ambient conditions or the user's sensory abilities.
   a. Use different modes (pictorial, verbal, tactile) for redundant presentation of essential information.
   b. Provide adequate contrast between essential information and its surroundings.
   c. Maximize "legibility" of essential information.
   d. Differentiate elements in ways that can be described (i.e., make it easy to give instructions or directions).
   e. Provide compatibility with a variety of techniques or devices used by people with sensory limitations.

[3] Connell, B., Jones, M., Mace, R., Mueller, J., Mullick, A., Ostroff, E., Sanford, J., Steinfield, E., Story, M., and Vanderheiden, G. (1997). The principles of universal design: version 2.0 https://go.umd.edu/Principles-of-Universal-Design.

5. **Tolerance for Error**: The design minimizes hazards and the adverse consequences of accidental or unintended actions.
   a. Arrange elements to minimize hazards and errors: most used elements, most accessible; hazardous elements eliminated, isolated, or shielded.
   b. Provide warnings of hazards and errors.
   c. Provide fail-safe features.
   d. Discourage unconscious action in tasks that require vigilance.
6. **Low Physical Effort**: The design can be used efficiently and comfortably and with a minimum of fatigue.
   a. Allow user to maintain a neutral body position.
   b. Use reasonable operating forces.
   c. Minimize repetitive actions.
   d. Minimize sustained physical effort.
7. **Size and Space for Approach and Use**: Appropriate size and space are provided for approach, reach, manipulation, and use regardless of the user's body size, posture, or mobility.
   a. Provide a clear line of sight to important elements for any seated or standing user.
   b. Make reach to all components comfortable for any seated or standing user.
   c. Accommodate variations in hand and grip size.
   d. Provide adequate space for the use of assistive devices or personal assistance.

As with all work on guidelines and principles, the goal of the Center was to help to create, contribute to, and promulgate guidelines and standards that were clear, concise, effective across disabilities, and practically implementable. These principles represent the most concise list of underlying principles and are particularly valuable since they apply across architecture, physical, and electronic products—fields that are rapidly converging.

5.3 User Needs Summary

In the 1990s and the early 2000s, the Trace Center created a systematic compilation of user needs across all types, degrees, and combinations of disabilities and all ICT interface techniques. This was used by the Trace Center in training its students and researchers, as well as in Trace's industry training. In 2005, the Trace Center submitted the user needs summary to the ISO/IEC JTC 1-SWA Special Working Group on Accessibility. At its April 2005 meeting, the Special Working Group formed an ad hoc committee to begin the process of turning it into an SWG-A technical report. Dr. Jim Carter later led an effort which resulted in its being adopted as ISO/IEC TR 29,138–1.[4]

[4] ISO/IEC TR 29,138–1:2009 Information technology—Accessibility considerations for people with disabilities—Part 1: User needs summary https://www.iso.org/standard/45161.html.

5.4 The Experience Lab

As part of its education program and work with industry, the Trace Center developed a set of 30 experience stations that allowed students and industry workshop participants to experience first-hand effect of good and bad designs on one's ability to use a product.[5] The stations were designed as paired stations with an accessible and an inaccessibly designed commercial product. In each case, both products were equally usable by people without disabilities, but one of them was essentially unusable by people with a disability. Different stations focused on different products and different disabilities. In order to experience the frustration of not being able to use the first (inaccessible) standard product, the participants had to use the products while blindfolded, or wearing sound-blocking headphones with white noise in them, or using a headstick, or wearing goggles that blurred vision, or removed the ability to perceive some colors, or had all labels visible but nonsense so they could not read them, etc.

The participants would first try the inaccessible product—and quickly found how unusable they were. They then tried the second product (which at first seemed identical to the first product they used) but were surprised that they had no problem completing the task with the second product.

While these activities did not simulate disability, the lab did help participants better understand some of the frustrations of people with different disabilities encounter in trying to operate standard products with bad designs. It also illustrated how sometimes a simple change in the product can make a difference in whether or not it can be used.

In addition to using the experience sessions in our industry training, it was offered as part of a workshop presented at several mainstream HCI conferences. From 2003 to 2018, the Experience Lab was offered primarily to the University of Wisconsin students, including pre-engineering students (as part of a required survey course focused on design) and students in a higher level elective course on Design and Human Disability and Aging, taught annually by Gregg Vanderheiden. The lab was also requested by many groups visiting the Trace Center. From the feedback of those going through the experience sessions, the change in understanding and empathy was quite remarkable.

5.5 The Trace Usability Screening Kit (TUSK)

To help companies to screen their own products for barriers, the Trace Center created the Trace Usability Screening Kit (TUSK), including most of the items developed for use in the Experience Lab, including the following:

[5] Jordan, J. B. and Vanderheiden, G. (2010). Accessibility experience lab: Discovering the impact of design on disabilities. In *Proceedings of the Human Factors and Ergonomics Society Annual Meeting*, September 2010, 54(19), 1396–1400. San Francisco. Santa Monica: Human Factors and Ergonomics Society. https://doi.org/10.1177/154193121005401909.

- **Blindfolds**—to screen for products that depended on vision.
- **Dark Pillowcase**—to allow non-sight use of smaller, non-light-emitting products without a blindfold.
- **Sound-Blocking Headphones** with built-in radios that can be tuned between stations for white noise—to screen for products where the product sounds are important to operation. (For example, some products provide no indication that they are operating other than the noise of their operation. Other products provide no feedback other than a beep to indicate that a button press was successful.)
- **Ear Plugs**—to use with the headphones for complete blockage for products with louder noise.
- **Mouthsticks**—that can be held to the face to simulate mouth or headstick operation.
- **Hand Splints**—to simulate inability to use hands.
- **Hand Dowels**—to use with splints to simulate typing with a dowel or single finger (which prevents any keyboard or control use that requires simultaneous operations).
- **Stickers with "blah blah"** printed on them of different sizes to paste over labels on controls to indicate problems in using products if one can't read the labels. (It was amazing to watch industry designers who were unable to operate their own company's products without seeing the labels.)
- **Goggles with different lenses** that provided:

  o Blurred vision—approximating 20/200 vision;
  o Tunnel Vision;
  o Color filters—to give them the inability to perceive certain colors (red, green).

- **Gloves with some fingers removed and others glued together** to eliminate their ability to manipulate, as a person with severe arthritis or missing fingers or severe spasticity would.
- **Different-sized audio plugs** can be inserted into the headphone jacks to cause any audio to be cut-off from coming out of a speaker.
- **Instructions on how to use the kit** both to create experience sessions and to screen products for embarrassing accessibility barriers before bringing in people with disabilities to test their products.

The kits were sold at cost and purchased both by industry and training programs. Yahoo used the kits to give experience sessions to new employees as part of their orientation and training (Fig. 5.1).

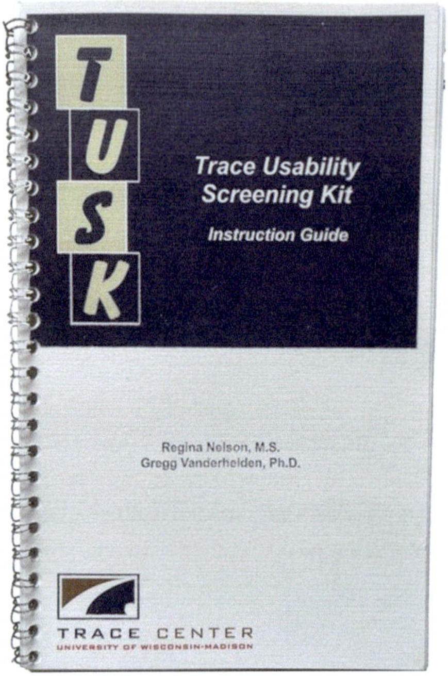

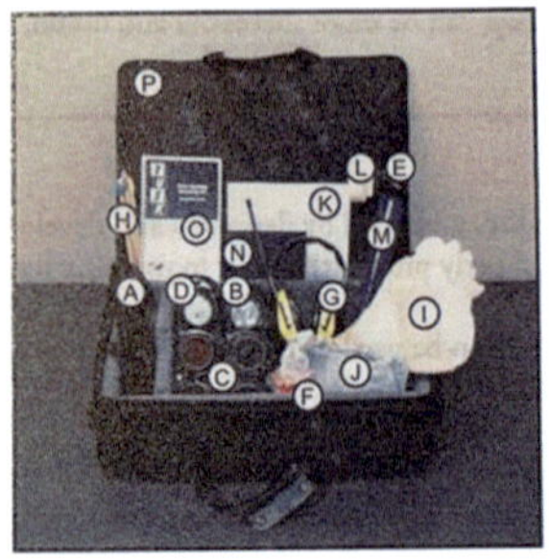

Fig. 5.1 Trace Usability Screening Kit (TUSK) manual and contents. Again, it must be emphasized that this kit does NOT simulate a disability. It simply imposes limitations (visual, physical, hearing, etc.) on developers that allow them to better identify weaknesses in their designs and remove them before testing them with people who have disabilities

5.6 Contributions of ICT Accessibility Information to Other Summative Studies

Trace has also participated in the creation of other summative and prospective publications by the National Research Council and National Academies on the current status and recommended directions of information technologies as they relate to people with disabilities.

The first was *More Than Screen Deep: Toward Every Citizen Interfaces to the Nation's Information Infrastructure* (1997),[6] a publication of the Computer Science and Telecommunications Board of the National Research Council. The Trace Center provided a position paper, "Nomadicity, disability access, and the every-citizen interface," for the workshop and a first draft for three of the six chapters in the final report: "Requirements

[6] National Research Council, Computer Science and Telecommunications Board. (1997). *More than Screen Deep: Toward Every-Citizen Interfaces to the Nation's Information Infrastructure*. Washington, DC: National Academies Press.

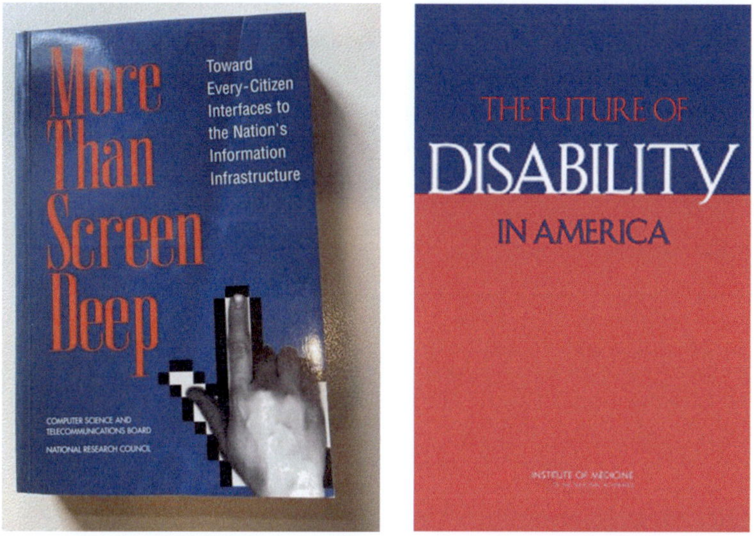

Fig. 5.2 Chapters in "More that Screen Deep" and "The Future of Disability in America" are two Trace contributions to the broader discussions of technology and disability

for effective every-citizen interfaces" (pp. 21–70); "Input/output technologies: Current status and research needs" (pp. 71–120); and "Nomadicity, disability access, and the every-citizen interface" (pp. 297–306) (Fig. 5.2).

The second was *The Future of Disability in America* (2007),[7] which summarizes an independent, two-phase study undertaken by the National Academies' Institute of Medicine (IOM) that represents a nonsystematic review intended to identify gaps in disability science and propose steps to strengthen the evidence base for public and private actions to reduce the impact of disability and related conditions on individuals and society in the United States. The Trace Center provided a first draft and chaired the subcommittee for the chapter "Assistive and mainstream technologies for people with disabilities" (pp. 7-1–7-31).

[7] Field, M. and Jette, A., (Eds.), and Committee on Disability in America, Board on Health Sciences Policy, Institute of Medicine of the National Academies. The Future of Disability in America [Internet]. Washington, DC: National Academies Press; 2007 [cited 2014 Mar 10]. Available from: http://www.nap.edu/catalog.php?record_id=11898.

The Trace Center also wrote two reports for the National Council on Disability:

1. *Access to the Information Superhighway and Emerging Information Technologies by People with Disabilities.* National Council on Disability (1996).
2. *Over the Horizon: Potential Impact of Emerging Trends in Information and Communication Technology on Disability Policy and Practice.* National Council on Disability (2006).

6 Web Access (1990–)

Even before Mosaic revolutionized the Internet and the Web by providing the first modern Web browser, the Trace Center was providing information via Gopher servers that used a text-based protocol that looked essentially like a searchable file directory mounted on the Internet. This protocol—released in 1991 by a team led by Mark P. McCahill[1] at the University of Minnesota—represented a new means of rapidly deploying information freely on the Web. Being largely text-based, it was also quite accessible. With the release of the Mosaic Web browser in 1993,[2] with its ability to embed graphics and rich text formatting, the Web took on a whole new, and much more attractive and friendly, personality. It also created new challenges for accessibility for people with disabilities.

6.1 First Web Accessibility Guidelines, 1995

To address this problem, the Trace Center created the first Web accessibility guidelines following the Second International World Wide Web Conference in Chicago in 1994 and drew from a Birds-of-a-Feather (BOF) gathering held at that conference, combined with research by the Trace Center. The guidelines were released in January 1995 and were titled "*Design of HTML (Mosaic) Pages to Increase their Accessibility to Users with Disabilities: Strategies for Today and Tomorrow* (Fig. 6.1)."[3]

Over the next 2 years, 39 distinct sets of guidelines (including Trace's own) were released by different organizations, leading to a fair amount of chaos in the field. As a result, Trace began working with the developers of different guidelines to come up

[1] Mark P. McCahill interviewed on the TV show Triangulation on the TWiT.tv network.

[2] https://en.wikipedia.org/wiki/Mosaic_(web_browser)#cite_note-mosaic_and_th_w3-10.

[3] https://trace.umd.edu/design-of-html-mosaic-pages-to-increase-their-accessibility-to-users-with-disabilities-strategies-for-today-and-tomorrow/.

G. Vanderheiden et al., *Technology and Disability*, Synthesis Lectures on Technology and Health, https://doi.org/10.1007/978-3-031-09214-5_6

DESIGN OF HTML (MOSAIC) PAGES
TO INCREASE THEIR ACCESSIBILITY TO USERS WITH DISABILITIES
STRATEGIES FOR TODAY AND TOMORROW

VERSION 1.0
1/31/95

Trace R& D Center, University of Wisconsin - Madison

Prepared under funding from
the National Institute for Disability Related Research (NIDRR),
Office of Special Education and Rehabilitation Services (OSERS), US
Dept. of Education
and in cooperation with the NCSA Mosaic Access Project.

(This is a living document. Comments and suggestions are solicited.
GCVander@Facstaff.wisc.edu)

Overview

When discussing the accessibility of Mosaic, it is important to break
the problem down into the three basic components: the source material,
the pipeline, and the viewer. Mosaic is actually a viewer, so
technically speaking, making Mosaic accessible really would apply only
to making the (Mosaic) viewer accessible. However, most users do not
differentiate between the different components, so making Mosaic
accessible would involve working to make the Mosaic software accessible

Fig. 6.1 First Web Accessibility Guidelines (1995)

with the *Unified Web Site Accessibility Guidelines*[4] that combined the best aspects of the different guidelines available at that time (Fig. 6.2). As new guidelines and additional information about Web accessibility emerged, the Unified Guidelines were continually revised—a total of eight times by 1996.

6.2 The W3C and the Web Accessibility Initiative (WAI)

In 1996, the National Institute on Disability and Rehabilitation Research (NIDRR) (the Trace Center's core funding agency) was contacted by the White House saying that they had received a request from the World Wide Web Consortium seeking funding to develop Web accessibility guidelines. Because the White House doesn't directly fund projects, they had asked if NIDRR thought it was a good idea and would like to fund it. This led to a call to the Trace Center asking whether that wasn't what Trace was already doing. The Trace Center's response was that the W3C was in a much better position to do this work authoritatively "and if the W3C did one third as good a job as Trace might, it would

[4] https://trace.umd.edu/central-reference-document-version-8-unified-web-site-accessibility-guidelines/.

1. Accessible Design for Users with Disabilities — Sun Microsystems
2. The Accessible Web: Web Access Through Adaptive Technology — Kevin Nguyen, University of Toronto
3. ACT Centre Accessible Web Design
4. All Things Web
5. ALT text recommendations, and notes on viewing situation — A.J. Flavell, University of Glasgow
6. Alternative Access to the World Wide Web — University of Toronto
7. Any Browser Table Format — Department of MIssions, Abilene Christian University
8. Best Viewed With Any Browser — Accessible Site Design
9. Compatibility & Accessibility — Towards the creation of an accessible, truly World-wide Web — All Things Web
10. Composing Good HTML — James "Eric" Tilton.
11. Design Considerations: Readers with Visual Impairments — Arthur R. Murphy
12. Designing Access to WWW Pages — Alliance for Technology Access.
13. Designing HTML Tables to Work with HTML 2.0 Browsers — Stanton McCandlish
14. DO-IT HTML Guidelines — University of Washington
15. Experiences Implementing Web Accessibility Guidelines in IBM — Phill Jenkins
16. For Web Page Designers — Microsoft
17. GSA HTML Accessibility Guidelines — Paul Fontaine
18. Guide to Writing Accessible HTML — University of Toronto
19. Guidelines on Universal Web-Site Accessibility — Treasury Board Internet Working Group on Internet Presentation, Style and Accessibility
20. Hints for designing accessible Websites — Royal National Institute for the Blind
21. IBM Web Design Guidelines
22. Increasing Access to World Wide Web Sites for Blind and Visually Impaired Computer Users — Dena Shumila, Jan Richards
23. InfoUse Web Accessibility Guidelines
24. Levelling the Road Ahead: Guidelines for the Creation of WWW Pages Accessible to Blind And Visually Handicapped Users, Judith M. Dixon, Ph.D., Consumer Relations Officer, National Library Service for the Blind and Physically Handicapped
25. The Lynx Manifesto — Dehanced for Lynx
26. Making Your Site Speech Friendly — Cathy Anne Murtha, Web Design and Access Specialist, Magical Mist Creations
27. NCSA Mosaic Access Page
28. Nimble Document Navigation Using Alternative Access Tools — Jutta Treviranus, University of Toronto
29. On-Line Examples of HTML Accessibility — Chuck Le Tourneau
30. Tables on non-table browsers — A.J. Flavell, Glasgow University
31. Unified HTML Accessibility Guidelines — Previous version of this document
32. Universal Accessibility — Government of Canada Internet Guide
33. Universal Design of WWW Pages — a DO-IT (University of Washington) Brochure
34. Universal Information Access on the WWW (COCA)
35. "Universal Specifications" Accessibility Standards for Web Design — New South Wales Attorney General's Department
36. Usability of Information and the WWW — UCLA Disabilities and Computing Program
37. Web Accessibility Guidelines — IBM
38. World Wide Web Access: Disability Discrimination Act Advisory Notes — Australia

Fig. 6.2 Thirty-eight guidelines referenced in the creation of the Trace Center Unified Website Accessibility Guidelines

be 10 times more effective than anything that Trace could accomplish." When told that NIDRR did not have any funding available for the effort, the Center offered to have its own core grant cut, and the funds redirected to the W3C at MIT to fund it if the W3C was interested in taking it on. Deliberations led to another White House meeting, including the Trace Center and the W3C, and again, the Trace Center strongly endorsed funding the W3C effort and again made the offer. Subsequently, MIT was funded to create a Web accessibility initiative (WAI) with funding from both NIDRR and the National Science Foundation (and fortuitously, without a cut to Trace's grant budget).

Volume 8 of the *Trace Center's Unified Web Accessibility Guidelines* (Fig. 6.3) was transferred to the W3C and became their central reference document[5] for the creation of the first draft of the Web Content Accessibility Guidelines (WCAG 1.0). The Trace Center then shifted from its own guidelines development effort to support the efforts of the W3C, providing one of the two co-chairs for the WCAG working group and two of the four editors, as well as research and logistical support.

The Trace Center contributed between one and two FTEs worth of effort and support continuously over the next 10 years to support the development of both WCAG 1.0 (released in 1999) and WCAG 2.0 (released in 2008). The Center's team collaborated with the Lighthouse for the Blind in carrying out the research and development for the contrast provision to accommodate both individuals with color blindness and individuals with low vision. It collaborated with Graham Harding from the United Kingdom (the primary researcher for photosensitive epilepsy research) and Cambridge Research Associates on the development of the measures and standards for the photosensitive epilepsy provisions in WCAG. The Trace Center also provided background research for other provisions as they came up, and provided one of the two reference implementations for all of the techniques, as required by the W3C at that time for the adoption of standards. In addition to working on the standards, the Trace Center expended considerable effort in creating the Techniques document and made substantial contributions to the "understanding WCAG 2.0" support document with the group.

The Trace Center also worked with the U.S. Access Board and European standards organizations, ISO and CEN/CENELEC, on their guidelines covering Web accessibility.

6.3 Tools to Support and Enable WCAG Provisions

As noted above, the Trace Center provided the research for, and developed or supported the development of, several tools in support of the WCAG guidelines development process. These tools were essential to the inclusion of key provisions in WCAG. It is not practical or appropriate to include required provisions in a standard if there is no measure available to determine success and/or if there is no (affordable) tool to carry out the measurement or fulfill the criterion.

[5] https://www.w3.org/WAI/GL/central.htm.

Central Reference Document - Version 8: Unified Web Site Accessibility Guidelines

ADVANCED DRAFT COPY

January 20, 1998

Compiled by:
Gregg C. Vanderheiden Ph.D., Wendy A. Chisholm, M.S.,
Trace R and D Center, University of Wisconsin - Madison
For the Web Accessibility Initiative Guidelines Working Group

(This is a final Trace Center Guidelines Document.
It is compiled in preparation for transfer of the Guidelines to the Web Accessibility Initiative of the W3C.
This guideline reflects recent work of the WAI as well as previous contributions of many other guidelines developers (listed in the appendix)).

Fig. 6.3 *Unified Web Accessibility Guidelines Version 8* used by the W3C WCAG working group as its initial Central Reference Document

In the development of WCAG, this problem arose around several provisions: contrast, photosensitive seizure disorder stimuli, and captioning. The Trace Center therefore launched research efforts into each and secured funding to create tools to address them.

6.3.1 Color Contrast Analysis Tool

Creating the Measure

The Trace Center worked with Dr. Aries Arditi, a vision researcher at the Lighthouse for the Blind, to develop a contrast measure that would provide equivalent contrast for text for those with low vision and also for color blindness. The international standard for people with normal vision at the time was 3:1. Using research with people who had low vision, it was determined that a contrast of approximately 4.5:1 would provide the same level of readability for people with low vision to normal size text with less contrast required for large text. 7:1 contrast was determined to be better and covered a wider range of low

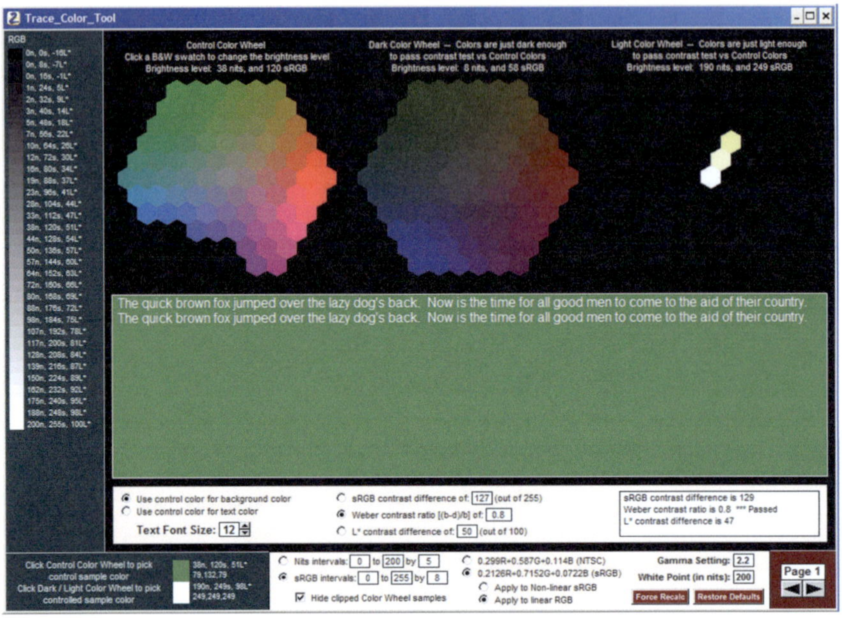

Fig. 6.4 Research on color contrast and low vision was carried out by Trace Center and Lighthouse for the Blind to support WCAG Success Criterion development

vision and was used in WCAG for the level AAA contrast provision. To address color blindness, the contrast provision was based on luminosity (lightness/darkness) rather than hue (color). This research was used by the working group to establish the success criteria.

Commissioning a Tool

In June 2007, the Trace Center commissioned the development of a contrast analysis tool (Fig. 6.4). It found an existing open-source tool and commissioned its developer to create a version that would test for both the AA- and AAA-level WCAG provisions for both regular and large text. This free tool is now updated and maintained by The Paciello Group (now TPGi), which continues to make it available free of charge.[6]

6.3.2 The Photosensitive Epilepsy Analysis Tool (PEAT)

The second area dealt with preventing Web content from causing seizures in people with photosensitive seizure disorders such as epilepsy. Again, a provision was desired but neither a measure for success nor a tool to evaluate content against that rule existed. At

[6] Colour Contrast Analyzer https://www.tpgi.com/color-contrast-checker/.

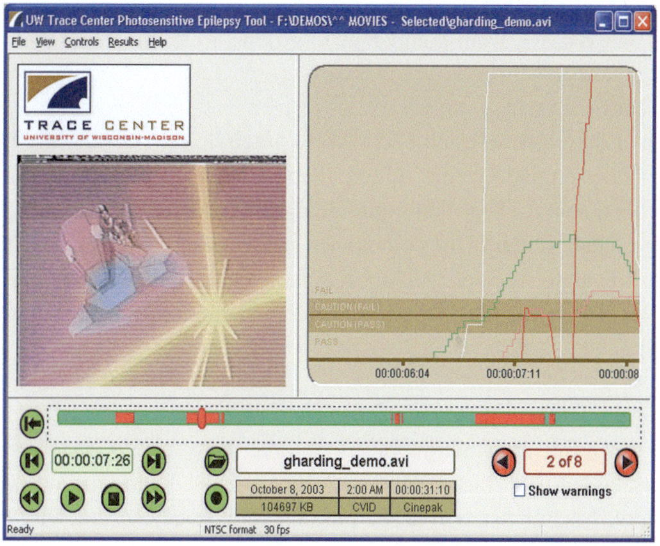

Fig. 6.5 Trace Center Photosensitive Epilepsy Analysis Tool, shown analyzing the Pokémon Clip that sent 350 children to the hospital in Japan. It was then shown on the evening news where it sent an additional approximately 350 children to the hospital.[7]

the time, the only tool for analyzing content for potential seizure-inducing material was designed for television content and cost $30,000.

Creating the Measure

To create a measure that would work for Web content the Trace Center drew on the expertise of Dr. Graham Harding from the United Kingdom (the primary researcher for photosensitive epilepsy research) and Cambridge Research Associates (who had worked with Dr. Harding on the development of the existing $30,000 tool for evaluating television content). Web content was different than television content in several key ways, including the fact that Web content users would be viewing the content at a much closer distance. The assumption for television was that viewers would be far enough away that their screen would fit entirely within their central vision (10°). It could therefore be evaluated as one "window." With Web content, screens are much closer and the central vision of the viewer (i.e., the area most sensitive to flashing stimuli) covers only a portion of the screen. As a result, every possible 10° window of the screen would need to be evaluated.

With input from Dr. Harding and Cambridge Research Associates, the criteria for both general and red flashes were created that could be used in the WCAG guidelines. However, the measure without a tool to evaluate content was not viable—and the cost of the only measurement tool, at $30,000, was far out of reach of the millions of Web authors who might want to use WCAG, from companies to groups, to teachers and their students.

Creating the Tool

The Trace Center therefore invested $200,000 to purchase the rights to use the Cambridge Research Associates engine (developed in collaboration with Graham Harding) and built-in (otherwise open-source) tool that could analyze Web content (and any non-broadcast and non-game-related content) for compliance with the new standard. Called the Photosensitive Epilepsy Analysis Tool (PEAT), it was made available as a free download from the Trace Center (Fig. 6.5). (A fully open-source version is now also under development. See Chap. 13.)

Captioning Tool

The third tool was a free captioning tool. At the time there was no free, user-friendly, captioning tool available. The Trace Center therefore proposed and was awarded funding to create such a tool. As a first step in developing the tool Trace checked with the Accessible Media program at WGBH. WGBH, the public television station in Boston, had extensive expertise in this area and their own captioning service but had previously said they were not interested in creating a free tool that would compete with their captioning service (which was why Trace had applied for funding to do its own). However, on checking in with WGBH, the Center's team learned that WGBH had changed their minds and had recently submitted a proposal to create such a tool, but it was not funded. Knowing that WGBH would be better at creating the tool than Trace, the Center sought permission from the funding agency to transfer the funding Trace had received to create a captioning tool to WGBH. It received permission and transferred these funds plus some additional funds to WGBH. This resulted in the development of the first MAGpie (Media Access Generator)[8] captioning tool. WGBH followed up with a MAGpie 2 under other funding and that has now evolved into their current captioning tool, called CADET (Caption and Description Editing Tool).[9]

Support for Other Tool Efforts

Other places where the Trace Center provided funding to other groups to support their efforts to create Web accessibility tools include support for:

- the "Bobby" Web accessibility verifier tool[10] (Center on Applied Special Technology—CAST);

[7] https://en.wikipedia.org/wiki/Pokémon_episodes_removed_from_rotation.

[8] MAGpie http://ncamftp.wgbh.org/ncam-old-site/invent_build/web_multimedia/tools-guidelines/magpie.html.

[9] CADET http://ncamftp.wgbh.org/cadet/.

[10] Bobby https://en.wikipedia.org/wiki/Bobby_(software).

- the A-Prompt Web accessibility verifier tool[11] (University of Toronto's Adaptive Technology Research Centre—ATRC, now the IDRC);
- the Accessibility Wizard for PowerPoint (University of Illinois); and
- the UI Options Plus (UIO+)[12] Web browser plug-in (Ontario College of Art & Design, Inclusive Design Research Center).

6.4 Universal Adoption of the Web Guidelines

Once the Web standards were established (and remembering what had happened with the first Web accessibility guidelines in 1995), the Trace Center worked carefully with both the U.S. Access Board and with the European and international standards bodies, CEN/CENELEC, ISO, and IEC, to ensure that the guidelines were adopted intact and in identical fashion by all. This was necessary so that Web developers did not have multiple sets of guidelines to meet. Fortunately, this was one time that the disability groups and the industry groups were in 100% agreement—that there should be only one set of Web accessibility guidelines and that it should be the one developed by the W3C.

6.5 Basic Contributions to WCAG Architecture and Design

There were two additional contributions of note that the Trace Center made to the Web accessibility effort. The first was in 2002 when Trace proposed the restructuring of the guidelines into its current Perceivable, Operable, Understandable, and Robust (POUR) organization. This re-organization was proposed by the Trace team to the WCAG working group at its meeting held in conjunction with the 17th Annual CSUN conference (2002) and was subsequently adopted and used in all of the WCAG guidelines since.

The second was the extensive effort and lobbying to keep the guidelines technology agnostic. Making them HTML-specific would have greatly simplified both the writing and readability of the guidelines. However, that would exclude many other (non-HTML and non-markup) technologies from being able to be used and meet the guidelines. These efforts to keep the guidelines technology-agnostic also led to the U.S. Access Board's being able to adopt the Web Content Accessibility Guidelines not only for Web content but also for electronic documents and for software (although for software, additional guidelines were needed to supplement WCAG in order to cover aspects of accessibility that would be addressed through the Web browser and, therefore, were not part of the WCAG guidelines).

[11] A-Prompt http://www.icdri.org/WebAccess/a_prompt.htm.

[12] UI Options Plus (UIO+) https://chrome.google.com/webstore/detail/ui-options-plus-uio%2B/okenndailhmikjjfcnmolpaefecbpaek.

6.6 Tapping the Web to Extend Accessibility in New Ways

In addition to website accessibility, the Trace Center also began, starting in 1996, to look at how the Web could enable a broader spectrum of services that could benefit people with disabilities. One of the early concepts explored in connection with Trace's work with the National Computer Science Alliance was the concept of personal services on demand. This approach used layering to provide services (Fig. 6.6). The default service would be provided by the local computing resources (i.e., using the CPU on the phone or computer). When these are not sufficient or accurate enough to handle the request, the user could press a "Try Harder" button that would kick the service up to online automated resources in the cloud. If these also proved insufficient or inaccurate, then another press of "try harder" could bring humans into the loop to assist. The objective of this layered approach was to minimize cost and maximize personal privacy by having the information process be handled locally if possible—but to have additional layers of (more expensive) resources available whenever local or automated cloud services were insufficient. An advantage of this approach is that it allows automated services to be used earlier than would normally be possible. Before automated (local or cloud) services are sufficiently good and accurate enough to be generally acceptable, they could be used by individuals or in situations where they would work. And any individual could use them for more privacy or lower cost—knowing that if they failed a button press would get them to a service that did work.

For example, such an approach as this could allow individuals who are deaf to accept automatic speech captioning or telecommunication relay services earlier and enjoy the privacy and speed if they knew that any time it would not work for them, they could push a button to instantly get more advanced services or a human interpreter.

6.7 Recent and Ongoing Work on Web Accessibility

More recent work (2015–2021) around the Web and accessibility has focused on creating exemplars of simpler interfaces. With Web 2.0 and rich content and apps, websites and webpages have become increasingly complex to the point where they can still meet guidelines, but be very hard for users (both with and without disabilities) to use. The Center is therefore working on strategies and tools that can be used with dynamic Web content to make it easier to use. In addition to the UI Options Plus support, the Center is also working on simple and ultra-simple interfaces to key Web functionality, such as with its Easy123 program[13,14] that allows the individual to have an extremely simple-to-use

[13] Zhou, J., Chourasia, A., and Vanderheiden, G. (2017). Interface adaptation to novice older adults' mental models through concrete metaphors. *International Journal of Human–Computer Interaction*, 33(7), 592–606. https://doi.org/10.1080/10447318.2016.1265827.

[14] Easy123 https://easy123.org.

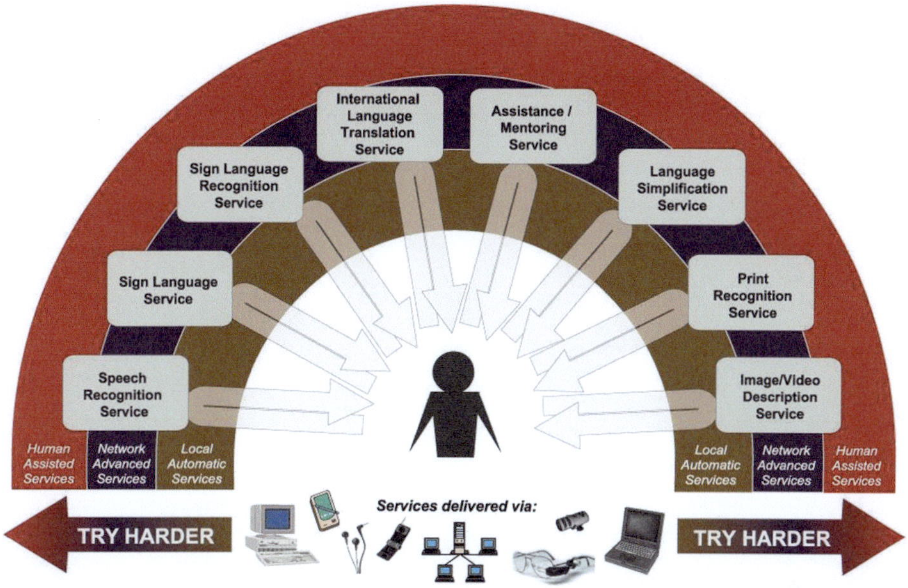

Fig. 6.6 Concept of a spectrum of layered services with "Try harder" that was introduced by Trace in the 1990s

interface for email, picture sharing, communication, and a subset of easy-to-use websites, that does not require any computer or browser expertise. It is also working on a simpler, friendlier version of Gmail, and the free Morphic tool that provides access to both computers and the Web for people with disabilities and those who just find computers and the Web too complicated.[15]

[15] Morphic https://morphic.org.

Telecommunication Access (1990–) 7

Beginning in 1999, the Trace Center partnered with the Technology Access Program (TAP) at Gallaudet University to propose the creation of the first Telecommunication Rehabilitation Engineering Research Center. The RERC grant was awarded, and the two centers carried out a joint program on Telecommunication Access for the next 15 years.

During this time, the Access Board twice revised its telecommunication accessibility rules, under Sect. 255, which were then adopted by the Federal Communications Commission (FCC). In both cases, the Access Board created a special Accessibility Advisory Committee. The first was the Telecommunications Access Advisory Committee (TAAC). The second was the Telecommunications and Electronic and Information Technology Access Advisory Committee (TEITAC). TEITAC also revised the Access Board's guidelines on Sect. 508,[1] later implemented by federal agencies to ensure IT accessibility for persons working within and interacting with those agencies. In both cases, the Trace Center was recognized for the extensive work it had carried out in supporting the committees with research and for working with consumers and industry to find commonly acceptable language.

In the development of the first set of guidelines for 255, the Trace Center also played an additional key role. Although the guidelines were first drafted by the Access Board, the Access Board has no regulatory authority in the telecommunications area. Instead, it is charged with creating recommended guidelines that are then forwarded to the Federal Communications Commission (FCC) for consideration. The FCC can then adopt them in whole or in part, or edit them as part of their review, deliberation, and adoption. In 1999, as the FCC was reviewing the rules sent to them by the Access Board, they were getting heavy lobbying from industry to weaken the rules, claiming that many of them "defied the laws of physics" or were not possible in a production phone. Consumer groups were so worried that they tried twice to work out a compromise with industry on a set of guidelines

[1] https://en.wikipedia.org/wiki/Section_508_Amendment_to_the_Rehabilitation_Act_of_1973.

G. Vanderheiden et al., *Technology and Disability*, Synthesis Lectures on Technology and Health, https://doi.org/10.1007/978-3-031-09214-5_7

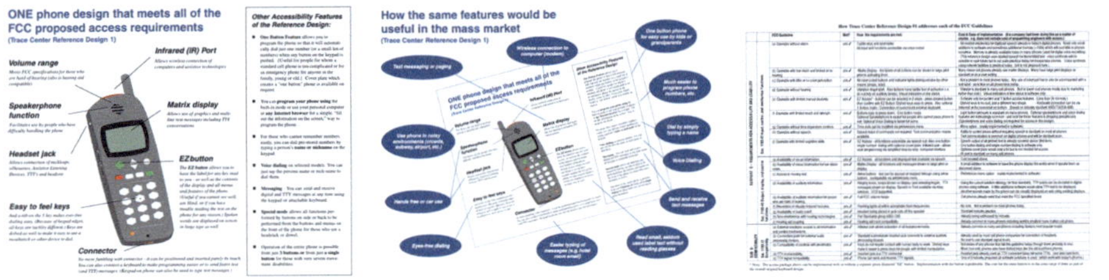

Fig. 7.1 Illustrations and spreadsheet from July 1999 comments. Full comments are in Appendix B

they thought would be better than what would otherwise come out of the FCC. In both attempts, they failed. To address this issue, the Trace Center created a reference design that showed how the requirements could all be met in a practical phone. To offset the criticism that the Trace Center was not a phone manufacturer and would not know what was possible, the Center included a chart showing how existing phones had demonstrated that the features could be implemented with current phone technologies. The design and notes were submitted to the FCC on July 7, 1999, as an *ex parte* comment (see Appendix B) (Fig. 7.1).

When the FCC released its Report and Order on September 29, 1999, it included the 255 rules from the Access Board intact. Trace Center comments were cited repeatedly in the final rule.

7.1 Caption Correction

A major problem faced by people who are deaf is mistakes in captions. Sometimes, it is a function of poor-quality captioning, but often it is attributable to the use of names or terms that are unfamiliar to the captioners or automatic captioning systems. Caption errors can cause the information presented to be wrong or uninterpretable, leaving deaf participants on a call unable to follow or participate. With funding from the National Science Foundation, the Trace Center developed the first local user-correctable, remote caption correction system. The system operated via high-speed Internet and allowed individuals in the audience to be able to correct errors when they saw them appearing in captions. This system was used with the grid telecommunication system of the NSF supercomputer National Computer Science Alliance. Later, under Rehabilitation Engineering Research Center funding, the caption-correction system was improved and designed to work with modern CART-based caption streaming services. The real-time captioning correction system was transferred to the IDEAL Group.

7.2 Trace Online Hand-Raising Utility (TOHRU)

After participating in many Web conferences that included individuals with disabilities, the Trace Center identified an unaddressed barrier to participation by people with disabilities who could not raise their hand or respond quickly enough. Two groups were impacted. The first group included people who could not physically respond quickly enough when the moderator would ask if anyone had a question. The second group were those who relied on captions, and who found that by the time the captions displayed the moderator's question ("Are there any questions?") or ("Does anyone else have a comment?"), too much time had passed, and the moderator had moved on. (There is often a delay between when the speech is audible and when the captions appear, and since the captioner would use the pause to catch up—there was usually no time delay between when the caption for "are there any questions" and the caption for "Ok, moving on" would appear on the caption display.) These participants were also unable to raise their hands during gaps in conversation for the same reason. To address these problems, the Trace Center developed the Trace Online Hand-Raising Utility (TOHRU) (Fig. 7.2).

This hand-raising utility not only helps moderators keep track of who raises their hand first and in what order but also allows individuals to raise their hands in four different ways:

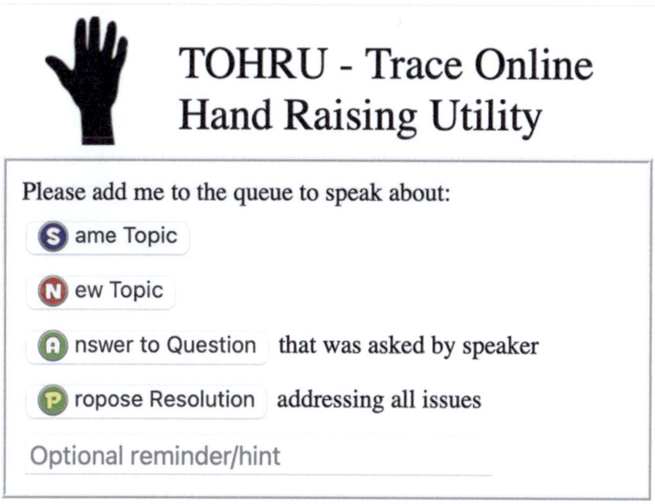

Fig. 7.2 TOHRU allows users to indicate why they are raising their hand—allowing moderators to determine the most efficient order to call on people during complicated or contentious meetings. It also facilitates participation by people with slow reflexes or communication rates

1. [C] to make a comment about the current topic;
2. [N] to get in line to talk about a different topic;
3. [Q] to respond to the question that was just posed by the person who is speaking:
   a. so that they can be called on before someone else changes the topic or the individual speaking has to yield to the next speaker with their question unanswered; and
4. [P] to indicate that they think they have a proposed resolution to the topic being debated that incorporates the concerns of the different parties and may help bring the discussion to an end.

Users are also able to leave a note for themselves and others as to why they have raised their hand so that when their time comes up, they are both reminded of it.

These features enable the moderator to better manage the meeting, allow discussions to occur in a more productive fashion, and avoid people having to wait in line to talk about a new topic—only to be told "we are still discussing the old topic" (and requiring them to raise their hand again—putting them at the end of the queue).

The greatest benefit, however, is that individuals who do not have quick reaction times can very easily raise their hand, get in line, and inject comments in a fashion that is compatible with their reaction time and abilities. It also allows those who are slow to pre-type the essence of their comment in advance.

The tool is open-source and free to use. It works for both phone conferences and video teleconferences. It has been used by the FCC for many years and continues to be used by them even though some basic hand-raising has now been added to teleconferencing systems.

The tool was transferred to Raising the Floor, which now maintains it. It can be used from the Raising the Floor server https://tohru.raisingthefloor.org or the open-source code can be downloaded from GitHub and freely installed and operated on any local server or incorporated into any commercial or non-commercial program without limit.

7.3 Combining 255 and 508: Impact of WCAG Being Technology Agnostic

An unexpected side benefit of the time that Trace spent in trying to ensure that WCAG was technology agnostic was the realization by the Access Board that the Web Content Accessibility Guidelines could (by just replacing the words "web page" with "electronic document" and "software") form the core of the 508 and 255 guidelines for all three (Web content, e-documents, and software). This was fortuitous in that as things were evolving it was becoming increasingly difficult to distinguish between the three. E-documents like PDFs were increasingly being used on the Web and displayed in browsers, making them Web content. But if downloaded they became e-documents. The line between Web apps and applications began to blur, and some applications (such as Microsoft Office) existed in both forms. Users often have a hard time distinguishing between the two. Having different guidelines for a document if it were online vs. if it were downloaded or attached to an email would have been problematic. Because the WCAG guidelines were designed to be technology agnostic, the Access Board could use the same guidelines across the technologies. The European accessibility standard EN 301 549 followed suit and, except for a couple of provisions, the Web, E-doc, and Software sections use the same accessibility provisions—with just the words Web, e-doc, and software swapped out—providing a unified set of guidelines and avoiding having to determine which set applies to ambiguous ICT.

7.4 Real-Time Text

With the demise of analog phones and the TTY, people who are deaf and those with speech disabilities have lost their only mechanisms for real-time text communication. While many have turned to messaging because of the ubiquity of it in telecommunication products, messaging is different from real-time conversation. Starting with the 1999 Rehabilitation Engineering Research Center, the Trace Center has worked with Gallaudet University and other deaf telecommunication researchers on the development of real-time text communication mechanisms. The work involved policy, technology, and standards development, and culminated in the FCC's December 15, 2016 Report and Order requiring the support of real-time text in mobile telecommunications devices. The Telecommunication RERC (Trace Center and Gallaudet) was again cited extensively in the Report and Order.

Kiosks and Information-Transaction Machine Access (1999–)

8

8.1 EZ Access

Trace's first efforts in the area of kiosks and ITM access occurred in the late 1990s. A kiosk vendor approached the Trace Center looking for accessibility techniques that could be used on public kiosks. This request posed a particular challenge in that the solution had to meet several criteria:

- It must require no instruction (or even familiarity), as all users would be novices.
- It must not require significant modifications to the kiosks, such as adding a keyboard.
- It must work across disabilities.
- It must be usable by individuals who are completely blind.

The first approach involved using a single button and gestures on the computer screen. The system (called "EZ Access"[1]) was deployed on a touchscreen kiosk at the Mall of America in Bloomington, Minnesota in 1999.

Subsequent testing, especially with blind users, showed that the on-screen gestures, although easily learned by some, were very difficult for some and impossible for others, including some of those who were blind.

In July 2000, a three-button EZ Access kiosk was featured at a special exhibit celebrating the 10th anniversary of the ADA at the National Museum of American History at the Smithsonian Institution in Washington, D.C. The kiosk contained all the information in

[1] Vanderheiden, G. C. (1997). Cross disability access to touch screen kiosks and ATMs. In *Proceedings of HCI International 97. 7th International Conference on Human Computer Interaction jointly with 13th Symposium on Human Interface*, August 24–29, 1997, vol.1 (pp. 417–20). San Francisco: Elsevier.

G. Vanderheiden et al., *Technology and Disability*, Synthesis Lectures on Technology and Health, https://doi.org/10.1007/978-3-031-09214-5_8

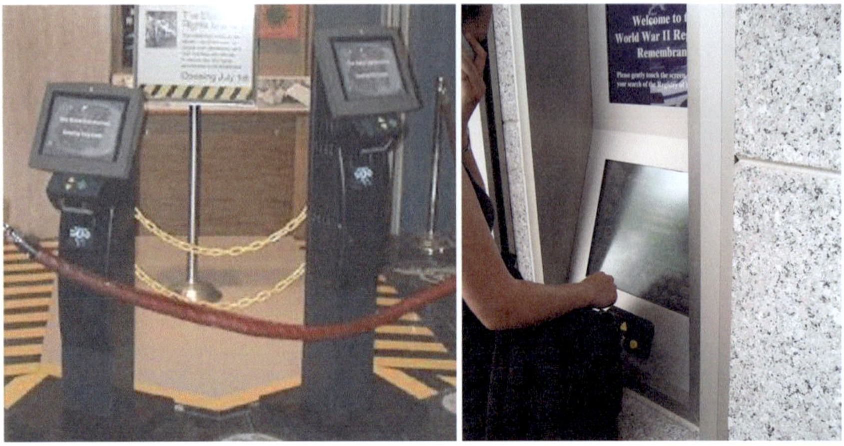

Fig. 8.1 Photo at left: EZ Access kiosk with a three-button interface at the special exhibit celebrating the 10th Anniversary of the ADA in the National Museum of American History at the Smithsonian Institution in Washington, D.C. Photo at right: EZ Access kiosk with a four-button version installed at the World War II Memorial on the U.S. Capitol Mall in Washington, D.C

the exhibit in a form accessible to people with disabilities, as part of the hands-on exhibit (Fig. 8.1).

A new four-button approach (up, down, confirm, and help) was developed and deployed at the World War II Memorial on the National Mall in Washington DC as well as in Automated Postal Centers deployed as self-service kiosks in post offices across the country (Fig. 8.2).

When some of the early four-button keypads could not stand up to brutal daily traffic, especially at the WWII memorial on the Capitol Mall, the Trace Center teamed up with Storm/Keymat in the UK and adapted one of their numeric keypad housings and keys to design a new keypad that was weatherproof and essentially indestructible—even if someone beat on it with their fist, hosed it down, or sprayed it liberally with cleaning fluid. Both five- and eight-key versions were designed to handle linear and page-like kiosks, respectively (Fig. 8.3).

At the same time, Trace also expanded the EZ Access collection of techniques, refining them to move from a modal model to a completely modeless cross-disability access package (i.e., all-access features available for all disabilities all the time). Being modeless, it could work completely in parallel with the touchscreen so that the touchscreen and EZ Access techniques could be used interchangeably from one selection to the next.[2] For example, someone with low vision could use the touchscreen directly for all things that were in large enough print for them to read them directly (or if they remembered the

[2] EZ Access https://trace.umd.edu/ez/.

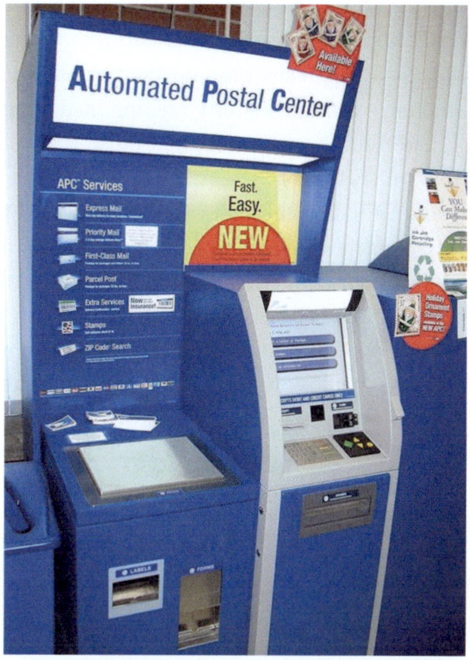

Fig. 8.2 U.S. Postal Service Automated Postal Centers with ruggedized four-button EZ Access keypad and techniques implemented on it. These kiosks enabled patrons to weigh packages and buy postage; they were operable by individuals with disabilities, including patrons who were completely blind

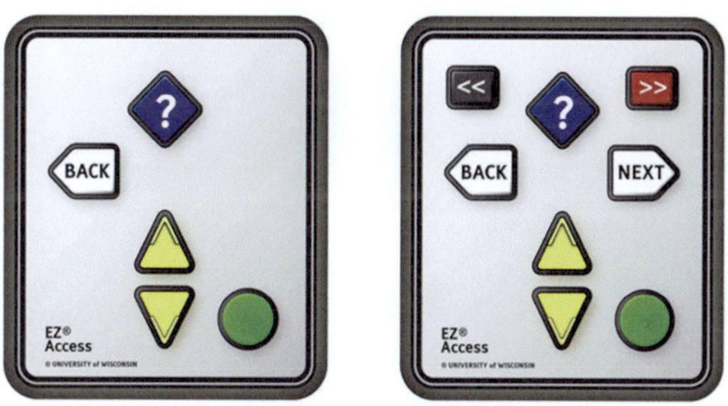

Fig. 8.3 The "square" five- and eight-button weatherproof, and user-proof, EZ Access Keypads

buttons from the last time the kiosk was used). But for buttons or text on screen that was too small for them to read (or that changed dynamically), they could use EZ Access.

This improved EZ Access set of techniques covered access by individuals who were blind, had low vision, had any type of difficulty reading, had cognitive disabilities, were deaf or hard of hearing, had trouble with reach, and those who used prosthetic hands to which kiosks were insensitive (Fig. 8.4).

When the kiosks became slimmer and there was no longer a place to locate the EZ Access keypad, the Trace Center developed a linear version of the access keypad that could be mounted easily just below the screen (Fig. 8.5). Two versions were developed. With the first version, pressing the buttons would actually press a tiny mechanical finger onto the extreme bottom edge of the touchscreen. This interface required no electronics and could simply be attached to the lower cowl of any touchscreen kiosk. There were concerns about dirt or debris falling into the area just below the mechanical touch fingers causing it to malfunction. So, the Center again worked with Storm/Keymat to create a second version of the linear keybar using the same switch technology used on the five- and eight-key EZ Access keypads.

Fig. 8.4 John Kemp using the new EZ Access Keypad on an IBM kiosk at the CSUN conference

Fig. 8.5 United Airlines ticketing kiosk with the linear EZ Access keypad

The Trace Center also consulted with Storm on a diamond-shaped array with a button in the middle that they had proposed in working with one of their clients, NCR. The Trace team confirmed that it also would be capable of implementing EZ Access but recommended changes in button colors to have buttons that contrast with their housing.

Variations on the EZ Access techniques and interfaces can now be found on Amtrak ticket machines, Homeland Security kiosks, airport check-in kiosks, the FDIC's history exhibit, post offices, voting machines, and many other applications (Fig. 8.6).

The Trace Center also worked with Smith-Kettlewell Eye Research Institute and a Wisconsin firm, Viking Electronics, to create the first cross-disability accessible building entry system which was deployed in a public housing complex in San Francisco and allowed access to the building directory and entrance security by individuals with low vision, blindness, physical disabilities, hearing impairments, deafness, and reading disabilities (Fig. 8.7).

Fig. 8.6 A sampling of kiosks using EZ Access with "square" EZ Access keypad. #1; Photo credit: Tasnim Shamma for WFAE; #3; Photo credit: U.S. Customs and Border Protection; #5; #6; #7

8.2 Cross-Disability Voting Prototypes

In 1999, the Trace Center developed cross-disability voting prototypes to demonstrate that a single machine could be designed that would work for all voters, including people with a variety of types, degrees, and combinations of disability and those without. Both kiosk and tablet prototypes were created (Fig. 8.8). These were shared with voting manufacturers over the years both in person and in different venues, including exhibits at National Institute of Standards and Technology (NIST) events and invited presentations such as

Fig. 8.7 EZ Access providing cross-disability access for Viking Door Intercom and Entry System. Here, a deaf individual is able to converse with residents using their portable TTY. (Today they would use their cellphone and text)

the Help America Vote Act (HAVA) Webcast (2003, May 13).[3,4,5,6] Manufacturers were encouraged to borrow ideas from the prototypes, and they did.

In 1999, the Trace Center Rehabilitation Engineering Research Center was invited to present its accessibility work with computers, telecommunications, and voting in the Grand Foyer of the White House (Fig. 8.9).

[3] Invited Presentation: "Demonstration of a Prototype Cross-Disability Accessible Voting Tablet," Help America Vote Act (HAVA) Webcast (2003, May 13).

[4] "A natural accessibility interface for voting systems" and "Future technology developments and domotics," *4th International Conference on Gerontechnology*. (2002, Nov. 9–12). Miami, Florida.

[5] Invited Presentation: "Ballot Design: Opportunities for November and Beyond," Voting Technology: Innovations for Today and Tomorrow, IT. (2004, Oct. 2). Boston, Massachusetts.

[6] Invited Presentation: "Changing the rules: Natural accessibility for voting systems and personal pluggable interfaces for everything," *Usability Professionals Association Annual Conference*. (2005, June 29). Montreal, Quebec.

Fig. 8.8 Trace Center's cross-disability mainstream voting tablet prototype. It was designed to be used with a card or with a ballot printer

Fig. 8.9 Trace Center director Gregg Vanderheiden demonstrating the Trace Center's accessibility work on computers, phones, and voting to President Bill Clinton and Vice President Al Gore (holding one of the exhibit phones). Photos courtesy of William J. Clinton Presidential Library

8.3 Secure USB

To support accessible voting, including the ability for voters to use their own special interfaces, the Trace Center developed an "unhackable" USB module (Fig. 8.10). This module would sit between the outside world and a standard USB port that would be secure inside the case. The module would allow the connection of USB-compatible switches and controllers as well as keyboards and assistive technologies acting as keyboards. The module was read-limited and would only accept the types of switch actions needed to

Fig. 8.10 Secure USB shown in case used for dissemination and testing

operate the voting machine and/or keyboard input for write-in votes, or control of the voting machine from the arrow keys on the keyboard. To test the "unhackableness" of it, a $10,000 reward was offered for anyone breaking it. No one collected.

Accessibility Infrastructure (2010–) 9

9.1 The Global Public Inclusive Infrastructure (GPII)

While wrapping up the development of the WCAG 2.0 guidelines in 2008, it became clear that the only way to write guidelines was to assume that consumers would be able to secure assistive technologies that were powerful enough to access the new generation of web technologies. However, at the same time, it was clear that not all people with disabilities had access to the assistive technologies they needed. In some cases, technologies that adequately address their types, degrees, and combinations of disability are not available. In other cases, the AT was not available in their country, in their language, or at a price they could afford. Still others were just not aware of solutions that might exist for them.

To address these issues, the Trace Center envisioned a National Public Inclusive Infrastructure—an infrastructure that could take a comprehensive approach to accessibility to facilitate the development, dissemination, and use of the AT needed by people who faced barriers to using ICT due to disability, literacy, digital literacy, or age.

Within a year it was clear that this effort needed to be global, so the focus shifted to creating a Global Public Inclusive Infrastructure (GPII). Three major needs were identified that led to the three major goals that became the pillars for the infrastructure effort.

1. **Awareness:** If a solution exists anywhere in the world for an individual, they should be able to find it.
2. **Availability when needed:** If the person knows what assistive technologies, accessibility features, or settings they need, those settings and technologies should be on, or appear at, every piece of ICT they encounter and need to use.
3. **Existence:** If a solution does not exist for an individual, the infrastructure should support the creation of new or improved solutions that could meet the person's needs.

G. Vanderheiden et al., *Technology and Disability*, Synthesis Lectures on Technology and Health, https://doi.org/10.1007/978-3-031-09214-5_9

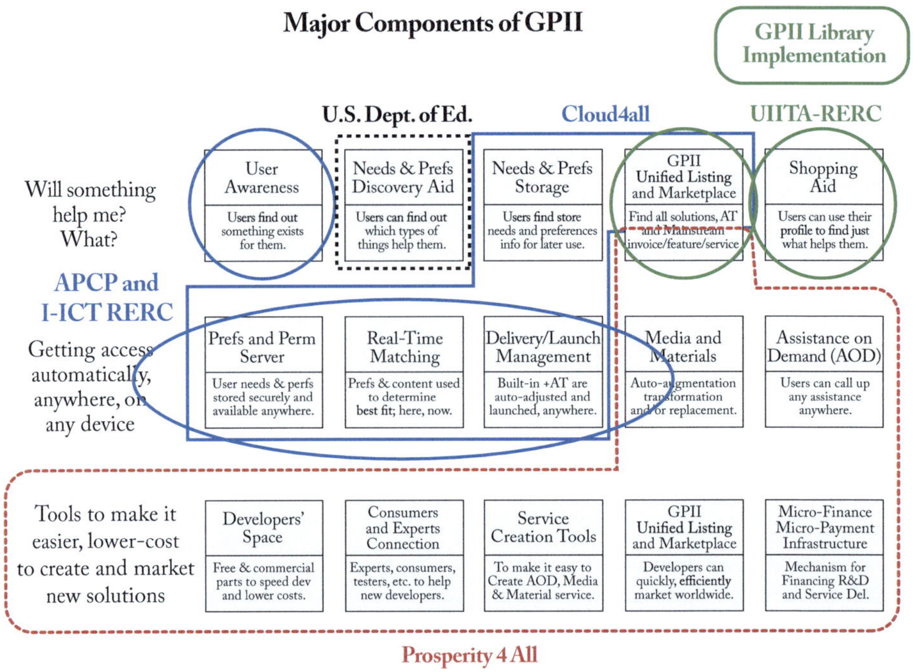

Fig. 9.1 The major components of the GPII as they were first proposed in 2010—along with the grants that were secured and executed to address them

Five key functions were identified to address each of these goals. Figure 9.1 shows goals and components as they were first proposed. Also shown in the figure are the different grants that were secured to explore and develop each of the components. These grants included the following:

- The Universal Interface and Information Technology Access RERC: Grants H133E090001 and H133E080022 from the National Institute on Disability and Rehabilitation Research (NIDRR), U.S. Dept of Education. Led by the Trace Center, University of Wisconsin-Madison.
- The Fluid/Flow Project: Funded through multiple grants. Led by the Inclusive Design Research Centre, Ontario College of Art and Design University.
- The Preferences for Global Access: Contract ED-OSE-12-D-0013 from NIDRR, US Dept of Education. Led by the Institute for Knowledge Management in Education (ISKME).
- Cloud4All: A large-scale Integrated Project Grant #289,016 from the European Union's 7th Framework Program. Led by Technosite, Spain and Raising the Floor-International, Geneva.

- Prosperity4All: A large-scale Integrated Project Grant #610,510 from the European Union's 7th Framework Program. Led by Fraunhofer IAO, Stuttgart, and Raising the Floor-International, Geneva.
- The Automated Personalization Computing Project (APCP), Grant H421A150005/6 from the Rehabilitation Services Administration, U.S. Dept of Education. Led by the Trace Center, University of Maryland, College Park.
- The Inclusive ICT Rehabilitation Engineering Research Center (RERC), Grant 90REGE0008 from National Institute on Disability, Independent Living, and Rehabilitation Research (NIDILRR), Administration for Community Living (ACL), U.S. Dept. of Health and Human Services. Led by the Trace Center, University of Maryland, College Park.

As a result of these projects, all 15 areas shown in Fig. 9.1 were addressed with at least initial implementations—and all 3 legs are serving people with disabilities (in sustainable form beyond the end of the grant funding) in the form of the Unified Listing (information availability), the DeveloperSpace (facilitating development of new or better solutions for unmet needs), and Morphic (providing both auto-personalization for assistive technologies and built-in accessibility features and Assistive Technology on Demand (AToD)).

9.2 Unified Listing

The **Unified Listing**[1] is an international listing of products for making communication aids, computers, and digital devices more accessible. It brings together data on products to provide access to information and communication technologies (ICT) access from 12 different databases in Europe, the United States, and Australia.

The Unified Listing provides four different searching techniques from guided searches to power searching to make it easier for people with all levels of knowledge and search skill to find products that might help them (Fig. 9.2).

The Unified Listing has several unique features that help manufacturers.

1. The Unified Listing automatically feeds all of its federated databases from around the world with any new information that it finds or receives. Manufacturers can therefore update the information in one place (the Unified Listing) and it will automatically be sent to all of the federated databases as well.
2. Users of the Unified Listing (consumers and manufacturers) can ask to be alerted by email if any new information on products from any category, manufacturer, or search is added to the listing. Thus, any time a manufacturer has a new product included in the Unified Listing, any Unified Listing users who are interested in that category of

[1] Unified Listing https://ul.gpii.net.

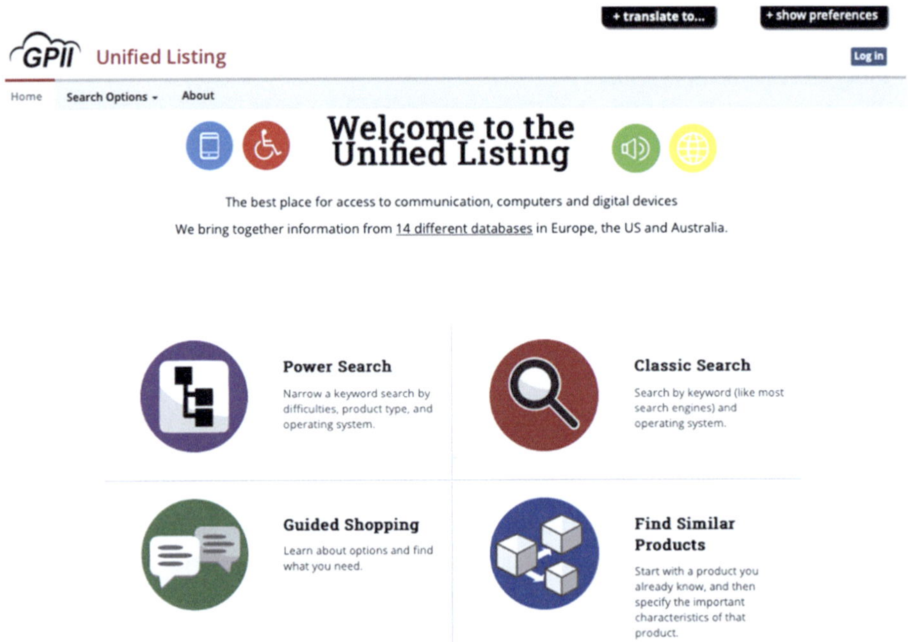

Fig. 9.2 Unified Listing home page with four search options

product can automatically have an email sent to them—without having to return and re-search the database.

3. There is also a feature that allows manufacturers to be automatically notified of any major changes to the listing of their products in the Unified Listing.

The Unified Listing is also part of the EASTIN Assistive Technology Database Collaboration. Trace is now launching a new effort, with EASTIN, Raising the Floor—International, the Global Alliance of Assistive Technology Organizations (GAATO), and others to develop an international data collaboration that can provide other countries, particularly in the global south, who do not have their own assistive technology databases, with the data and tools to allow them to very cost effectively create databases of assistive technologies created in or supported within their country, at costs appropriate to their country, and supporting the language of their country. As this occurs the Unified Listing would be merged into this even broader infrastructure project.

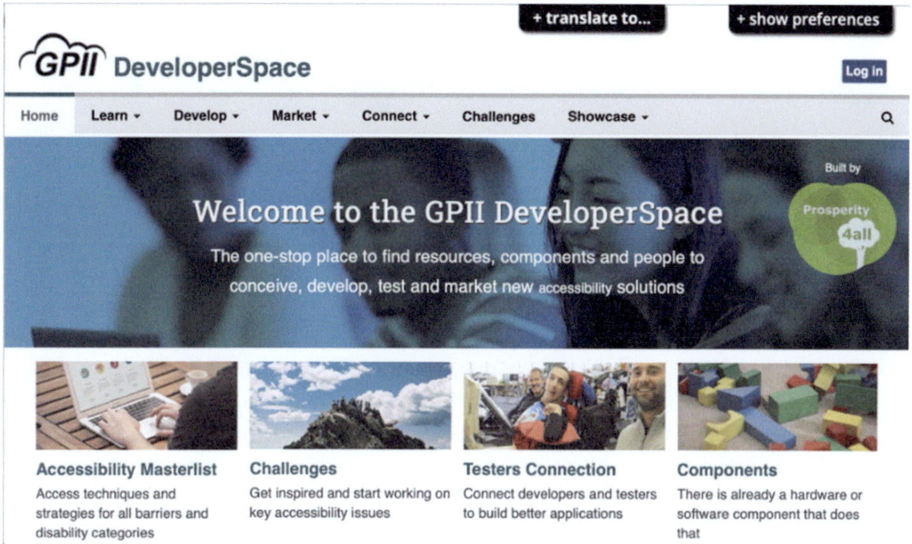

Fig. 9.3 Home page of the DeveloperSpace—a free online resource for developers of assistive technologies and accessibility features in mainstream products

9.3 DeveloperSpace

The DeveloperSpace is designed to provide a one-stop place to find resources, components, and people to conceive, develop, test, and market novel accessible solutions (Fig. 9.3).[2]

The Trace Center also worked collaboratively with 20 other organizations in Europe in the creation of the DeveloperSpace, an online resource that makes it easy to find information on accessibility and open-source tools, components, and more. The goal is to make it easy for new individuals to learn about all the different dimensions of accessibility and to find any existing open-source tools and components they might use in creating their own solutions.

The **Master List of Accessibility Strategies**, one of the tools from the Trace Center that is available on the DeveloperSpace, is a comprehensive listing of all the different accessibility strategies known at this time. Each strategy has its own page branching off of it that provides a description of the strategy, how it benefits different disability groups, a listing of open-source, free, free-to-try, and commercial programs that use this particular technique. It also provides a list of research papers on the technique as well as other resources related to the technique in the DeveloperSpace.

[2] DeveloperSpace https://ds.gpii.net.

Fig. 9.4 Morphic logo

The Master List has been vetted and added to by experts in different disabilities. It is also kept evergreen through a $50 reward to anyone who finds a technique not covered by the existing compendium and five dollars for each new research reference for any of the techniques.

In addition to the MasterList and other information resources in the DeveloperSpace, it also provides a user-friendly, live, dynamic compilation of all of the open-source accessibility projects and components on GitHub, and challenges for developers and other resources to help people get started, become more informed, or find tools for creating new and better solutions.

9.4 Morphic

Morphic is the latest tool from the Trace Center and was developed as a collaborative effort with groups in the U.S., Canada, and Europe. Morphic is an extension to the Windows and Macintosh operating systems that provides four functions that together provide a range of benefits for computer users who need assistive technologies or who just have trouble using computers (Fig. 9.4).

1. Provides easier discovery and access to built-in features
   - Morphic makes it easy to discover and activate both built-in and third-party accessibility and usability features via its MorphicBar and menu.
2. Provides customized and simplified experiences
   - Morphic allows people to create customized MorphicBars with just the functions, apps, and websites needed. Users can create these for themselves. Morphic also makes it easy for a person to create custom MorphicBars for their students or clients, friends or family members, who have trouble using computers or who cannot otherwise use the computer at all.
3. Provides "Anywhere AT/Accessibility"
   - Allows essential assistive technologies and accessibility features that a person needs to show up (i.e., they will be automatically installed and configured for the user) on any computer they need to use at school, a tutor's house, work, library, community center, family's or friends' house, etc.—and then disappear when the user is finished and signs off.

4. Instant Setup
   - Allows a new computer at an internship, new job, or even a replacement computer to be automatically set up in minutes with all of the assistive technologies and computer settings needed to make it accessible for that user.

In developing Morphic, the Trace Center also established a new model for privacy. This involved the creation of an external Privacy and Data Ethics Council made up of international privacy and security advocates and experts. This Council oversees all privacy policies and practices for Morphic.

Morphic is open-source software that is available free from https://morphic.org, a website of the collaborating nonprofit organization, Raising the Floor, to which Morphic has been transferred.

9.4.1 New Definition of Accessibility

As noted above, any computer with Morphic is capable of supporting Assistive Technology on Demand (AToD). This new capability, coupled with the fact that Morphic is open source and can be installed on any computer free of charge, allows, for the first time, people with disabilities who need assistive technology to be able to sit down to any/all of the same computers as their peers, and have the computers be accessible to them. An "accessible library" could now mean that the entire library and its computers, labs, and programs are accessible. (Not just a couple of computers in a resource room upstairs that may or may not have the necessary AT).

Move to University of Maryland (2016) 10

In August 2016, the Trace Center moved from the University of Wisconsin-Madison, where it had begun and flourished for 45 years, to the University of Maryland, College Park. The move was inspired by an invitation from Ben Shneiderman to consider bringing the Trace Center out to the University of Maryland (UMD)—or at least come visit the iSchool at the University of Maryland and meet the students, staff, and dean. From the first ad hoc visit (UMD was just a subway ride away from a meeting in Washington), it was clear that the iSchool—and its joint HCI Lab with Computer Science—was a perfect environment for Trace. In addition to Ben Shneiderman and his group, UMD was also home of Paul Jaeger and other faculty with strong interests and many contributions to accessibility. With UMD being located just a subway ride away from the consumer groups and industry associations that Trace worked with, as well as the government agencies working on accessibility, the University of Maryland's location also was ideal for the extensive stakeholder work that has been important in Trace's activities and effectiveness. Although the University of Wisconsin had been very supportive of the program, the programs and people at the University of Maryland looked to provide a much richer environment for the Trace Center going forward.

Ordinarily, moving a center would be a major disruption of program and people. However, over the last decade, the Trace Center had expanded its program and moved from a model of "recruiting the best local people with the skills needed" to a virtual design where Trace engaged the best people no matter where they were located. As a result, the majority of the Trace Team was in other locations around the U.S. and abroad, so only a few people actually needed to relocate to Maryland.

Shortly after moving to UMD, Dr. Amanda Lazar and Dr. Hernisa Kacorri came to UMD, and Dr. Jonathan Lazar (no relation to Amanda) moved to UMD from nearby Towson University to join Trace as Associate Director. These additional faculty further enhanced the Trace Center, allowing it to expand and strengthen its work in aging,

G. Vanderheiden et al., *Technology and Disability*, Synthesis Lectures on Technology and Health, https://doi.org/10.1007/978-3-031-09214-5_10

artificial intelligence, cognition, and policy. With Dr. Bern Jordan's almost 20 years in standards and design, and the rich environment of collaborators (for example, affiliated faculty Abhinav Shrivastava, Ana Palla, Elizabeth Marie Bonsignore, Eun Kyoung Choe, Galina Madjaroff, Gulnoza Yakubova, Niklas Elmqvist, Paul T. Jaeger, Rachael Bradley-Montgomery, and Ursula Gorham-Oscilowski), the benefit of moving the Trace Center to the University of Maryland was borne out.

10.1 Passing of the Gavel

In October 2021, the 50th anniversary of the trip out to the school that began Trace's evolution, the Co-Founder and Director of the Trace Center, Gregg Vanderheiden, passed the Directorship over to Dr. Jonathan Lazar.[1] Dr. Vanderheiden continued his research and development work, concentrating his focus on issues that will be created by next-next-generation user interfaces, as well as potential ways new evolving technologies might be used to completely reinvent our concept of and approach to accessibility.

[1] https://trace.umd.edu/news/jonathan-lazar-named-director-of-the-trace-rd-center/.

Elements that Have Defined the Trace Center 11

Over the first 50 years, there have been a number of elements that have defined the Trace Center and are believed to be responsible for its successes. Many of these were developed as the result of lessons learned along the way around what did and didn't work. They are captured here for others interested in what drove the Trace Center program and what seemed to work, at least for this group.

11.1 Forecasting the Future: Skating to Where the Puck Will Be

The Center is perhaps best known for its ability to look at mainstream and assistive technology trends and developments, predict where technology will be going, and to both identify gaps in what is needed and to capitalize on opportunities. This was the primary strength mentioned by both David Capozzi (former Executive Director of the U.S. Access Board) and Judy Brewer (Director of the W3C's Web Accessibility Initiative), when discussing the contributions of the Trace Center at a panel on Trace's 50 years at the ASSETS Conference in October 2021.[1] During the panel discussion David related a time in 1998 when Dr. Vanderheiden, during a presentation at the Access Board, pulled out a cardboard mockup (having forgotten his plastic mockup) of what he said would soon be used by everyone and that the Access Board needed to start preparing for. The mockup was a touchscreen-only device that would be used for all telecommunication and also web access. It had just two buttons for volume, two for other control, and dual miniature cameras. Dr. Vanderheiden presented the same prototype (which he dubbed a "Window to the World") at Microsoft Accessibility Days in February 1998. Figure 11.1 shows two frames from a short animation that was used at that presentation and Fig. 11.2 shows the handout from the presentation. David Capozzi commented that he remembered

[1] https://www.youtube.com/watch?v=AHm3VjGOPko.

G. Vanderheiden et al., *Technology and Disability*, Synthesis Lectures on Technology and Health, https://doi.org/10.1007/978-3-031-09214-5_11

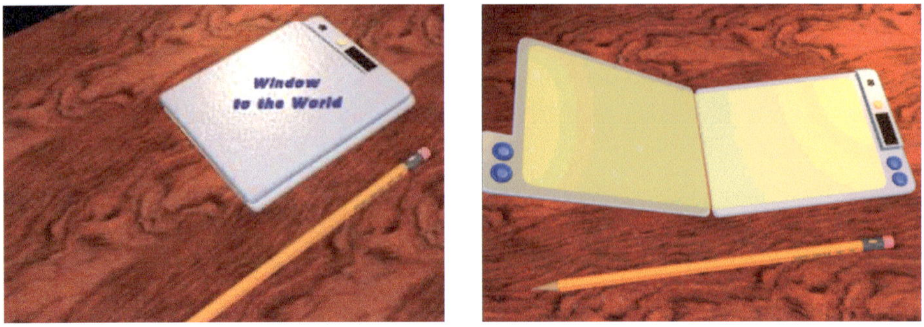

Fig. 11.1 Trace Center's "Window to the World" prediction of future telecom and mobile computing made in 1998

the 1998 presentation in 2008 (10 years later), when the iPhone was introduced. (The iPhone was also all touchscreen except for 4 buttons, two for volume, and a camera.) In 2018 (20 years later), Samsung introduced a folding phone that looked even more like the original prediction.

Below are other examples of Trace's predictions and efforts launched to create solutions and awareness of problems so that people with disabilities could have access at or near the introduction of technologies when they became widespread for mainstream users.

- Trace's focus in the early 1980s on "transparent access" (i.e., techniques to allow access to all mainstream software—rather than writing special programs for people with disabilities).
- Trace's "Information Super-Highway" special experience room at CSUN for 5 years starting in the late 1990s to help the field, including both developers and practitioners, to learn about the Web in order to be better prepared, and to prepare for it entering all aspects of their lives.
- The focus on designing WCAG to be technology agnostic so that it would continue to be relevant and effective as the Web quickly evolved from HTML to many different technologies.
- Work with Larry Scadden and Frank Bowe to create the first White House conference (in 1984) to facilitate the engagement of mainstream computer companies to work on accessibility in their products, a decade before requirements began to emerge that would require it.
- Working with Rick Foulds (in 1983) to convince NIHR the Rehabilitation Engineering Research Center program to expand beyond physical rehabilitation topics to include an RERC on Augmentative Communication.

Window to the World
Presentation at
Microsoft Accessibility Days 98,
February 18, 19 & 20, 1998.

By Gregg Vanderheiden Ph.D.

∀ Access anything – anywhere (that you have permission)
  o Short link to local net
∀ Two way telecommunication
∀ Auto translation
∀ 2 cameras
  o Take pictures
  o Take movies (never run out of film)
  o Video phone
  o Show people things
  o ZOOM in - enlarge
  o Mirror
∀ Capture/Read
  o Lookup
  o Translate
  o Stitch images
∀ Talk to it – it to you
∀ Earbud – (wireless)
  o Hands free
  o Eyes free
∀ Heads Up Display
∀ Touchscreen
  o Silent operation
∀ Instant help - with picture if needed (remember you can show people things)
∀ Knows where you are
  o "Where is the closest....?"

Blind – All Verbal
∀ Capture read
∀ Stitch images: Poor aim
∀ Visual assistant on demand
  o Environment
  o Documents

Low Vision
∀ Enlarge text
∀ Use as magnifier
∀ Capture and read

Deaf
∀ All silent operation
∀ Captions anywhere
∀ You sign – speech comes out of device

Hard of Hearing
∀ Export sounds for translation into text (captions anywhere)
∀ Hand device to person (or lecturer) and have them talking in your ear

Physical
∀ Buttons are "soft" so can enlarge
∀ Speech control
∀ Speech re-voicing service
  o Auto or "Try Harder"

Cognitive
∀ Assistance on demand
∀ Knows where you are
∀ Text capture and read
∀ See companion assistant on demand

Fig. 11.2 Trace Center's "Window to the World" presentation handout at Microsoft Accessibility Days 1998

- Convincing NIHR to further expand the Rehabilitation Engineering Research Center program into computers and information technologies—fields with no counterpart in medical rehabilitation.
- In partnership with Gallaudet University, expanding the Rehabilitation Engineering Research Center program to include an RERC on Telecommunication Access.
- For several more examples, see Chap. 13.

11.2 Identifying and Filling Gaps

In addition to working with consumers, industry, and researchers to identifying (current and future) gaps, the Trace Center also sought to step into those gaps and fill them. Some examples included the following:

- In the early days of augmentative communication, when AT manufacturers had few resources, Trace not only created new interface techniques but carried through to prototypes and even production design, complete with PC board art and part lists to get new AT onto the market when AT manufacturers lacked the resources. The Center stepped back from this activity when AT manufacturers were more established and could do this work themselves.
- When there were no accessibility guidelines for computers—Trace created them.
- When there were no accessibility guidelines for consumer products—Trace created them.
- When there were no accessibility guidelines for the Web—Trace created them.
- When there were dozens of guidelines for the Web—and the field needed something that harmonized them—Trace worked with different authors to create the Unified Web Accessibility guidelines (seven versions).

    o When the W3C stepped up to work on web accessibility, Trace created an 8th version for the W3C, passed it to them, and stepped back, ceasing all work except to support the W3C.

- When a tool for measuring contrast was needed so that a provision could be included in WCAG requiring contrast—Trace partnered with low vision experts to create a standard and then with others to create a free tool to measure it.
- When the only tool for evaluating dangerous flashing that could cause seizures cost $30,000, and a requirement could not be included if that was the only tool, the Trace Center raised $200,000 to license an engine and create a tool that could be made

available free for web content evaluation—thus allowing a provision to be included in accessibility standards.

- When there was no free, easy-to-use captioning tool, Trace secured funding for this purpose and then passed the funds on to WGBH to create one.

11.3 Addressing Needs of Consumers, Clinicians, Developers, and Industry

Another important component of the Trace Center's approach is to maintain ongoing discussions with stakeholders before and throughout its projects.

The Center has engaged in a variety of activities to serve and engage all stakeholder groups from consumers to industry to government agencies. These include providing summative information, creating resource sites, developing free tools, assembling data repositories, teaching workshops and seminars, writing scores of chapters in industry, academic, and consumer-oriented books, acting as expert consultants to all stakeholders, and mediating conflicts.

The Center has focused on building consensus across stakeholder groups, trying to communicate the needs and constraints of each "side" to the other, and trying to find language that all can "live with." One example is the work on the Web Content Accessibility Guidelines (WCAG). Although it took many years of effort, in the end the WCAG 2.0 guidelines were passed—not with general consensus, but with unanimous consent and without any formal objections from within the group or from the field. This is almost unheard of.

11.3.1 Work on Standards

Anyone who has worked on standards knows the enormous amount of time and effort it takes to create or even update one standard. It is uncommon for a standard to take less than 5 years to create, and many take longer. Few will take the time or have the patience to work on them. And for each standard there needs to be one or a few people who work 8–10 times harder.

The Trace Center led a number of accessibility standard efforts and served as the main support center for many others, providing research, drafting, and tools support for them. The reason that Center invested so much time and effort in these standards is the impact they can have. Although not all standards see extensive use, others have literally changed the accessibility landscape for information and communication technologies

(ICT). And even standards that seem to come before their time (and are not now heavily referenced) were often important for developing the concepts that were used in later landmark standards.

Both the U.S. and Europe look to standards whenever they can when building their accessibility laws and regulations. And companies usually look to the regulations to determine what they should be doing to make their products more accessible. So, research and development can change what is known and what is possible. But standards can have a greater impact on what the person with disabilities actually sees in their everyday life. The ideal is to have major investments in both. Unfortunately, we typically only have funding programs for research. Another advantage of the Rehabilitation Engineering Research Center program is the ability to combine research and such enabling activities as guidelines and standards.

Some of the standards the Trace Center has led or provided major support for included the following:

- SET and Multi-Switch Standards: Created by Trace.
- Canadian Standards Association: Disability Standards Working group (member).
- WCAG 1.0 Working group: Provided one co-chair and two of four editors.
- WCAG 2.0 Working Group: provided one co-chair and two of four editors (plus one Trace alum working at W3C). Trace also did the research that led to quantification of two success criteria—and created or commissioned the development of three tools, the Photosensitive Epilepsy Analysis Tool (PEAT), the Contrast Analysis tool, and a Captioning Tool, to make WCAG provisions practical/adoptable.
- ISO 9241-151 "Ergonomics of human-system interaction: Part 151: Guidance on World Wide Web user interfaces"—expert on Working Group.[2]
- ISO 9241-171 "Ergonomics of human-system interaction: Guidance on software accessibility"—expert on Working Group.
- ANSI/HFES 200 Human Factors Engineering of Software User Interfaces, Part 2: Accessibility: chair and editor.
- Internet Engineering Task Force IETF RFC-4103: standard on real-time text used in multiple accessibility standards (Trace-Gallaudet RERC).
- CEN/CENELEC on its accessibility standard EN 301 549: "Accessibility requirements suitable for public procurement of ICT products and services in Europe"—Trace Center expert on Working Group representing European Disability Forum.

Unified ICT Accessibility Standards Comparison Tool.

Trace is currently leading the development of a comprehensive tool for comparing, contrasting, and harmonizing all of the existing ICT accessibility standards' provisions.

[2] ISO 9241-151:2008(en). Ergonomics of human-system interaction—Part 151: Guidance on World Wide Web user interfaces https://www.iso.org/obp/ui/#iso:std:iso:9241:-151:ed-1:v1:en.

Called the Unified ICT Accessibility Standards Comparison Tool,[3] this compendium contains all of the provisions of all of the accessibility standards and guidelines internationally, presenting them in a manner that allows researchers, students, and policymakers to easily compare the provisions of all of the standards in a side-by-side, topic-by-topic fashion. The compendium has two goals. The first is to facilitate comparing and contrasting the different versions of the same provision in different standards. The second is to work toward better harmonized standards and ensuring that new standards both build off of older standards using the established language from the past—or all use the same, better, language going forward. The first test of this tool will be its use in creating the much-needed Kiosk and ITM guidelines.

11.3.2 Work with Policy Creating Agencies

In addition to having both a representative and a second as a member on the following committees—the whole Trace Center worked to support the following accessibility committees, providing information, compiling drafts, and conducting research as needed for the committees.

- TAAC: Telecommunications Access Advisory Committee: U.S. Access Board; led to Section 255 Telecommunications Accessibility Regulations.
- EITAAC: Electronic and Information Technology Accessibility Advisory Committee: U.S. Access Board; led to first Section 508 Accessibility Regulations for Electronic Information Technologies.
- TEITAC: Telecommunications and Electronic and Information Technology Advisory Committee: U.S. Access Board; led to revisions of both the Section 508 Accessibility Regulations for Electronic Information Technologies and the Section 255 Telecommunications Accessibility Regulations.
- TAC: Technological Advisory Committee—FCC: composed of engineers from major ICT companies—to provide FCC with advice on new technologies on the horizon.
- EAAC: Emergency Access Advisory Committee—FCC: to provide input to the FCC on its development of regulations regarding Telecommunication in Emergencies.

Trace also regularly provides answers to queries and public comments on proceedings of the Access Board (ATBCB), the Federal Communications Commission (FCC), the Department of Justice (DOJ), the Department of Transportation (DOT), and the Federal Election Commission.

[3] Unified ICT Accessibility Standards Comparison Tool https://go.umd.edu/unified-ict-a11y-stds-comp.

11.4 Supporting Others in the Field

Much of the Trace Center's efforts over the years has focused on supporting the other players in the field. For many years, the Trace Center was the only federally supported Research and Development Center in its field. First, for Augmentative Communication, then for Computer and ICT Access, and then for Telecommunication Access. As such, the Trace team felt it was its responsibility to support and foster the development of the whole field and everyone in it. Over time, as more centers were funded and the field grew and also received support from other funding agencies, this was less needed. Still, the Center was unique in thinking of itself as a central reference point for the fields in which it was working—and in trying to provide resources and support (and fill gaps) in those fields.

Activities in support of others included the creation of summative information, giving workshops aimed at people coming into the field, providing advice and consultation to groups without charge, carrying out research on areas of interest to consumers that were hard or expensive or time-consuming to do, creating tools for clinicians, helping both consumers and researchers to more effectively interface with and impact industry, and helping to find and disseminate fugitive literature (i.e., important information that is not otherwise found in catalogued research publications).

The ResourceBooks (and their electronic counterpart, the Co-Net CDs) were an example of the large-scale summative information efforts that were the sole source of summative information before the Web and Google came into being. The Unified Listing of ICT assistive technologies, the DeveloperSpace, and the MasterList of accessibility strategies are some of the more recent examples.

The National Workshop Series (first for Augmentative Communication and then for Computer Access) were examples of attempts to spread the word and start up new efforts across the nation. And the industry workshop series attempted to inject expertise directly into industry at a time when there were few people with accessibility knowledge within companies.

11.4.1 Helping Fund the Efforts of Others

Trace has also been unique in its funding of the efforts of others. On numerous occasions the Trace Center sought permission from its funding agency to redirect funds awarded to the Trace Center for an activity—to another organization when it discovered one that was in a better position to carry out some needed work. (Several examples of this have already been mentioned above.)

The Center has also stepped in to help save other programs in the U.S. or abroad that got into trouble due to misadventure, holding special fund-raising events or covering costs that another organization encumbered but was unable to cover, or engaging a researcher when another program lost funding so that that researcher would not be lost from the field.

The Center has even written letters of support for younger research programs that were submitting grants in competition with Trace (but did not know that Trace was submitting when they asked for a letter of support). It also provided advice to groups that were competing with Trace, helping them to better understand how to write effective grants and how to understand particular funding agencies.

11.5 Moving Ideas into the Hands of People with Disabilities and Practitioners

Finally, the Center is known for the number of developments that were actually moved into the hands and lives of people with disabilities.

A core part of the Trace Center, one might even say one of its core principles, has been its focus on technology transfer—the movement of ideas from conception and research all the way through to either commercial production or common clinical practice.

Technology transfer is perhaps the hardest part of the Trace Center's work. Much research and development falls victim to what NSF has called the Valley of Death (see Fig. 11.3).

By making knowledge and tech transfer a core value, the Trace Center has been able to create what has been called by many a remarkable transfer track record.

A review of the technology transfer records of RERCs, conducted by the Technology Transfer RERC (Lane 2008), provides an evaluation of the Trace Center IT RERC's technology transfer performance as well as suggesting some of the reasons for the Center's success.

> The two RERCs managed by the Trace Center at the University of Wisconsin-Madison are clearly operating at a level of success unmatched by the other nine RERCs. Both of these RERCs record nearly 100% congruence between the planned and actual results of development and transfer projects.
>
> The Trace Center's two RERCs' proposals are distinctive from the other nine in that they describe a thorough plan for accomplishing the transfer outcome for development project outputs. ...the Trace Center's two proposals describe the development and transfer process as one that is entirely different than the process used for conducting research projects. The narrative sets realistic goals, acknowledges limitations and describes the RERCs' role in an ambiguous and constantly changing application environment.
>
> The [Trace Center's] model is the most detailed of the 11 RERC proposals studied, showing the highest awareness of the complex process involved.

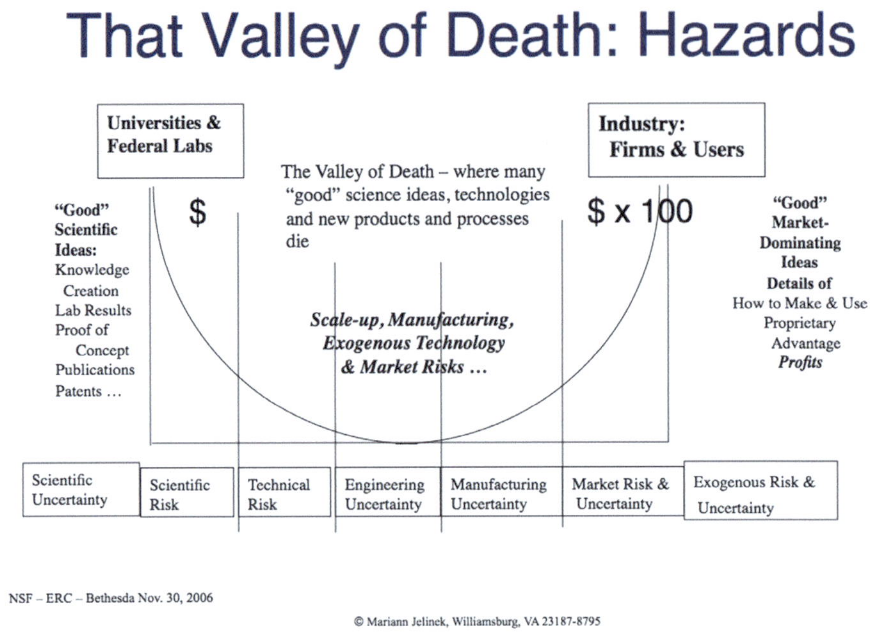

Fig. 11.3 "Valley of death" (Jelinek 2006)

> Of the RERCs studied, the two operated by the Trace Center demonstrated the most innovative approach to applying the standard methodologies of new product development and transfer. The Trace Center's ... model is embedded in the singular goal of accomplishing the transfer of the internal innovation through an external partner, and then out to the target audience. Its ability to begin with the end in mind goes beyond even the business model's definition of transfer "to" the external partner, and instead sees them as a necessary intermediary to impact the lives of people with disabilities (Lane 2008).[4]

And again in 2015:

> There are excellent and oft-cited examples where an individual academic is well versed in both the enabling technology and the requirements of the niche market, and where the market timing allows them to make critical contributions as the mainstream market evolves. Vanderheiden (2013) at the University of Wisconsin, Madison is one such person. His sustained efforts ensured that every Microsoft and Apple product now contains key accessibility features

[4] Lane, J.P. (2008) Delivering on the D in R&D: Recommendations for increasing transfer outcomes from development projects. *Assistive Technology Outcomes & Benefits, suppl. SPECIAL ISSUE*; Chicago (Fall 2008): 1–60.

and usability interface options for persons with sensory, physical, or cognitive impairments (Lane 2015).[5]

This coincides with the conclusion of Sauer et al. (2000),[6] who evaluated different models for public–private partnerships: "The Trace Center at the University of Wisconsin, Madison, presents the best example of successful transfer of design to the marketplace."

11.5.1 Types of Technology Transferred

This technology transfer process has taken many forms—corresponding to the different forms of technology being transferred.

- Some were transferred into standards—mainstream and accessibility.
- Some were transferred into clinical practice.
- Some were transferred to the assistive technology industry as a product.
- Some were transferred as techniques that were incorporated into assistive technologies or mainstream products.

Some were serendipitous and unexpected. According to Bobby Silverstein who along with Rud Turnbull drafted the Technology-Related Assistance Act of 1988 (Tech Act) which provides resources to all of the states for assistive technology resources, the language in the Act was inspired by a paper written by the Trace Center[7] and discovered later by congressional staff.

Some were by invitation. For example, Trace was invited to help design the first digital talking book player for the National Library Service for the Blind and Print Disabled, Library of Congress. Specifically, the Trace Center was tasked with the aspects dealing with accessibility by people with physical disabilities and with the cognitive-aging aspects of the player (Fig. 11.4).

---

[5] Lane, J.P. (2015). Aligning policy and practice in science, technology, and innovation to deliver the intended socio-economic results: the case of assistive technology. *International Journal of Transitions and Innovation Systems*, 4 (3/4), 221–248. https://doi.org/10.1504/IJTIS.2015.077191.

[6] Sauer, M., Wallace, J. F., Knorr, K. H., Yoder, D. E., Moulton, G. M., Trachtman, L. H., and Jones, M. L. (2000). Public and private partnerships: The future for assistive technology. *Technology and Disability*, 12(1) pp. 29–40. https://doi.org/10.3233/TAD-2000-12105. https://doi.org/10.3233/TAD-2000-12105.

[7] Vanderheiden, G. C. (1987). Issues in planning a statewide technology service delivery program for special education. In C. A. Coston (Ed.), *Planning and Implementing Augmentative Communication Service Delivery [Proceedings of the National Planners Conference on Assistive Device Service Delivery]* (pp. 24–29). Washington, DC: RESNA.

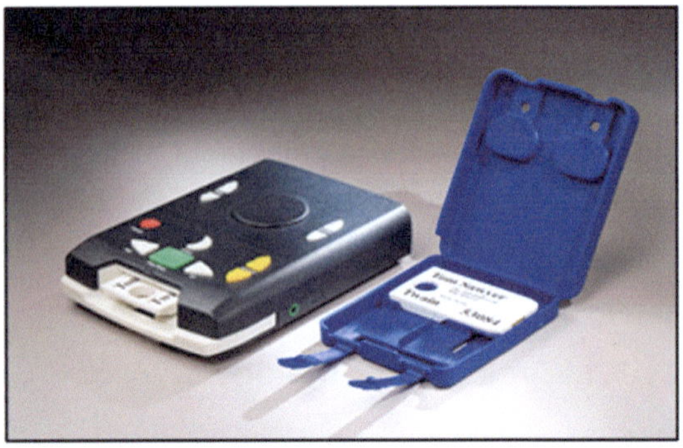

Fig. 11.4 Advanced version of the digital talking book player developed for the National Library Service, Library of Congress Talking Book Program

Mostly, however, the work transferred was from R&D carried out to address problems faced by people with disabilities—or those working with them—or creating new accessibility solutions for them. That is, developments that were driven by stakeholder input or by trying to predict the problems that would be faced by one stakeholder group or another as technology evolved.

Today, Trace Center developments can be found in billions of ICT products including all products that use Windows, iOS, or macOS operating systems and most that use Android or Linux. It can also be found in the U.S. Postal Service Automated Postal Centers, airline check-in kiosks, Amtrak ticket machines, museum and memorial kiosks and exhibits, Homeland Security kiosks, phones, voting machines, computer workstations, and assistive technologies. In all Trace has worked with more than 50 companies, helping them to develop better assistive technologies and more accessible mainstream products.

Most of what Trace learned regarding tech transfer is summarized in the paper "Technology Transfer—Lessons Learned" that was prepared for the Technology Transfer Center and available from https://go.umd.edu/TC-TechTransfer which included the 10 Laws of Technology Transfer in Appendix C. (Appendix D contains a partial list of Trace Center products.)

11.6 Perseverance

Another aspect the Trace Center was known for was perseverance. If its research and/or stakeholder work indicated the need for something—the Center would stay on it for decades if necessary. Although known for its success rate, few are aware that most successes came after a string of failures—sometimes a long string of failures stretching out more than a decade. In fact, almost none of the major accomplishments of the Center occurred in less than 5 years. Sometimes it was possible to demonstrate success with a prototype or research result, but then take many years and many times the effort and cost to bring that idea to mass adoption or availability. This takes both dedication to ideas by the Center and the ability to secure sustained funding for long periods—at least at some level. This type of sustained effort is difficult in a funding or academic environment that favors new funding of new ideas and publishing of new concepts over continued refinement of an idea or the investment to develop an idea or technology to the point where it can be successfully transferred (hence the "valley of death").

The Center has addressed this through the continual introduction of new ideas while simultaneously devoting considerable effort and looking for ways to support the ongoing work needed to fully evolve, debug, reimagine, reimplement, and refine older ideas that look to be important if it can be figured out how to make them work in the real world. It also takes a large tolerance for failure and ability to recognize it—pivot—and come at it again.

Toward this end, the Trace Center has been quite fortunate to have a program like the Rehabilitation Engineering Research Centers at the National Institute on Disability, Independent Living, and Rehabilitation Research (NIDILRR) and to have been successful in securing contiguous competitive renewals that allowed the Center to be able to carry out the long-term efforts needed for successful transfer and impact.

11.7 Impact

Overall, what the Trace Center is best known for (and the primary focus of its program) is Impact; impact on the lives of people with disabilities, on their families and friends, on those working with them, and on others in the field, especially those starting out. As the Center moves forward, impact continues to be its primary focus.

12 Some Lessons Learned from Trace's First 50 Years

These are lessons that needed to be, or were serendipitously, learned by the Trace team over the years. They are shared here as reminders for more experienced researchers, and to younger researchers in hopes that they will not need to all be learned through personal experience. They are loosely grouped by topic.

12.1 Success

- Success comes from failure—lots of them. Do not fear failure—for that is where you learn the most—and most of us have so much to learn. The Trace Center continued to fail frequently throughout its efforts but just kept trying again, and trying something else. This took confidence by the group members—but also confidence and space and support (and sometimes patience) from those around them.

  o We also draw your attention to John Cleese and Gorden the Guided Missile[1] for lessons in both successive failure and the importance of constant and early communication.

- Question and examine your successes as much as your failures. There is a tendency to think we know why we succeeded when we succeed (because we were right—or brilliant). If we don't always succeed, however, then our success in this instance may be due to something else, some external factor, some confluence of factors, or something we accidentally did. Figure out why you succeeded—and learn from it.

[1] https://www.openculture.com/2016/01/john-cleese-on-the-importance-of-making-and-embracing-mistakes.html.

G. Vanderheiden et al., *Technology and Disability*, Synthesis Lectures on Technology and Health, https://doi.org/10.1007/978-3-031-09214-5_12

- Take your pride from what you accomplished, and the change you effected or helped effect. Working for awards is empty in the long run—fun for a moment and forgotten. And many who do the most are not recognized. But the times you see your work helping people—those you remember for a lifetime.

12.2 Choosing Which Projects to Tackle

- Don't limit the scope of your work or dreams to just those areas **where work is currently ongoing, or where funding agencies are currently funding**.

  o It is possible to convince funding agencies to support good ideas in areas they currently do not fund. This occurred with the United Cerebral Palsy Research Foundation, with the National Science Foundation (NSF) and the National Institute on Disability, Independent Living, and Rehabilitation Research (NIDILRR) multiple times. It often takes a long time—but not always. However, it never happens if it is not attempted.

- Look to clinicians and other practitioners (of all types) if you would like a tremendous resource for ideas and problems needing practical solutions. Solving the problems they face is a much better way to have a broad impact than relying on the inventiveness of engineers and researchers to *imagine* what would be useful to practitioners. The same applies for people with disabilities (and for industry).
- Shared practitioner–researcher and user–researcher conversations can both uncover simple elegant solutions to unmet needs and also identify forward-looking solutions to problems that might not occur to either group alone.
- Do good work that is useful to others—and they will find ways to show appreciation.

12.3 Working with Industry

- Get your designs into commercial production if you want to really solve a problem. Creating a solution for an individual helps only that individual. Publishing a paper on an idea only advances the literature and not what is available to people with disabilities **unless** you can figure out how to get that idea into commercial or clinical practice.
- If you want to influence industry practices, work with them early on, involving them in all aspects of planning and problem exploration. Understand what it looks like from their side and build from there—not from an ideal side.

- If possible, find an industry leader and get them to change practice. Then a second. And then progress. Success breeds success. Leader adoption brings credibility. This applies not just to industry but to all areas of endeavor.
- Always involve companies directly in solving the problem when you can. The Center never would have expected DEC to change the motherboard of their commercial product to address a need of the Center. But when exploring the problem with them, it was a DEC engineer, when he could find no other way to solve our problem, who suggested a last-minute change to an upcoming circuit board revision to the DECtalk—and also a modification to the program in the boot ROM—to solve the problem. This was similar to the Apple Engineer who amazingly had a custom keyboard encoder chip made for the Apple IIe to support a StickyKeys feature for one-finger/one-hand/headstick operation of the Apple IIe. There were many other examples over the years.
- Telling the story in the right ways—with both a strong people component and clear practical paths for achieving something—can have a tremendous effect on success. The view that industry ignores anything other than the just bottom line is not completely accurate. Though profit is a major and perhaps **the** major driver (after all most companies are owned by stockholders—and their primary driver for owning a company's stock—or hiring a CEO—is profit) it is not the only factor. And anything you can do to minimize impact on profit—or to increase it—will increase your chance of success.
- The fact that an accessibility feature will increase profits will not ensure that it will be adopted or implemented by a company.

    - First—it does not matter whether it will or won't increase profits. The only operable thing is whether they **believe** it will or not.
    - Second—an accessibility feature that costs X in money or people or time to market and makes Y additional profit will not be implemented (even if Y is greater than X) if the same expenditure of X in money or key people, or time would generate two or three times as much profit. Companies have limited resources and will invest them where the payoff is greatest—not just where it is positive.

- Relying on pride is much more successful than trying to shame. Praise any success rather than accusing a company of being uncaring. And remember to hamburger your critiques. Start with praise, then present the meat of your complaint including your understanding of their problems they face in solving it, and then end again with praise.
- For many companies (and organizations), there is a fear of being the first to do something. The perceived risks often cause them to delay or not act. Getting the first company to implement an idea is the hardest and most important. The more of a leader they are, and the more they are respected, the better chance you have of breaking the barrier and getting others to follow. Put all your efforts there—and work toward broader acceptance after. (Though you can't always predict which company or organization will go first—and it will often surprise you.)

- Employees within a company who have disabilities can be one of the strongest forces for advancing accessibility of a company's products. They both bring expertise into the company and also break down two important barriers: (1) an attitude that accessibility is something done out of charity for unfortunate people (rather than being done for equity among colleagues) and (2) changing "us and them" thinking (they have a problem and we need to fix it) into some of us thinking (some of us have a problem and we need to solve the problem by working together).
- (The lessons learned by Trace in the area of technology transfer are summarized in the paper "Technology Transfer—Lessons Learned" that was prepared for the Technology Transfer Center and is available from https://go.umd.edu/TC-TechTransfer. See also Appendix C.)

12.4 Partners and Colleagues

- Always watch out for fellow colleagues in the field and their projects and priorities. It is the right thing to do. You never know when it will come back to benefit you—but don't count on it or do it for that reason.
- In any partnership—always expect to put in more than you get out. Successful partnerships usually result from situations where **both sides think they are giving 75% and getting 25%** and are happy with that since they are both working toward the same goal. It is the nature of things to always feel you are giving more than you are getting. If you always expect to give more than you get—you will be happier—and your endeavors more successful. This leads directly to the next lesson....
- Pick partnerships where you share goals. That way, you always succeed even if you put in most the effort. You will have at least gotten extra effort from the other partner to help you meet your common goals. And sometimes you will find they put in the most.
- No matter how much you do, or how great your work is, the best way to advance the field is to disseminate the work of others whenever you can. It is an adage that no matter how much a company invests in research, most innovation will occur elsewhere. The same occurs in research groups. No matter how good you are—the best work in your field will also come from other places. Disseminate that information too (and support it when you can).
- Getting the funding to the right people will result in much better outcomes than trying to just do a better job with the local team. This proved true in every instance where the Center funded another group that had more specialization in an area than Trace did.

- o This experience also led the Trace Center to move from a pure local team to a new model where the Trace Center team was extended and local-virtual. That is, when adding new people, Trace would find the best people and engage them where they were rather than relying only on people who were local or would relocate.

12.5 Working on Standards

- Standards are hard, grueling, and, by necessity, nitpicking. They also consume enormous amounts of time. Do not engage in standard making unless you are willing to sit patiently for long periods of time listening to others, picking out the wisdom from confusion and misunderstanding—and consuming a significant portion of your life and energies for the period of time you are on the committee—which will be much longer than you think.
- However, the impact of a good standard cannot be compared to almost any other work in enabling things to work together (compatibility standards) or change policy (accessibility).
- In order to develop good standards and regulations—one needs to have both consumer and industry involvement. You also need to listen, and if something differs from what you believe—then assume you are missing something first—and ask, and listen more. Only when you completely understand the other person's point **and you can voice it back to them as well or better (better in their opinion—not yours)** should you venture to have them understand yours.

  - o One, it will save you from many a mistake.
  - o Two, you will be much wiser—and even if it turns out you are right, you will be able to communicate your point of view better—and in their language and from their point of view.
  - o Three, they will listen to you when they know you listened to them.
    - They may not agree—but it is much more likely that they will listen and understand.
  - o And it is the best way to find a common ground—and look wise as well—since you combine the wisdom of others in your ideas.

- It is important to develop rules and standards that are **principle** or **outcome** based (as WCAG 2.x series is) and not **technique** or **technology** based (as WCAG 1.0 was) in order for them to not become rapidly outdated.
- If accessibility guidelines can be made technology agnostic—they also can be applied across technologies (as WCAG 2.x has been) and will survive technology advances better.

12.6 The Importance of Tools

- Tools are the key to implementing ideas. Many ideas are published or advocated for. But without tools to make them easy to do, they often live out their lives in literature.
- In the disability field, especially in the early years, assistive technology manufacturers were short of resources. Pre-designed tools and pre-coded techniques greatly aided assistive technology manufacturers in moving ideas to market. Today, a much broader market and ability to reach it via the Internet has allowed assistive technology manufacturers to do more development themselves. But new ideas without instant broad markets still need a development boost to get them out.
- Free or very low-cost tools are important to users implementing accessibility. Most employers of those developing content (Web or video) often do not value accessibility as much as content creation and do not provide support for the accessibility tools needed if they cost much (except where it is driven by fear of a lawsuit if they are not accessible).

12.7 From Our Experience in Designing Accessible Public Kiosks/ITMs

- Designers of public ITMs (and designers of accessibility for techniques for them) need to assume: (1) people will come with no experience and expect them to be operable without instruction; (2) the ITMs need to take a beating equivalent to being pounded on with a rubber mallet (and keep on ticking); and (3) they need to work after having food, cotton candy, and Coke dumped on them, and then cleaned by someone using industrial strength cleaner, sprayed robustly on them, and then scrubbed.
- Enormous educational effort not only needs to be expended to get across that kiosk accessibility is not just wheelchair access and reach range, but also includes the design of the software and the ability to operate it with disabilities. This includes not assuming that attaching an accessible keypad like the EZ Access keypad would make a kiosk accessible.

    o For example, a kiosk at the White House had an EZ Access keypad on it—leading one to assume it was accessible. However, the up and down arrow keys were wired to (silently) scroll the list of menu items up and down. And the page forward and backward buttons were used to "silently" spin the image of the White House for a 360° view.

    o Another kiosk was deemed accessible to people who were blind because it had a braille sign on it. When a blind person was asked to read what was on the braille sign, they reported that it said "All of the information on this [24 h] kiosk is available from 8–noon and 1–4 at [a location 200 miles away]."

o NOTE: Progress toward this is underway by the Access Board and the Kiosk Industry Association itself is working hard on this. But everyone involved needs to help them. Not everyone is connected. The industry is very disbursed.

12.8 People and Teams

- Success comes from interdisciplinary and diverse groups that bring different skills and backgrounds to the table—and from different **personality** types.
- Each programmer has their own style and pace. Have patience. Accommodate differences. One of our brightest engineers, when facing a programming deadline, was known to walk around the halls staring at the ground for weeks or more without writing a single line of code before he sat down and created some of the most amazing and tight code. Like a program for DOS-ABLEDATA that ran in 480 K of RAM (so there was room for a screen reader in a 640 K total RAM computer) yet could find all of the records with a word NEAR another word in a database of 20,000 records in less than a second—on a computer running at 3 MHz (that's megahertz, not gigahertz).
- Always give your team members enough leash to be able to spend at least some of their time exploring and trying new things and new ideas. Some of the best advances come from inventive people who are just presented with problems and left to think. Or discover problems on their own. All of our lead programmers made advances in the field that are used by people throughout the world today by trying things on their own and then moving them into projects when they succeeded.
- Never underestimate the potential of students—even undergraduate students.
- If you don't tell a student that no one has figured out how to do something—the student can often succeed where much more senior researchers have failed.
- A talented student's true potential is best achieved, especially in early stages, when there is unselfish support from individuals around them at the University (faculty and administration) to allow them latitude, and to challenge, and support them.
- To students: Learn the rules and learn how systems work. Rules often seem like encumbrances and bureaucracy. But they were put there for a reason—often to protect you—sometimes to protect others. Learn them and learn how to support and work well with them.
- Administrators: When students seem to be flouting the rules, don't assume that they know them or understand them. Sometimes they seem to be brazen and disregard the rules, but it may be simply because they are young and don't know rules exist—or why. This may be true even when you can't see how they could not know. Assume ignorance and teach both the rules **and the reasons**.

13 Trace's Focus for the Next Decade(s) (2021–)

Trace is now entering its 6th decade with an expanded team of researchers and a new home. The basic mission and values remain the same—but the capabilities have expanded. The current program scope of activities is briefly summarized here.

13.1 Mission

Trace's mission continues to focus on maximizing the potential of people with disabilities by harnessing evolving technologies while also working to prevent barriers created by the same.

Trace Mission Statement

> Our mission is to capitalize on the potential that technologies hold for people experiencing barriers due to disability, aging, or digital literacy, and to prevent emerging technologies from creating new barriers for these individuals.
>
> In doing this, we bring together disciplines such as information science, computer science, engineering, disability studies, law, and public policy. We engage in research, development, tech transfer, education, policy, and advocacy.

Its approach is both interdisciplinary and full spectrum to maximize real-world impact, with special attention to

- understanding and addressing user needs;
- identifying and preventing emerging technology barriers; and
- capitalizing on technology advances wherever possible to help address both.

G. Vanderheiden et al., *Technology and Disability*, Synthesis Lectures on Technology and Health, https://doi.org/10.1007/978-3-031-09214-5_13

13.2 Current Focus Areas

Although Trace continues to work across the full spectrum of user needs (all types, degrees, and combinations of disability), and across all types of information and communication technologies, the Center is particularly focusing on the following nine areas for the near future.

13.2.1 Dementia

Dementia is an umbrella term that refers to conditions such as Alzheimer's disease and vascular dementia. The prevalence of dementia increases with age and includes changes beyond cognitive impairment. These changes vary from individual to individual and can include sensory, emotional, sense of time, and hallucinations. There is tremendous variability to the experience of dementia, with different symptoms, experiences, and courses of the condition (some dementias progress from mild to advanced in a year or two, and some over decades). Social relationships and societal attitudes greatly impact the experience of living with dementia, and stigma and fear of the condition majorly limit the ability of people with dementia to fully participate in society.

The Center's work is focusing both on understanding the different needs and abilities people with dementia have, and on exploring better ways in which technology can help individuals experiencing dementia stay independent and participate in life longer. A key component is identifying and learning from the innovations that people with dementia themselves make to their environments and routines to continue using technology and the strategies of those who engage life in the face of inaccessible technologies and the changes that they experience. The Center is also looking at ways to keep new technologies from introducing new barriers to this group.

13.2.2 Cognitive, Language, and Learning Disabilities

The area of cognitive, language, and learning disabilities is an under-addressed area. We see this area as a key domain for next-next-generation work to address, as it requires new approaches and advances. For example, standards as we currently envision them are incredibly challenging to create for cognitive, language, and learning disabilities given the variability between individuals experiencing these disabilities, the intersecting nature of some of these disabilities (e.g., ADHD often co-occurring with learning disabilities), and the relative lack of assistive technology and accommodation strategies for these disabilities.

Trace Center researchers are investigating approaches that can improve the interaction across a wide range of technologies and devices. This includes focusing on specific disabilities (such as dementia and Down syndrome) as well as the combination of cognitive and sensory changes with technology and how they interact. Many of the techniques sometimes thought of as being for one group of users, provide solutions for many groups of users. For instance, technologies for reading digital content aloud are useful for users who are blind, but also for people who have trouble manipulating, or who have trouble reading text for any of a wide variety of reasons. Older adults can also experience a range of normal age-related changes that affect cognition, language, and learning that affect technology use. For example, voice assistants that are based on how younger users speak may not provide sufficient time for an older adult who needs more time to recall a word, and may time out before they are finished. This can also be a problem for people using augmentative communication aids with voice output where it can take more time to construct a verbal response than a device allows. As a result, the Center is focusing on ensuring that, as a field, there is better inclusion and coverage of cognitive, language, and learning disabilities, but is looking for solutions that make this coverage be a natural part of the coverage of the needs of mainstream younger and older users, without and with all types and combinations of disability.

Efforts include both developing new methods, and assessing the efficacy of existing methods. The Center is also continually exploring new ways to include people with cognitive disabilities even more directly as partners in defining agendas and conducting research—something that is particularly difficult with individuals experiencing more advanced cognitive disabilities.

13.2.3 Low Digital Affinity

Different from low intellectual abilities, other learning disabilities, or computer literacy is something the Center has named "Digital Affinity," the ability to easily learn, remember, and use technologies. Digital affinity is different from intellectual ability since there are some individuals who are brilliant and at the top of their field but who struggle with technologies even when they use them daily. It is also different from digital literacy, which is a measure of skill. People with high digital affinity pick up digital skills easily and can learn new technologies quickly. People with low digital affinity have trouble learning and using digital technologies, even when they work at it. People with very low digital affinity have trouble or are unable to use digital technologies at all.

Low digital affinity should also not be confused with what has been termed crystallized intelligence. As we age our intelligence gets less flexible and it is harder to learn new things. Some people reach a stage where their intelligence is largely crystallized. They are still as bright and knowledgeable as ever about things they have learned before, but they have great difficulty in learning and remembering anything new. Some people also lose intellectual abilities as they age. But these are different than digital affinity—the talent for learning and using technology.

People with low digital affinity exist throughout society and at all ages. They are people who have trouble with new technologies, use technologies in limited ways, and are disrupted by any changes. For some with very low digital affinity, it is a severe barrier to their ability to be successful in education, employment, and participation due to the increasingly pervasive digital interfaces on everything and our reliance on computers for so many aspects of education, employment, and living.

The Center's ongoing work in this area is focusing on identifying strategies and developing tools to make interfaces simpler and easier to understand and to find industry-practical ways to provide alternate interfaces that are understandable and usable by those who do not have high levels of digital affinity, and cannot handle, or can no longer understand and handle the standard interfaces on mainstream computers and other digital technologies.

13.2.4 Inclusive AI

Artificial intelligence (AI) is increasingly informing high-stake decisions. This is despite evidence that AI models can be biased or based on spurious data patterns and annotation artifacts. In fact, data are often claimed to be at fault; data often lack representation and quality with noisy data collection and curation pipelines leading to systematic misalignment between benchmark and real-world tasks. Thus, Trace's efforts in promoting inclusive AI begin by increasing representation of people with disabilities and older adults in AI datasets and machine learning models. Datasets are central to innovating, benchmarking, and mitigating bias in AI. However, datasets sourced from people with disabilities and older adults are scarce. Even when such datasets are collected and are publicly available, it is often difficult to locate them.

To help with the scarcity and difficulty in finding accessibility data, Trace researchers are building IncluSet,[1] a dataset surfacing repository. Beyond promoting AI models that include data from people with disabilities, the goal is to contribute toward best sharing practices in our community. This means both reflecting on challenges and opportunities related to locating and sharing accessibility datasets and calling for technical, legal, and institutional dataset collection and privacy frameworks that are more attuned to concerns from the disability community.

Due to the "edge" nature of disability data, just including accessibility data in datasets alone will not necessarily have the desired effect, since models employing deep neural networks, typically used in widely deployed AI-infused systems, struggle to learn rare phenomena. Therefore, work on the underlying models is needed to ensure that AI will cover and work for sparse, dispersed populations, and individuals distributed at the edges.

[1] https://incluset.com.

13.2.5 Teachable Interfaces

Teachable interfaces enable end-users with no machine learning expertise to innovate and build AI-infused systems by explicitly training their models with user-generated data and labels. Thus, it is no surprise to see them applied in accessibility as they can enable individuals with disabilities to personalize data-driven assistive technologies. By significantly constraining the conditions of the machine learning task to a specific user and their environment, such applications can achieve higher robustness in real-world scenarios. Contrary to automatic personalization, the end-user is called to consciously provide training examples and actively interact with the machine learning algorithm to increase its accuracy.

A primary goal of Trace researchers' work on teachable interfaces is putting control of AI back into the hands of users with disabilities. An example is the use of teachable object recognizers, where blind users can personalize their mobile phone or smart glasses to recognize objects of interest in their surroundings just by providing it a few photos for each object—taken the way they take pictures—so that the AI can recognize the objects when a blind user is aiming the camera. Work here is bi-directional with the user and AI working together to train each other how to come up with the most accurate results in real-life use by real-life users with very different skills and abilities.

13.2.6 AI and Privacy

There are many privacy and ethical concerns associated with AI in the context of disability as people who have distinct data patterns may be more susceptible to data abuse and misuse. Trace researchers are exploring some of these concerns in the context of AI data from people with disabilities. Naturally, the risk of deduction can increase when reporting data on smaller populations. Given that some disability communities can be very small, the effectiveness of privacy-preserving techniques can also be affected, calling for novel approaches. Even when re-identification is not a risk, consent and disclosure can be, as disability status is sensitive. In addition to these challenges, there is another thread at the intersection of AI and accessibility that raises privacy concerns. This time not only from the perspective of the users of AI-infused assistive technologies, but also of bystanders who may be recorded by these technologies. Together, with collaborators, Trace has started exploration of this topic in the context of pedestrian detection with wearable cameras like smart glasses for blind users. The broader question is: How to navigate the delicate act of balancing competing needs? Can technologies be designed that meet both the access needs of people with disabilities (e.g., a blind person recognizing people they meet from "memory" or a photo given to them) with bystanders' privacy needs?

13.2.7 Easier Conformance—Easier Accessibility

In order to create more real accessibility in the world as experienced by people with disabilities, the Trace Center is focusing on a PUSH–PULL approach; both pushing current understanding and the rules for making ICT accessible, and making it easier and more rewarding for companies to create accessible products.

The research efforts above are designed to help discover ways to create accessible products that are more accessible to more people in ways that are easier and more practical for industry. To augment these efforts, Trace is also working on the development of better tools including the following:

- tools for the creation, analysis, and improvement of accessible documents and media;
- a fully open-source tool for the evaluation of media to ensure it is safe for people with photosensitive seizure disorders; and
- tools for better understanding accessibility laws, standards, and regulations.

Trace will also continue updating the MasterList of accessibility strategies, which catalogs all of the known strategies for making ICT accessible, along with a resource page for each showing its impact on people with different disabilities, products (free, free to try, and commercial) that implement each strategy and any known research and resources regarding that strategy.

Trace is also helping the nonprofit Raising the Floor—International in maintaining the collaborative DeveloperSpace (ds.gpii.net) that exists to make it easier to find information and resources for creating new accessibility solutions and improving existing products and solutions. The MasterList of Accessibility Strategies is one resource available through the DeveloperSpace.

13.2.8 Better Accessibility Standards, Policy, and Law

Accessibility standards, policy, law, and regulations are powerful tools that have been proven with time to be necessary for actual system change around accessibility. However, as necessary as rules may be, they are by their nature limiting. It is essential therefore that they be designed well in order to have maximum benefit without limiting the innovation that has driven technology forward or the effectiveness of the ICT for users who do not have a disability. Time and industry have shown that properly designed standards/policy/regulations do not necessarily impede innovation but can actually encourage innovation, resulting in more usable interfaces and products by the entire population of technology and digital content users.

As seen in previous sections, the Trace Center has devoted considerable effort over the years to help ensure that policymakers have the best information in order to help find the sweet spot for maximum accessibility that is commercially practical—and works across disabilities and for mass market users.

In addition to continuing the work of the past on informing the development of technical standards, regulations, and policies, the Center is also expanding its efforts:

- to quantify the impact of accessibility (or lack thereof) to assist policymakers and regulators in decisions about cost–benefit analysis. The goal of this work is to better understand the impact to people with disabilities, both of the cost of inaccessible interfaces and the benefits of accessibility;
- to create a compendium and analysis tool for Accessibility Standards Worldwide that will make it easier to compare similar provisions across accessibility standards, to define design specifications that will simultaneously meet the different standards, and to develop better language for future accessibility standards;
- to create targeted guidelines for specific industries or product types when none already exist—to make it easier for product designers (most of whom will always be new to accessibility) to sort out which guidelines apply to them—and to have a shorter set of guidelines to sort through; and
- to work at the intersection of the technical and legal aspects of digital accessibility, including investigating and proposing legal and technical solutions to the existing gaps between digital accessibility statutes and regulations (which often don't acknowledge the actual guidelines and tools and usage) and the guidelines and tools (which conversely don't acknowledge the statutes and regulations).

13.2.9 Re-imagining Society's Entire Approach to Accessibility Policy and Practice

Society is currently reaching the limit of what can be done with the current approach to accessibility; trying to create accessibility guidelines for each different type of ICT and include provisions for each different person with their type, degree, and combination of disability. There have been increasing efforts with decreasing new progress in the last few years—and key disability groups are still not being addressed well. People are also asking how the current guidelines would be applied to new technologies such as agent-oriented interfaces, gesture-based interfaces, or virtual environments (what are the accessibility guidelines for xR devices and environments to make them accessible to people who are blind)—questions to which no one has come up with good answers and some fear there are no good answers—especially using traditional approaches.

Trace is mounting a collaborative effort to step back, question all current assumptions and approaches, and, taking into account the power and opportunities of new technologies, rethink the whole approach to accessibility. There are several reasons to believe this is necessary—and possible.

- First, the current guidelines approach doesn't match the future—it doesn't address next-generation ICT and HCI (see xR and blindness example above).
- Second, society is stalling out on addressing cognitive, language, and learning disabilities with current approach.
- Third, new and emerging technologies are presenting the field with new tools and capabilities that will allow us to create new types, and stronger types, of assistive technologies for all disabilities—and also suggest new approaches that can provide more access for less effort by web page designers.

Although early in the process, one approach discussed is the use of AI, deep learning, cloud-based AT, "try-harder" hybrid-assistive technologies, verbal- and agent-oriented interfaces, auto-personalization, and more that does not yet exist but will in the future to create sort of super-AT that can directly take as input the standard interfaces of mainstream technologies (as long as they are understandable and usable by the median person with median abilities) and present as their output an interface designed specifically for each individual with their abilities (including anything currently classified as a disability). This super-AT would consist of an **Info-Bot** like entity coupled with Individual User Interface Generators (IUIGs) that would create familiar, accessible, and understandable interfaces for each person. Although called super-AT here, they would in fact be designed to be used by the large portion of the population who have any trouble with interfaces that continually change, or that are different on different devices that do the same thing, or that are simply different from what the user has seen before, or are difficult to use for any reason.

Appendix A: Resources for Learning About Assistive Technologies Available Pre-Internet

For communication and writing aids in the 1960s and 1970s see:

- *Aids for the Severely Handicapped* (1974)—edited by Keith Copeland.[1]
- *Non Vocal Communication Techniques and Aids for the Severely Physically Handicapped* (1976)—Gregg Vanderheiden and Kate Grilley (includes many citations and photos from Copeland '74, with permission).[2]

For all communication aids, environmental controls, switches, adaptive software and computer access aids available for each year in the 1970s, 1980s, and 1990s see:

1. ***Trace Resourcebooks*** published in a three-ring binder form in 1978, with update inserts approx. annually, then in book form in 1987 (three books), 1988 (update to three-book version), 1989–90 (one combined book), 1991–92, 1993–94, 1996–97.
2. **Trace Center Co-Net CDs** containing ABLEDATA and all Trace Information (see Thread 9) issued in June 1989 (Co-Net 1) through 1998 (Co-Net 11).

All versions of both are available from Trace Center Archive[3] and the DeveloperSpace.[4]

A Taste of the Web

- When Co-Net 10 and 11 were released in 1997–98, many in the disability community were not yet connected to the Web or knew exactly what riches it could provide. An extra CD titled "A Taste of the Web" was therefore included in Co-Net 10 and

[1] Copeland, K. *Aids for the Severely Handicapped*. London: Spector Publishing Co., Ltd. 1974.

[2] Vanderheiden, G. C. and Grilley, K. (Eds.). *Non-Vocal Communication Techniques and Aids for the Severely Physically Handicapped*. Baltimore: University Park Press, 1975.

[3] Trace Archive https://go.umd.edu/trace-archive.

[4] DeveloperSpace https://ds.gpii.net.

G. Vanderheiden et al., *Technology and Disability*, Synthesis Lectures on Technology and Health, https://doi.org/10.1007/978-3-031-09214-5

11. Readers are encouraged to see what the Web looked like in those days and what disability information was available on the Web. *A Taste of the Web* (which also included all of ABLEDATA and the Trace Website among other disability sites of the time) can be viewed by downloading the 1997 or 1998 *Taste of the Web* from the "Taste of the Web" folder[5] in the Trace Archives. A description of the Taste of the Web CD can be found in the "Taste of the Web Readme."

Publications of the time.

- A bibliography of publications covering research, clinical practice, and the commercial market at the time (1978) can be found in Appendix B.

[5] Taste of the Web Folder https://go.umd.edu/taste-of-the-web.

Appendix B: Reference Design in Comments to FCC July 1999

Before the
Federal Communications Commission
Washington, D.C. 20,554.

	)	
In the matter of	)	
	)	
Implementation of Sect. 255 of the	)	
Telecommunications Act of 1996	)	
	)	WT Docket No. 96–198
Access to Telecommunications Services	)	
Telecommunications Equipment, and	)	
Customer Premises Equipment	)	
By Persons with Disabilities	)	
	)	

Ex parte Comments
Reference Design

Gregg C. Vanderheiden Director,
Trace R&D Center
Dept of Industrial Engineering
University of Wisconsin
5901 Research Park Blvd
Madison, WI 53,719
608–262-6966
July 7, 1999

G. Vanderheiden et al., *Technology and Disability*, Synthesis Lectures on Technology and Health, https://doi.org/10.1007/978-3-031-09214-5

Attached for the Commission's general information is a reference design that we are working on at the Trace Center for a cellular telephone. This design meets all of the specifications in the FCC/Access Board Guidelines. This design is intended to show how a single phone can be designed so that it would be cross-disability accessible as well as usable and attractive to mass market customers.

This design uses only technologies that are already found in today's cell phones (although the software in the telephones today may not currently be written to use these technologies in an accessible fashion). The only exception to this is hearing aid compatibility with digital wireless phones. This design assumes that industry will develop a solution to this problem in conjunction with ANSI C63 and that solution would be incorporated into this design.

The cost to implement these features is nominal. Basically, it involves the addition of a single button to the keypad on the front of the phone and changing the software instructions that tell the phone how to behave. (A design which does not require the addition of the extra button is also possible.) All of the technologies described and used in this phone are already present in other cell phones today. Most of them are in low-cost phones. A couple technologies are currently only found in mid-range phones today, but we expect these technologies to be available in the inexpensive phones shortly (except where there are marketing reasons for companies to reserve some features for higher end phones for product differentiation rather than cost reasons).

You should find the following pages attached:

1. A brief description of the Reference Design 1 cell phone which meets all of the FCC guidelines.
2. Notes as to how the access features on page 1 are actually related to a standard product feature that would be desirable by mass market users.
3. A table listing each of the FCC guidelines, how the guideline is met in the proposed reference design, and a comment about cost of implementation.

You will note that in almost all the cases there are already cell phones on the market that either provide the capability or have the technology necessary to provide the capability. All that would be necessary would be to change the software in the phone that governs its behavior.

Additional and related information to this and other reference designs will be at http://www.trace.wisc.edu/world/telecomm/.

ONE phone design that meets all of the FCC proposed access requirements

(Trace Center Reference Design 1)

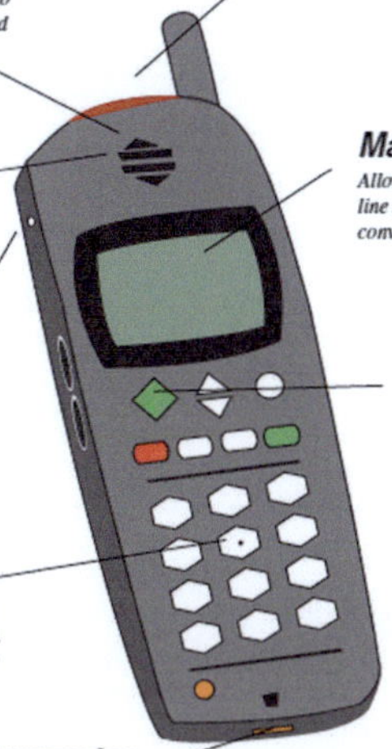

Volume range

Meets FCC specifications for those who are hard of hearing (also is hearing aid compatible)

Speakerphone function

Facilitates use by people who have difficulty handling the phone

Headset jack

Allows connection of neckloops, silhouettes, Assistive Listening Devices, TTY's and headsets

Easy to feel keys

And a nib on the 5 key makes eyes-free dialing easy. (Because of keypad edges, all keys are tactiley different.) Keys are dished as well to make it easy to use a mouthstick or other device to dial.

Infrared (IR) Port

Allows wireless connection of computers and assistive technologies

Matrix display

Allows use of graphics and multi-line text messages including TTY conversations

EZbutton

*The **EZ button** allows you to have the label for any key read to you - as well as the contents of the display and all menus and features of the phone. (Useful if you cannot see well, are blind, or if you have trouble reading the text on the phone for any reason.) Spoken words are displayed on screen in large type as well.*

Connector

No more fumbling with connector - it can be positioned and inserted purely by touch. You can also connect a keyboard to make programming easier or to send faster text (and TTY) messages. (Keypad on phone can also be used to type text messages.)

Other Accessibility Features of the Reference Design:

- **One Button Feature** allows you to program the phone so that it will automatically dial just one number (or a small list of numbers) when any button on the keypad is pushed. {Useful for people for whom a standard cell phone is too complicated or for an emergency phone for anyone in the family, young or old.} Cover plate which creates a "one button" phone is available on request.
- You can **program your phone using** the built-in mode or use your personal computer or **any Internet browser** for a simple, "fill out the information on the screen," way to program the phone.
- For those who cannot remember numbers easily, you can dial pre-stored numbers by typing a person's **name or nickname** on the keypad.
- **Voice dialing** on selected models. You can just say the persons name or nick-name to dial them.
- **Messaging** - You can send and receive digital and TTY messages at any time using the keypad or attachable keyboard.
- **Special mode** allows all functions performed by buttons on side or back to be performed from the buttons and menus on the front of the phone for those who use a headstick or dowel.
- Operation of the entire phone is possible from just **3 buttons or** from just **a single button** for those with very severe movement disabilities.

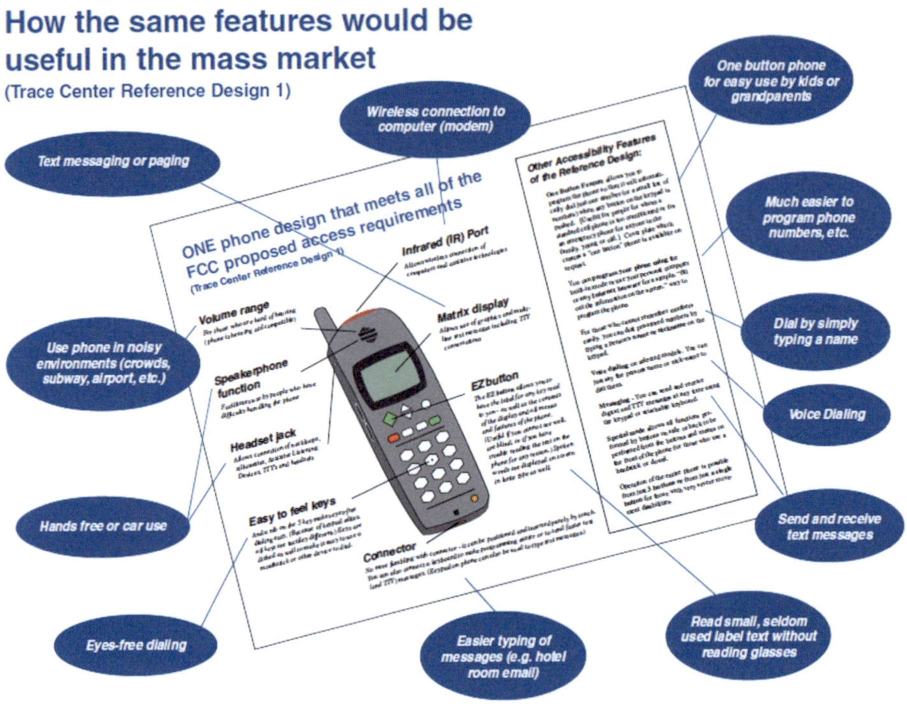
How the same features would be useful in the mass market
(Trace Center Reference Design 1)
Text messaging or paging
Wireless connection to computer (modem)
One button phone for easy use by kids or grandparents
Much easier to program phone numbers, etc.
Use phone in noisy environments (crowds, subway, airport, etc.)
Dial by simply typing a name
Voice Dialing
Hands free or car use
Send and receive text messages
Eyes-free dialing
Easier typing of messages (e.g. hotel room email)
Read small, seldom used label text without reading glasses
ONE phone design that meets all of the FCC proposed access requirements
(Trace Center Reference Design 1)
Infrared (IR) Port
Volume range
Matrix display
Speakerphone function
EZ button
Headset jack
Easy to feel keys
Connector
Other Accessibility Features of the Reference Design:

How Trace Center Reference Design #1 addresses each of the FCC Guidelines

		FCC Guideline	Met?	How the requirements are met.	Cost & Ease of Implementation (If a company had been doing this as a matter of course. e.g. does not include cost of acquainting engineers with access.)
SUBPART C – REQUIREMENTS FOR ACCESSIBILITY AND USABILITY	Sec. 1193.41 Input, control, and mechanical functions.	(a) Operable without vision.	yes ✓	Tactile keys and landmarks All input and functions accessible via voice output	- All needed electronics for digitized speech already in today's digital phones; Need only small additions to software and sometimes additional memory (~100k) which will cost little in phones tomorrow. Memory is already available today in many phones (used for digital voice recording). - (This reference design uses spelled speech for transmitted text - voice synthesis will be possible in near future but is not quite practical today for inexpensive phones. Voice synthesis using network facilities is practical today - but is not proposed here.)
		(b) Operable with low vision and limited or no hearing.	yes ✓	-Matrix Display - the labels of all buttons can be shown in large print prior to activating them.	Many newer cell phones already use matrix displays. Many have large print displays as standard or as a user setting.
		(c) Operable with little or no color perception.	yes ✓	All color coded buttons and indicator lights distinguishable by other means (shape, label)	- Not a problem in most phones today. Any use of color just has to also be accompanied with a text label - as is true on all phone keys today.
		(d) Operable without hearing.	yes ✓	Vibration ringer alert. Also buttons have tactile feel of activation (i.e. do not rely on auditory beeps). Visual indication of line status.	- Vibrator is standard in many cell phones. [Not in lower cost phones mostly due to marketing rather than cost.) Visual indication of line status is software only.
		(e) Operable with limited manual dexterity.	yes ✓	EZ Access* - buttons can be selected in 2 steps - press desired button then confirm with EZ Button; Dished keys easy to press; Also optional 1-Button mode ; Connection of customized external keyboard.	- Software only for confirm and 1 button access features. (Less than 2k memory.) - Dished keys is no cost, just a different key shape. - Keyboard connection can be via Infra-red or the connector on bottom (Based on industry standard ANSI/TIA/EIA-688)
		(f) Operable with limited reach and strength.	yes ✓	Buttons easy to press down; One button mode. Optional Speakerphone is easier for people who cannot place phone to ear; Optional Voice Dialing is faster for some.	- Light button pressure is standard on many phones. Optional speakerphone and voice dialing features are increasingly common - and cost for these features is dropping precipitously. (Speakerphone and voice dialing not required for access in this design).
		(g) Operable without time-dependent controls.	yes ✓	Time-outs can be modified via preferences menu	- Menu option. (easily implemented in software)
		(h) Operable without speech.	yes ✓	Speech input of commands not required; Text communication modes available.	- Ability to control phone without requiring speech is standard on most all phones. - Text communication is common on digital phones and will be standard soon.
		(i) Operable with limited cognitive skills.	yes ✓	EZ Access - all functions accessible via speech out; Also one-button / single number dialing with optional cover plate; Infrared port - allows user programming via simplified step-by-step computer interface	- Speech output of all printed text is already covered above (first item). - One button dialing and single number dialing is software only. - Optional cover plate would cost a bit but is not needed for access. - IR port is standard on many cell phones
	Sec. 1193.43 Output, display, and control functions.	(a) Availability of visual information.	yes ✓	EZ Access - all functions and displayed text available via speech	- Cost covered above.
		(b) Availability of visual information for low vision users.	yes ✓	Matrix Display - all functions and messages shown in large print on display	- A small addition to software to have the phone display the words when it speaks them as discussed above.
		(c) Access to moving text.	yes ✓	Arrow buttons - text can be paused or stepped through using arrow buttons - configurable via preferences menu	- Preferences menu option (easily implemented in software)
		(d) Availability of auditory information.	yes ✓	Ringing tones, beeps shown on display (and vibrating ringer). TTY messages shown on display. Speech to Text available via relay services. VCO supported.	- Using the Lucent solution strategy (or final standard), TTY codes can be decoded in digital phones using software. A little additional software would allow TTY text to be displayed. - All other sounds made by the phone can be visually displayed as well using existing displays.
		(e) Availability of auditory information for people who are hard of hearing.	yes ✓	Full FCC volume range.	- Cell phones already exist that meet the FCC specified levels
		(f) Prevention of visually-induced seizures.	yes ✓	Flashing lights all within acceptable flash frequencies.	- No cost. Not a problem on most phones today.
		(g) Availability of audio cutoff.	yes ✓	Headset being placed in jack cuts off the speaker	- Standard industry practice.
		(h) Non-interference with hearing technologies.	yes ✓	Per Standards group ANSI C63	- Already being addressed by industry.
		(i) Hearing aid coupling.	yes ✓	Hearing aid t-coil compatibility	- Already common in many phones including world's smallest mass market cell phone.
SUB D - COMPATIBILITY	Sec. 1193.51 Compatibility.	(a) External electronic access to all information and control mechanisms.	yes ✓	Infrared port allows activation of all features remotely.	- Already common in many cell phones including Nokia's most popular model.
		(b) Connection point for external audio processing devices.	yes ✓	Standard subminiature headset jack connects to external auditory processing devices	- Already used by most cell phone companies for connection of headsets. - No cost to use standard signal levels.
		(c) Compatibility of controls with prosthetics.	yes ✓	Keys do not require contact with human body to work. Dished keys make it easier to press keys for people with limited manipulation.	- Not aware of any phones that fail this guideline today (though there probably is one). - Most (non-cell) phones also have dished keys like the old touchtone phones.
		(d) TTY connectability.	yes ✓	Headset jack is a TTY connector	- Headset jack already used as TTY connector today for some TTYs. (see also next item)
		(e) TTY signal compatibility.	yes ✓	Phone can send and receive TTY signals.	- One of 3 industry proposed all software solutions is used. (which work with today's phones.)

* Note: The access package above can be implemented with or without a separate green diamond "EZ" button. Implementation with the button is preferable. The cost for the extra button is in the cents range if done as part of the overall original keyboard design.

Appendix C: Trace's 10 Laws of Technology Transfer

In our experience with the transfer of ideas from a university-based research center to the marketplace, we have learned some important principles that can be of use to new inventors/developers. These laws can be bent in specific situations, but we have found that they can't be ignored.

1. **An idea or device is of little value to anyone (except its creator) if a manufacturer is not willing and able to make it**.
   - Do not proceed with development of a product until a manufacturer is identified who is willing and able to produce it.
   - Find one (or more) manufacturer(s) early in the R&D process and work with them.
2. **Remember that people will care for their own child, and invest in their child's future, more than they will in their neighbor's child. This holds true even if they have been given charge of the neighbor's child**.
   - Be willing to give up control of your product and its development to the manufacturer if you want them to nurture it. They need to feel it is their child now.
3. **People prefer to adopt young children (sometimes at birth—sometimes just out of diapers)**.
   - Don't hang on to your idea too long. Transfer your idea as early as possible—as soon as they are willing to take over developing it. Let the manufacturer shape the product to fit their needs/product line.
4. **What is most important to transfer is the idea—the soul of the product—and not the actual "inventor rendition**."
   - Spend your time developing, testing, and researching the idea rather than doing production design (unless you have to in order for the manufacturer to take it on).
5. **An extension of an existing product or product line is sometimes easier to sell to a manufacturer**.
   - Be willing to see your idea incorporated as an extension of an existing product rather than insisting that it be a product itself.
6. **Listen to and believe manufacturers concerning their own capabilities and limitations; offer your ideas and opinions, but listen**.

G. Vanderheiden et al., *Technology and Disability*, Synthesis Lectures on Technology and Health, https://doi.org/10.1007/978-3-031-09214-5

- Businessmen have a better understanding of their own companies' affairs than university researchers. There are few academicians who could successfully run a business—even businesses that they are very valuable consultants to.
- Your credibility increases as you demonstrate your willingness to listen and gain an understanding of the manufacturer's issues.
- Listen and learn even if you disagree. You can't change their minds if you don't understand their point of view completely.
- Understand that, in the end, manufacturers must and will act according to their best understanding and judgment—not yours.

7. **Work with the manufacturer to design a product which will fit into that company's product line and be manufacturable, supportable, and marketable**.
   - Remember that some new ideas may lead a manufacturer to totally re-scope, reorganize, or redirect their product line or other basic business strategies. Thus, they need time and warning to examine, plan, and implement such drastic change. The key again is to get them involved early in the process.
8. **Keep the design as simple as possible**.
   - Remember that simple designs are easier to manufacture and support.
   - Features are nice, but too many can be confusing and scare people (including manufacturers) away.
   - Complex products result in longer user training periods and more questions and support from dealers and manufacturers.
   - Trained sales forces are very hard to maintain. Complex products aggravate the problem (and increase the cost or even jeopardize their acceptance in the market).
9. **Once burned; twice cautious**.
   - Don't oversell your idea or its market. You may convince a manufacturer to take on your idea, but you will have a very hard time in the future if the idea doesn't live up to your hype.
10. **Provide all possible (requested) assistance to the manufacturer's efforts in developing, marketing and supporting the product**.

Gregg C. Vanderheiden Ph.D. Trace Center (1998).

See also "Technology Transfer—Lessons Learned" available from https://go.umd.edu/TC-TechTransfer.

Appendix D: Partial List of Products of Trace Center

	Result	Project
1	Commercial Transfer	AutoCom—First Portable User-Programmable and Correctable Communication Aid
2	Commercial Transfer × 2	TRINE—first portable communication writing and computer access aid
3	Commercial Transfer	Simple Electronic Transducer standard (SET) (now used for all AT)
4	Commercial Transfer	Keyboard Emulating Interface standard (KEI)
5	Commercial Impact	Portable DecTalk—First "portable" (wheelchair mountable) synthesizer
6	Commercial Transfer	Ten Branch, QuicKey, and SpeedKey
7	Commercial Transfer + Std	StickyKeys
8	Commercial Transfer + Std	MouseKeys
9	Commercial Transfer × 2	Long-Range High-Resolution Optical Head Pointer (LROP)
10	Commercial Transfer	One Screen
11	Commercially Published	The Trace Resource Books 1, 2, 3 (then Rbooks 1986–1994 self-published annually)
12	Published on Disk, CD	Hyper-ABLEDATA
13	Published on Disk, CD	DOS-ABLEDATA
14	Published on Disk, CD	Service Delivery Directory
	Published on Disk, CD	Co-Net Cooperative Library
15	Commercial Transfer + Std	SlowKeys
16	Commercial Transfer + Std	BounceKeys

G. Vanderheiden et al., *Technology and Disability*, Synthesis Lectures on Technology and Health, https://doi.org/10.1007/978-3-031-09214-5

	Result	Project
17	Commercial Transfer + Std	ToggleKeys
18	Commercial Transfer + Std	SoundSentry
19	Commercial Transfer + Std	ShowSounds, Show Captions
20	Commercial Transfer	General Input Device Emulating Interface standard (GIDEI) Used in T-TAM, Microsoft Windows, IBM AccessDOS, AccessX, more
21	Commercial Transfer	Trace Transparent Access Modular (T-TAM)
22	Commercial Transfer	Access-X from Disability Access Committee for X (DACX)
23	Standard	Serial Control Standard
24	Commercial Transfer + Std	SerialKeys
25	Commercial Transfer	EZ Access 1
26	Standard	Wireless Remote Console Communication Protocol (ISO 24752)
27	Commercial Transfer	Cross-disability accessible electronic voting techniques and prototype
28	Commercial Transfer	First cross-disability accessible web kiosk
29	Commercial Transfer	EZ Access 2
30	Commercial Transfer	Viking cross-disability building security and door control system
31	Commercial Transfer	Cross-disability accessible ATM
32	Commercial Transfer	T-Trans—Locally Editable Remote Transcription
33	Free Tool	MAGpie 1—Free Captioning Tool (Funded by Trace)
34	Free Tool on Web	A-Prompt Web Accessibility Verifier Tool (Partial Funding by Trace)
35	Free Tool on Web	Photosensitive Epilepsy Analysis Tool (PEAT)
36	Free Tool on Web	Color Vision Analysis Tool for WCAG (Funded by Trace)
37	Commercial Transfer	Real-Time Text/Instant Messaging (AOL)
38	Commercial Transfer	Real-Time Text CODECs
39	Transferred—Free Website	Unified Listing of ICT assistive technologies and access features
40	Transferred—Free Website	DeveloperSpace
41	Transferred - Free Website	IncluSet repository surfacing accessibility datasets
42	Commercial Transfer	Morphic

	Result	Project
Accessibility Guidelines		
43	Free on Web	Trace Center Consumer Access Guidelines
44	Commercial Transfer	Apple Accessibility Guidelines and Intern Report Cards
45	Commercial Transfer	Software Accessibility Guidelines ITF
46	Commercial Transfer	IBM Accessibility Guidelines 1987
47	Published	Microsoft Intel PC system guidelines (chapters in their manuals)
48	Web Published	First Web Accessibility Guidelines 1995
49	Transferred to W3C	Unified Web Accessibility Guidelines (8 versions)
50	Commercial Transfer	The JAVA Accessibility Report
51	Facilitation	New VoIP Accessibility Recommendations
52	Incorporated in Standards	Quantitative Color Vision and Sensitive Contrast Guideline

Appendix E: Bibliography of Early History of Aug Com and Assistive Technology from 1st Trace ResourceBook (1978)

This is not a current bibliography of the fields that Trace has worked in. A 50-year bibliography—or even meaningful bibliographies of each of the fields that Trace is working in today—would be overly lengthy and quickly outdated. Rather, this is an historical reference—providing a snapshot of what was available back in 1978 since there is no easy electronic record of this today.

Note that this snapshot includes both journal/book references and references to "fugitive" literature, which made up much of the information in the early days of the field. Items with *'s were recommended reading for those just getting started in the field. Double asterisks were doubly recommended.

Additional information on publications for other years in the 1980s and 1990s can be found in the back of the Trace ResourceBooks published in those years. (See Appendix A for links to electronic scanned versions of the ResourceBooks.)

Note: This bibliography was scanned from old paper documents so will have OCR errors in it.

Bibliography of Early History of Aug Com and Assistive Technology (1978)

This bibliography is broken down into the following sections:

1. Summary Information
2. Direct Selection: Manual Communication Boards
3. Direct Selection: Other Aids
4. Scanning Communication Aids
5. Encoding Communication Aids
6. Fitting and interfacing Communication Aids
7. Special Language systems/Techniques
8. Manual Communication: A Selected Bibliography for the Multihandicapped
9. Other Related Information

G. Vanderheiden et al., *Technology and Disability*, Synthesis Lectures on Technology and Health, https://doi.org/10.1007/978-3-031-09214-5

1. Summary Information

Abelson, C. and Pfeiffer, D. Communication aids for the non-verbal severely handicapped child-A multidimensional challenge. *Canadian Journal of Occupational Therapy*, Winter 1975, 42(2), 141–144. https://doi.org/10.1177/000841747504200402.

Cohen, L. K. *Communication Aids for the Brain Damaged Adult*. Sister Kenny Institute, 1800 Chicago Ave., Minneapolis Minnesota 55,404.

Cohen, L. K. *Communication Problems after a Stroke*. Sister Kenny Institute, 1800 Chicago Ave., Minneapolis Minnesota 55,404.

*Copeland, K. *Aids for the Severely Handicapped*. London: Spector Publishing Co., Ltd. 1974.

Department of Health and Social Security (England). Electronic environmental control systems for the severely physically disabled. Jonway, 1977. Available from: Scientific and Technical Branch. DHSS 14 Russell Square, London WC1B5EP, England.

Egerton, S. W. Technical aids for the disabled. *The B.C. Professional Engineer*, July 1976, 27(7), 25–27.

Equipment for the disabled. Communications, 1975. Compiled by the Oxford Regional Health Authority on behalf of The Department of Health and Social Security. To order: 2 Foredown Drive, Ports lade, Sussex BN42BB, England.

Fothergill, Jana, Vanderheiden, Gregg C., Holt, Craig, and Luster, Mary Jo. Illustrated digest of nonvocal communication and writing aids for severely physically handicapped individuals. In Gregg C. Vanderheiden (Ed.), *Non-Vocal Communication Resourcebook*. Baltimore: University Pak Press, in press, 1978.

Harris, Deberah, Lippert, Janet C., Yoder, David E., and Vanderheiden, Gregg C. BlissSymbols: An augmentative symbol/communication system for non-vocal severely handicapped children. In R. York and E. Edgar (Eds.), *Teaching the Severely Handicapped*, Vol. IV. Seattle: American Association for the Education of the Severely Physically Handicapped, 1978.

Harris-Vanderheiden, D. and Vanderheiden, G. Basic considerations in the development of communicative and interactive skills for non-vocal severely handicapped children. In E. Sontag and N. Certo (Eds), *Educational Programming for the Severely and Profoundly Handicapped*. Reston, Virginia: CEC Division on Mental Retardation, 1977.

*Harris, Deberah and Vanderheiden, Gregg C. Enhancing the development of communicative interaction in non-vocal severely physically handicapped children. In R. Shiefelbusch (Ed.), *Non-Speech Language Intervention Processes*. Baltimore: University Park Press, in press.

Harris, Deberah. *A Survey of Critical Factors in Evaluating Communication Aids*. The Trace Center, Madison WI 53,706, 1975.

Holt, C. and Vanderheiden, G. *Master Chart of Communication Aids*. Trace Center, University of Wisconsin, Madison, 1974. (Please note: this edition is superseded by Vanderheiden, Brown, and Fothergill, same title, same source, 1978, listed in this bibliography.)

Kafafian, Haig. *Study of Man–Machine Communication Systems for the Handicapped* (3 vols). Washington: Cybernetics Research Institute, Inc., (1970–1973).

Kavanagh, R. N., Holmlund, B. A., and Krause, A. E. Communications systems for the physically handicapped. *Digest of the Canadian Medical and Biological Engineering Conference*, Ottawa, September 1966.

Kolstoe, B J. Assisting the non-verbal to "talk". *Journal of Physically Handicapped, Homebound, and Hospitalized*,(Council for Exceptional Children), 1976, _3(1), 18–21.

LaBlanc, Maurice A. What do you do if you can't talk with your voice or your hands? Rehabilitation Engineering Center at Children's Hospital at Stanford. Palo Alto, California. Presented at *Communication Enhancement Institute*, Michigan State University, August 25–27, 1976, and *Conference of Systems and Devices for the Disabled*, Boston, June 10, 1976.

Larson, Thalia. *Communication for the Non-Verbal Child*. Johnstown, Pennsylvania: Maj ex Associates, Inc., 1975.

**Lloyd, Lyle (Ed.) *Communication Assessment and Intervention Strategies*. Baltimore: University Park Press, 1976.

Lywood, D. W. and Vasa, J. J. A brief survey and classification of available systems. *Proceeding of the Seminar on Electronic Controls for the Severely Disabled*, 1974, 7–11.

McNaughton, Shirley. Electronic aids in Blissymbol communications. In P. Nelson (Ed.) *Proceedings of the Workshop on Communication Aids*, June 1977. Canadian Medical and Biological Engineering Society, c/o National Research Council, Ottawa, Ontario, Canada KIA 0R8, 1978.

National Center for Deaf Blind Youths and Adults. *Communication and Sensory Aids for the Deaf Blind*, report of a workshop. New Hyde Park, New York, 1973. (Appendix lists 26 communication and sensory aids.)

Nelson, Peter (Ed.) *Proceedings of Workshop on Communication Aids*. June 1977. Canadian Medical and Biological Engineering Society, c/o National Research Council, Ottawa, Ontario, Canada KIA 0R8, 1978.

Renfrew, C. and Murphy, K. (Eds.) The child who does not talk. *Little Clubs Clinics in Developmental Medicine*, No. 13. London: Spastics Society Medical Evaluation and Information Unit in association with Wm. Heinemann Medical Books, Ltd., 1964.

Robenault, I. P. *Functional Aids for the Multiply Handicapped*, Evanston: Harper and Row, 1973.

**Schiefelbusch, Richard L. *Non-Speech Language and Communication Intervention*. Baltimore: University Park Press, in preparation 1978.

Silverman, F. H. *A Bibliography of Literature Relevant to Nonspeech Communication Modes for the Speechless*. Communicative Disorders Program, Marquette University, 619 North 16th St., Milwaukee, WI 53,233 (includes gestural, gestural assisted, and neuroassisted modes), 1976.

**Vanderheiden, Gregg C. (Ed.), *Non-Vocal Communication Resourcebook*. Baltimore: University Park Press, 1978.

Vanderheiden, G. C. *Synthesyzed Speech as a Communication Mode for Nonvocal Severely Handicapped Individuals*. The Trace Center, Madison WI 53,706, 1976.

Vanderheiden, G. C. Evaluation and further development of the Automonitoring Communication Board as an educational aid for severely handicapped children: Summary final report. *Report to the National Science Foundation*, EC-40316, 1975. The Trace Center, Madison, WI 53,706.

Vanderheiden, G. C. Excerpt from final report to the Bureau for the Education of the Handicapped: Overview of grant activities BEH/OE OEG-O-74–7461. September 1974 to November 1976. The Trace Center, Madison WI 53,706, 1976.

*Vanderheiden, Gregg C., Brown, Warren P., and Fothergill, Jana. Master chart of communication aids. In Vanderheiden (Ed.), *Non-Vocal Communication Resourcebook*. Baltimore: University Park Press, 1978. Or separately from The Trace Center, Madison WI 53,706.

Vanderheiden, Gregg C. and Grilley, Kate (Eds.). *Non-Vocal Communication Techniques and Aids for the Severely Physically Handicapped*. Baltimore: University Park Press, 1975.

Vanderheiden, Gregg C., and Harris, Deberah. Developing effective modes for response and expression in non-vocal, severely handicapped children. In P. Mittler (Ed.), Research to practice in mental retardation. *Proceedings of the 4th Congress of IASSMD*, Volume 2. Baltimore, Maryland: University Park Press, 1977.

Vanderheiden, Gregg C., Kelso, David, Holt, Craig S., and Raitzer, Gerald S. A teacher modifiable portable microprocessor based communication aids for non-vocal severely physically handicapped individuals. The Trace Center, Madison WI 53,706, 1976.

Vanderheiden, G. C., Kelso, D. P., Holt, C. S., and Raitzer, G. A. Cost reduction in the development of new communication aids through use of a common control system: A case example, the Blisscom. In P. Nelson (Ed.), *Proceedings of Workshop on Communication Aids. Medical and Biological Engineering Society*, c/o National Research Council, Ottawa, Ontario, Canada KIA 0R8, 1978. Also from The Trace Center, Madison WI 53,706.

**Vanderheiden, Gregg C. and Luster, Mary Jo. Non-vocal communication techniques and aids as aids to the education of the severely physically handicapped: A state of the art review, 1975. The Trace Center, University of Wisconsin-Madison, Madison, WI 53,706.

Vicker, Beverly (Ed.) Non-oral communication system project 1964/1973. Iowa City: Campus Stores, 1974.

Wagner, Ethel. Augmentative and alternative communication for the severely handicapped (a bibliography.) 1621 Greenwich Lane, Janesville, WI 53,545, 1977.

2. Direct Selection: Manual Communication Boards

Davis, G. Albyn. Linguistics and language therapy: The sentence construction board. *Journal of Speech and Hearing Disorders*, May 1973, 38, 205–214. https://doi.org/10.1044/jshd.3802.205.

Dixon, C. Communication without speech. *Nursing Times*, August 13, 1970, p. 1032.

Dixon, C. Some thoughts on communication boards. *Cerebral Palsy Journal*, April 1965, 26, 12–13.

Dixon, Carmen C. and Curry, Barbara. Some thoughts on the communication board. *Journal of Speech and Hearing Disorders*, February 1973, 38, 73–88. https://doi.org/10.1044/jshd.3801.73.

Feallock, B. Communication for the non-verbal individual. *American Journal of Occupational Therapy*, 1958, 12, 60–63.

Fox, Joshua. Breaking communication barriers. *Special Education*, September 1969, 23–26.

*Goldberg, Herman R. and Fenton, Joseph. Aphonic communication for those with cerebral palsy: Guide for the development and use of a conversation board. New York: United Cerebral Palsy of New York State, 1960.

Green, Carol N. Help me to help myself. *Hospital Progress, Official Journal of the Catholic Hospital Association*. January 1974, 86.

Help for patients with language and visual problems. *Physical Therapy, Journal of the American Physical Therapy Association*, 1974, 54, 69. https://doi.org/10.1093/ptj/54.10.1094.

Help me to help myself. *Hospitals, Journal of the American Hospital Association*, 1 December 1973.

Holmland, B.A. and Kavanagh, R.N. Communication aids for the handicapped. *American Journal of Occupational Therapy*, November–December, 1976, 21, 357–361.

*McDonald, Eugene T. and Schultz, Adeline R. Communication boards for cerebral palsied children. *Journal of Speech and Hearing Disorders*, February 1973, 38, 73–88. https://doi.org/10.1044/jshd.380 1.73.

McDonald, E.T. Design and application of communication boards. In Vanderheiden & Grilley (Eds.), *Non-Vocal Communication Techniques and Aids for the Severely Physically Handicapped*. Baltimore: University Park Press, 1976.

Patient Handbook: Illustrated Booklet Helps Patients Communicate with Nurses/Physicians. Health Care Product News, December 1974, H15.

Roe, H. The Hall Roe conversation board. Ghora Khan Grolto, 2245 Fremont Ave., St. Paul, Minnesota, 55,119.

*Sayre, Joan M. Communication for the non-verbal cerebral palsied. *Cerebral Palsy Review*, November–December 1963, 3–8.

Schurman, J. Custom designing communication board frames: The role of the occupational therapist. In Vieker (Ed.) *Non-Oral Communication System Project 1964/1973*. Iowa City: Campus Stores, 17 West College Ave., Iowa 52,242, 1974.

Sklar, Maurice, £ Bennett, Daphne Nicholson. Initial communication chart for aphasics. *Journal of the Association of Physical and Mental Rehabilitation*, March–April 1956, 10, 43–53.

United Cerebral Palsy Association. Aphonic communication for those with cerebral palsy. 220 West 42nd Street, New York, New York.

*Vicker, Beverly (Ed.) *Non-Oral Communication System Project 1964–1973*. Iowa City: Campus Stores, 1974.

When speech is impossible. *Hearing and Speech News*, March–April 1974, 24.

3. Direct Selection: Other Aids

Adams, Martin R. Communication aids for patients with amyo-trophic lateral sclerosis. *Journal of Speech and Hearing Disabilities*, 1966, 31, 274–5. https://doi.org/10.1044/jshd.3103.274.

Anderson, Ken. An eye position controlled typewriter. In P. Nelson (Ed.), *Proceedings of Workshop on Communication Aids*, Ottawa, June 1977. Canadian Medical and Biological Engineering Society, c/o National Research Council, Ottawa, Ontario, Canada KIA OR8, 1978.

Boulton et al. A typewriting system for the seriously handicapped. *Digest of the International Electronics Conference*, Toronto, October 1969, 48–9.

Bullock, Ann, Dalrymple, George F., and Danca, Janice M. Communication and the non-verbal multihandicapped child. *American Journal of Occupational Therapy*, March 1975, 29, 150–152.

Bullock, Ann, Dalrymple, George F., and Danca, Janice M. The Auto-com at Kennedy Memorial Hospital: Rapid and accurate communication by a multi-handicapped student. *American Journal of Occupational Therapy*, 1975.

Butler, O. I., and Fouldes, J. F. Typing aid remote controlled (TARC). Presented at the *Biological Engineering Society on Remote Controlling Devices to Assist the Disabled*, London: July 1972.

Colby, Kenneth Mark, Christinoz, Daniel, and Grahm, Santiago, Jr. A personal, portable, and intelligent speech prosthesis. *Working Paper*, Department of Psychiatry, University of California School of Medicine, Los Angeles, California 90,024. Algorithmic Laboratory of Higher Mental Functions, UCLA Department of Psychiatry, Memo ALHMF-9.

Crooks, Maxwell. Special typewriter keyboard charts and instructions for handicapped typists. Sussex, England: National Fund for Research into Crippling Diseases, 1 Springfield Road, Horsham RH 12 2 PN.

Dalrymple, George F.; Bullock, Ann, and Danca, Janice M. The Auto-com at Kennedy Memorial Hospital: Rapid and accurate communication by a multi-handicapped student. *Proceedings of the Conference of Engineering Devices in Rehabilitation*, May 2–3, 1974.

Englehart, T. W. A computerized typing system for the handicapped. M.S. thesis, University of Alberta, 1971.

Heller, Jack. How to master touch typing step by step (For persons with. loss of fingers or hand function.) Wantagh, New York: Special Education Step by Step, Inc., 2947 Bayside Court, 11,793.

Henkel, J. E. A micro-processor-based gesture entry non-vocal communication system. In *Proceedings of the Fourth Annual Conference on Systems and Devices for the Disabled*, Seattle, June 1977. Sponsored by Department of Rehabilitation Medicine, University of Washington. Available from Continuing Medical Education, University of Washington, School of Medicine, E303HSB SC50, Seattle WA 98,195.

Hill, Suzanne D., Campagna, Debra Long, Munch, Joell, and Naecher, Sharon. An explanation of the use of two response keyboard as a means of communication for the severely handicapped child. *Perceptual Motor Skills*, 26, June 1968, 699–704. https://doi.org/10.2466/pms.1968.26.3.699.

Levy, Ronald. *Optical Pointer*. 1977 (head mounted pen light) For information: Ronald Levy, Ph.D., Clinique de Design, Faculte de l'Amenagement, University de Montreal, Case Postale 6128, succursal 'A', Montreal. P.Q. H3C 3J7, Canada.

Lywood, D. W. and S Vasa, J. A communication system for the severely handicapped, including computer terminal operation. *Digest of the Canadian Medical and Biological Engineering Conference*, Halifax, September 1970, 9–9a.

Newell, A. F., Beynon, J. D. E., Brumfitt, P. F., and Houssain, K.S. An alphanumeric display as a communication aid for the dumb. *Medical and Biological Engineering*, January 1975. https://doi.org/10.1007/BF02478192.

Newell, A. F., Beynon, J. D. E., Brumfitt, P. J., and Houssain, K.S. The talking brooch—a new communication aid. Paper presented at the *5th International Conference on Rehabilitation*, London, England, July 1974.

Newell, A. F. The talking brooch, a communication aid. In Keith Copeland (Ed.), *Aids for the Severely Handicapped*. London: Sector Publishing, Ltd., 1974.

Nicol, E. Breakthrough to communication. *Special Education*, December, 1972.

Perron, J. V. Typewriter control for an aphasic quadraplegic patient. *Canadian Medical Association Journal*, 1965, 92, 557–559.

Rinard, George. An ocular-controlied video terminal. In P. Nelson (Ed.), *Proceedings of Workshop on Communication Aids*, Ottawa, June 1977. Canadian Medical and Biological Engineering Society, c/o National Research Council, Ottawa, Ontario, Canada, KIA OR8, 1978.

Samson, D. A communication device for patients unable to speak. *Medical and Biological Engineering*, January 1975.

Silverman, H. and Kelso, D. The Bliss-com: A portable symbol printing communication aid. In *The Proceedings of the Fourth Annual Conference on Systems and Devices for the Disabled*. Seattle, June 1977. Sponsored by the Department of Rehabilitation Medicine, University of Washington. Available from: Continuing Medical Education, University of Washington, School of Medicine, E303 HSB SC50, Seattle WA 98,195.

Soede, M. and Stassen, H. G. A light spot operated typewriter for severely disabled patients. *Medical and Biological Engineering*, 1973, 641–644. https://doi.org/10.1007/BF02477412.

Soede, M., Stassen, H. G., Van Lunteren, A., and Luitse, W. J. A light spot operated typewriter for severely physically handicapped patients. *Ergonomics*, November 1973, 829–844. https://doi.org/10.1080/00140137308924574.

Stassen, H.G., Soede, M. J., and Luitse, W. J. The light spot operated typewriter: The evaluation of a prototype. *5th International Seminar on Rehabilitation*. London, England, 1974, 1–21.

Vanderheiden, Gregg, Raitzer, Gerald A., Kelso, David P., and Geisler, C. Daniel. A portable non-vocal communication prosthesis for the severely physically handicapped. Trace Center, University of Wisconsin-Madison, 53,706, 1975.

Vanderheiden, Gregg C, Volk, Andrew M., and Geisler, C. Daniel. An alternate interface to computers for the physically handicapped. *AFIPS Conference Proceedings of the 1974 National Computer Conference*, 43, 115–121.

Vanderheiden, Gregg C., Volk, A. M., and Geisler, C. D. The auto-monitoring technique and its application in the auto monitoring communication board (Auto-com), a new communication device for the severely handicapped. *Proceedings of the Carnahan Conference on Electronic Prosthetics*, Lexington, Kentucky, November, 1973, 47–51.

Vasa, J., and Lywood, D. W. A typing aid for the severely handicapped. *Digest of Canadian Medical and Biological Engineering Conference*, Winnipeg, September 1972, 72a–72b.

Wardell, Ron. Development of the Eyewriter. In P. Nelson (Ed.), *Proceedings of Workshop on Communication Aids*, Ottawa, June 1977. Canadian Medical and Biological Engineering Society, c/o National Research Council, Ottawa, Ontario, Canada KIA 0R8, 1978.

Wendt, Eugene. Habilitation: A team approach to communication. *Teaching Exceptional Children*, Fall, /1975.

Ziskind, A., and Ziskind, R. Remote control typewriter for paraplegics. *Journal of American Medical Association*, January 3, 1959, 169, 459–460. https://doi.org/10.1001/jama.1959.73000220001009.

4. Scanning Communication Aids

Boydell, R. G. Possum-I can. *Spastic News*, May 1964, 6.

Brulisaur, Peter. Maling rehabilitation systems. *Proceedings of the Seminar on Electronic Controls for the Severely Disabled*. Vancouver, British Columbia, Canada: 1974, 37–39.

Bruun, Georg, Jarkler, Bjorn, Speldt, Peter, and Sorenson, Arne Nybroe. Communication display/printout aid with a memory. In Keith Copeland (Ed.), *Aids for the Severely Handicapped*, 116–118. London: Sector Publishing Ltd., 1974.

Charbonneau, J. R., Cote, C., and Roy, O. Z. NRC's 'Comhandi' communication system, technical description and application at the Ottawa Crippled Children's Treatment Center. *Proceedings of the Seminar on Electronic Controls for the Severely Disabled*. Vancouver, British Columbia, Canada: 83–88, 1974.

Crochetiere, J. W., Foulds, R.A., and Sterne, R.G. Computer-aided motor communication. *Proceedings of the 1974 Conference on Engineering Devices in Rehabilitation*. Boston, Massachusetts: 1–5, 1974.

Dixon, C. Electronic aids for the severely physically handicapped. *Dist. Nursing*, August, 1971.

DUFCO. Matrix communicator: A versatile communication aid for the speechless. Cambria: DUFCO, 1975.

Foulds, R. A. The Tufts interactive communicator. *Proceedings of the 1972 Carnahan Conference of Electronic Prosthetics*. Lexington, Kentucky: 16–24, 1972.

Foulds, Richard A., Baletsa, Gregory, and Crochetiere, William J. The effectiveness of language redundancy in non-verbal communication. *Proceedings of the Seminar on Devices and Systems for the Disabled*. Philadelphia, Pennsylvania: 82–86, 1975.

Foulds, Richard A. and Gaddis, Earl. The practical application of an electronic communication device in the special needs classroom. *Proceedings of the Seminar on Devices and Systems for the Disabled*. Philadelphia, Pennsylvania: 77–80, 1975.

Fox, J. Breaking communication barriers. *Special Education*, September 1969, 23–26.

Harding, P. J. R., Kingma, V. J., Kozak, A. J., Stromore, K. A., and Vaneldik, J.F. Typewriter for teaching severely handicapped children. *Proceedings of the Carnahan Conference on Electronic Prosthetics.* Lexington, Kentucky, 1973, 43–46.

Holt, C. S., Raitzer, G. A., Harris, D., and Vanderheiden, G. Formative evaluation/design of a low cost scanning aid. The Trace Center, Madison WI 53,706, 1976.

Jefcoate, Roger. Possum-Its significance to multiple sclerosis patients. *M.S. News*, Christmas, 1970.

Jenkin, Rosemary. Possum: A new communication aid. *Special Education*, March, 1967, 9–11.

Jones, Morris Va. Electrical communication devices. *American Journal of Occupational Therapy*, May–June, 1961, 15, 110–111.

Maling, R. G. and Clarkson, D. C. Electronic controls for the tétraplégie (POSSUM). *Paraplegia*, 1963, 161–174. https://doi.org/10.1038/sc.1963.15.

Miller, John. Electronics for communication. *American Journal of Occupational Therapy*, January–February 1964, 18, 20–23.

Physically handicapped children learn to communicate. *Science Dimension*, April, 1973, 8–13.

Roy, O. Z. Technical note: A communication system for the handicapped. *Medical Electronic and Biological Engineering* (Vol. 3), 427–429. Great Britain: Pengamon Press, 1965. https://doi.org/10.1007/BF02476138.

Sampson, D. A communication device for patients unable to speak. *Medical and Biological Engineering*, January 1970, 99–101. https://doi.org/10.1007/BF02551755.

Tolstrup, I.M. VIDIALOG: A TV-based communication system for the motor handicapped. *Proceedings for III Nordic Meeting on Medical and Biological Engineering.* Tampere, Finland, 1975.

Vasa, J. J. and Mansell, M. Queen's communication aids. *Proceedings of the Seminar on Electronic Controls for the Severely Disabled.*

5. Encoding Communication Aids

Block, R. Design considerations for an environmental control system for the severely handicapped. *Proceedings of the Seminar on Electronic Controls for the Severely Disabled.* Vancouver, British Columbia, Canada: 1974, 25–33.

Calculator, Stephen N. Design and revision of non-oral systems of communication for the mentally retarded physically handicapped: A discussion of the unicolor binary visual encoding board with general implications for communication. *Working Paper 101*, Department of Communicative Disorders, University of Wisconsin-Madison, 53,706.

Clement, M. Morse code method of communication for the severely handicapped cerebral palsied child. *Cerebral Palsy Review*, September–October, 1961, 15–16.

Jack H. Eichler: Builds communication device. Case Alumnus. Cleveland: Case Institute of Technology Alumni Association, 211, (June 1973): 2.

Hagen, Chris, Porter, Wyne, and Brink, Joyce. Non-verbal communication: An alternated mode of communication for the child with severe cerebral palsy. *Journal of Speech and Hearing Disorders*, November 1973, 38, 448–455. https://doi.org/10.1044/jshd.3804.448.

Jenkins, Rosemary. POSSUM: A new communication aid. *Special Education*, 1967, 56(1), 9–11.

Johnston, H. B., Manning, R. P., and Lappin, J.S. A communications prosthesis for a quadriplegic. *Proceedings of the Carnahan Conference on Engineering Devices in Rehabilitation*, Lexington, Kentucky, November 1972, 27–29.

Kafafian, H. *Study of Man–Machine Communication Systems for the Handicapped* (3 vols.) Washington: Cybernetics Research Institute, Inc., 197–1973.

Newell, A. F. and Nabaui, C. D. VOTEM: The voice operated typewriter employing Morse Code. *Journal of Scientific Instruments*, Series 2, 2, 1969. https://doi.org/10.1088/0022-3735/2/8/314.

POSSUM introductory description, and POSSUM-Control system for severely disabled, general description. *P.O.S.M. Research Project*, Aylesbury, England, 1967.

Rosen, M., Drinker, P., and Dalrymple, G. A display board for non-verbal communication encoded as eye movements. Department of Mechanical Engineering, M.I.T., Cambridge, Massachusetts, 1976.

Ross, A. and Flanagan, K. Communication system using Morse Code to printed English translation. In *Proceedings of the Fourth Annual Conference on Systems and Devices for the Disabled*, Seattle, June

1977. Sponsored by Department of Rehabilitative Medicine, University of Washington. Available: Continuing Medical Education, University of Washington, School of Medicine E303 HSB SC50, Seattle WA 98,195.

Traynor, C. D. A breath-controlled computer data system. In *Proceedings of the Fourth Annual Conference on Systems and Devices for the Disabled*, Seattle, June 1977. Sponsored by the Department of Rehabilitative Medicine University of Washington. Available: Continuing Medical Education, University of Washington, School of Medicine E303 HSB SC50, Seattle WA 98,195.

6. Fitting and interfacing Communication Aids

Beesley, Margrit. The importance of positioning and seating for the cerebral palsied child. In P. Nelson (Ed.) *Proceedings on Workshop on Communication Aids*. June 1977. Published by Canadian Medical and Biological Engineering Society, c/o National Research Council, Ottawa, Ontario, Canada KIA OR8.

Hanson, Sue, The use of headgear for the physically handicapped: An occupational therapy viewpoint. *Adaptive Therapeutics Systems*, Inc. 162 Ridge Road, Madison Connecticut 06,442, 1973.

Holt, Craig, Buelow, Dave, and Vanderheiden, Gregg. Interface switch profile and annotated list of commercial switches (1976). In Vanderheiden (Ed.), *Non-Vocal Communication Resourcebook*. Baltimore: University Park Press, 1978. Also available separately from the Trace Center, Madison WI 53,706.

Levy, Irwin. Psycho-educational summary of headgear and its implications. Adaptive Therapeutics Systems, Inc.,1973. Madison, Connecticut 06,442.

Lowman, E.W. and Klinger, Judith L. *Infra Red "Sight Switch", Aids To Dependent Living*, pp. 558. New York: McGraw-Hill, 1969.

Muller, Bruce. Review and analysis of the Mancino adaptive headgear with respect to standardized psychological testing. Adaptive Therapeutics Inc., Madison Connecticut, 1973.

N.A.S.A. and S.W. Research Institute. Breath puff switch. Reported in *Medical Post*, July 11 × 1972.

Newell, P. H. and Bour, J. S. Voice operated powered devices. *Biomechanics*, 4, 45–48, 1971. https://doi.org/10.1016/0021-9290(71)90015-7.

Ring, Nigel. Specification of interfaces for communication aids. In P. Nelson (Ed.) *Proceedings of Workshop on Communication Aids. Canadian Medical and Biological Society*, c/o National Research Council, Ottawa, Ontario, Canada, KIA OR8, 1978.

Torok, Z. and Hammond, P. H. On the performance of single motor units as sources of control signals. *Proceedings of the Conference of Human Locomotor Engineering*, University of Sussex, pp. 35–44, September 1971.

7. Special Language systems/Techniques

Bliss, Charles. *Semantography*. Sydney: Semantography Publications, 1965.

Blissymbolics Communication Foundation Bulletin Volumes 1 to - BCE 862 Eglington Avenue E., Toronto, Ontario, Canada M4G2L1.

Bricker, D., Dennison, Vincent-Smith, L., and Watson, L. Language training program for young developmentally delayed children, institute on Mental Retardation and Intellectual Development: *Behavioral Science Monograph* No. 2, 1973.

Carrier, J., Jr. Nonspeech usage training with severely and profoundly retarded children. *Journal of Speech and Hearing Research*, 1976.

*Carrier, J. K., Jr. Application of a non-speech language system with the severely language handicapped. In Lloyd, L. (Ed.) *Communication Assessment and Intervention Strategies*. Baltimore: University Park Press, 1976.

*Chapman, Robin and Miller, Jon F. Analyzing language and communication in the child. In R. Shiefelbusch (Ed.), *Nonspeech Language Intervention Strategies*. Baltimore: University Park Press (in press).

Clark, C. and Woodcock, R. W. Graphic systems of communication. In Lloyd (Ed.), *Communication Assessment and Intervention Strategies*. Baltimore: University Park Press, 1976.

Cronin, J. M. (Ed.) Language stimulation activities for the non-verbal physically-disabled child. In *Preschool Learning Activities for the Physically Disabled: A Guide for Parents*. Springfield, Ill: Illinois Office of Education, Special Education Division (no date).

Dalrymple, G. F. Final report: Development and demonstration of communication systems for the blind and deaf/blind. Sensory Aids Evaluation and Development Center, M.I.T., February 26, 1973.

Dubner, Harriet W. A speech pathologist talks to the parents of a nonverbal child. *Rehabilitation Literature*, 1969, 30(12), 360–362. Chicago: National Easter Seal Society for Crippled Children and Adults, 2023 W. Odgen Avenue, 60,612.

Fristoe, Macalyne (Summary Chapter). In R. Shiefelbusch (Ed.), *Nonspeech Language Intervention Strategies*. Baltimore: University Park Press (in press).

Hammond, Jill and Bailey, Patricia. An experiment with Blissymbolics. *Special Education Forward Trends*, September 1976, 3(3), 21–22. https://doi.org/10.1111/j.1467-8578.1976.tb01073.x.

Harris-Vanderheiden, D. BlissSymbols and the mentally retarded. In Vanderheiden and Grilley (Eds.), *Non-Vocal Communication Techniques and Aids for the Severely Physically Handicapped*. Baltimore: University Park Press, 1976.

Harris, D., Lippert, J., Yoder, D., and Vanderheiden, G. Blissymbols: An augmentative symbol communication system for non-vocal severely handicapped children. In R. York & E. Edger (Eds.), *Teaching the Severely Handicapped* (Vol. IV) (in press).

Irwin, Orvic C. A comparison of the vocabulary of use and of understanding of cerebral palsied children. *Cerebral Palsy Journal*, 1966, 27(3), 7–11.

Kates, B. and McNaughton, S. The first application of Blissymbolics as a communication medium for non-speaking children. *History and Development 1971–1974*, Toronto: Blissymbolics Communication Foundation, 1975.

Kates, B., McNaughton, S., and Silvermann, H. *Handbook for Instructors, Users, Parents, and Administrators*. Blissymbolics Communication Foundation, 862 Eglington Ave. E., Toronto, Ontario, Canada, 1977.

** Lloyd, Lyle (Ed.) *Communication Assessment and Intervention Strategies*. Baltimore: University Park Press, 1976.

Lynes, George. *Mr. Symbol Man* (film of Charles Bliss and the use of BlissSymbols). Montreal: National Film Board of Canada, 1974. (film)

McDonald, Eugene T. Conventional symbols of English. In G. Vanderheiden and K. Grilley (Eds.), *Non-Vocal Communication Techniques and Aids for the Severely Physically Handicapped*. Baltimore: University Park Press, 1976.

McDonald, Eugene T. Nonspeech expression for children at risk for developing intelligible speech. In R. Shiefelbusch (Ed.), *Non-speech Language Intervention Strategies*. Baltimore, University Park Press (in press).

McLean, L. and McLean, J. A language training program for non-verbal autistic children. *Journal of Speech and Hearing Disorders*, 1974, 39, 186–193. https://doi.org/10.1044/jshd.3902.186.

McNaughton, S. BlissSymbols - alternate symbol systems for the nonvocal prereading child. In Vanderheiden & Grilley (Eds.) *Non-Vocal Communication Techniques and Aids for the Severely Physically Handicapped*. Baltimore: University Park Press, 1976.

McNaughton, S. Response to common misconceptions regarding Blissymbolics as a communication medium for non-speaking physically handicapped children. Ontario Crippled Children's Centre, Toronto, Ontario, Canada, 1975.

McNaughton, S. and Kates, B. Visual communication system for non-speaking persons. In R. Shiefelbusch (Ed.), *Non-Speech Language Intervention Strategies*. Baltimore: University Park Press (in press).

McNaughton, Shirley and Kates, Barbara. Visual symbols: Communication system for the pre-reading physically handicapped child. Paper presented at the *American Association of Mental Deficiency Annual Meeting*, Toronto, Ontario, 5 June 1974.

Moore, Mary Virginia. Binary communication for the handicapped. *Archives of Physical Medicine and Rehabilitation*, November 1972, 53, 532–533.

Ontario Crippled Children's Centre BlissSymbol Project Team, Ontario Crippled Children's Centre Symbol Communication Research Project 1972–1973. Toronto: Ontario Crippled Children's Centre, 1973.

Paget, G. and Gorman, P. *A Systematic Sign Language*. London: Association for Experiments in Deaf Education, 1969. (mimeographed).

Paget, G. and Gorman, P. *A Systematic Sign Language*. London: Association for Experiments in Deaf Education, 1972. (mimeographed).

*Scheafer, Benson. Spontaneous language through signed speech. In R. Shiefelbusch (Ed.), *Nonspeech Language Intervention Strategies*. Baltimore: University Park Press (in press).

**Shiefelbusch, R. (Ed.) *Nonspeech Language Intervention Strategies*. Baltimore: University Park Press (in press).

Symbol coordination committee newsletter. Toronto: Ontario Crippled Children's Centre, 1974.

Vanderheiden, Deberah, Brown, Warren P., MacKenzie, Paula, Reinen, Steve, and Schiebel, Claudia. Symbol communication for the mentally handicapped—An application of BlissSymbols as an alternate communication mode for non-verbal mentally retarded children with motoric impairment. *Mental Retardation*, February 1975, 13, 34–37.

8. Manual Communication: A Selected Bibliography for the Multihandicapped

This section of the bibliography represents selected entries from the resource list by M. Fristoe and L.L. Lloyd in *Mental Retardation*, October 1977, 15, 18–21.

Abrams, Paula. Simultaneous language program for non-verbal pre-school children. Dysfunctional Child Center, Michael Reese Medical Center, 2915 S. Ellis Avenue, Chicago, IL 60,616, 1975.

Andreas, Judy, Bell, David, Bentley, Janice, Buck, Ginger, and Klee, Dolly. *Let Your Fingers Do the Talking: A Teaching Manual for Use with Nonverbal Retardates*. Department of Communication Disorders and Education Training, Craig Developmental Center, Sonyea New York 14,556, 1975. Subsequently distributed by ERIC Document Reproduction Center, P.O. Box 190, Arlington, VA 22,210 (Document No. ED 121,034).

Creedon, Margaret Procyk (Ed.). *Appropriate Behavior Through Communication: A New Program in Simultaneous Language for Non-Verbal Children*, 2nd ed. Dysfunctioning Child Center, Michael Reese Medical Center, 2915 S. Ellis Avenue, Chicago IL 60,616, 1975. (See chapters by Candy Haight and Candy H. Smith).

Elwyn Institute. *Signs for Everyday*: Books 1 and 2. Elwyn Institute, Elwyn, Pennsylvania, 19,063, 1975.

Foster, Elizabeth. *Programmed Language Workbooks for Multiply Handicapped Deaf Children*. Indiana School for the Deaf, 1200 E. 42nd Street, Indianapolis, Indiana 46,205, 1972.

Foster, Elizabeth. *Programmed Language Workbooks for Multiply Handicapped Deaf Children*. Indiana School for the Deaf, 1200 E. 42nd Street, Indianapolis, Indiana 46,205, 1971.

Foster, Elizabeth, Levy, Joyce, and Cullison, Sammy. *Learning Activities for Multiply Handicapped Deaf Children*. Indiana School for the Deaf, 1200 E. 42nd Street, Indianapolis, Indiana 46,205, 1972. (Two booklets identified as Parts 1 and 2.)

Fristoe, Macalyne. *Language Intervention Systems for the Retarded*. State of Alabama Department of Education. (Order from Language Intervention Systems for the Retarded, L.B. Wallace Developmental Center, P.O. Box 2224, Decatur, Alabama 35,602), 1976. (This resource lists training programs using manual communication and systems developed to teach manual communication to the retarded.)

Hinkle, Carroll. *We Have Hands: A Teaching Manual for those Concerned with Our Deaf*. Green Valley Developmental Center, Greeneville, Tennessee 37,743, 1974.

Huffman, Jeanne, Hoffman, Bobbi, Granssee, David, Fox, Ann, James, Juanita, and Schmitz, Joseph. *Talk With Me: Communication with the Multi-Handicapped Deaf*. Joyce Motion Picture Company, 8320 Reseda Boulevard, Northridge, California 91,321, 1974. (This is the same as *Sign Language for Everyone* by the same authors and publisher, except for the addition of a chapter, "Suggested Activities", pp. 219–269.)

Lake, Sandra J. *The Hand-Book*. Communication Skill Builders, Tucson Arizona, 85,733, 1976.

Larson, Thalia. *Communication for the Non-Verbal Child*. Marfex Associates, Inc., Box 519, 90 Cherry Street, Jamestown Pennsylvania 15,907, 1975.

Lloyd, Lyle L. (Ed.) *Communication Assessment and Intervention Strategies*. University Park Press, Baltimore, Maryland 21,202, 1976. (See chapters by Ronnie Bring Wilbur; George A. Kopchick, Jr. and Lyle L. Lloyd; and Charlotte Clarke and Richard W. Woodcock. In addition, chapters by Joseph K. Carrier, Jr., and by Gregg C. Vanderheiden and Deberah Harris-Vanderheiden present other non-vocal communication systems.)

Mayberry, Rachel. If a chimp can learn sign language, surely my nonverbal client can, too. *Asha*, 1976, 18, 223–228. (This article reviews briefly a number of sign systems and then discusses teaching manual communication to persons without significant hearing loss.)

Owens, Michael and Harper, Beryl. *Sign Language: A Teaching Manual for Cottage Parents of Non-Verbal Retardates.* Pinecrest State School, P.O. Drawer 191, Pineville, Louisiana, 1971.

Robbins, Nan, Cagan, Janice, Johnson, Carol, Kelleher, Helen, Record, Jocely, and Vernacchia, Jan. *Perkins Sign Language Dictionary: A Sign Dictionary for Use with Multi-Handicapped Deaf Children in School*. Perkins School for the Blind, Watertown, Massachusetts 02,172, 1975.

Skelly, Madge; Schinsky, Lorraine; Smith, Randall W., and Fust, Rita Solovitz. American Indian sign (Amerind) as a facilitator of verbalization for the oral verbal apraxic. *Journal of Speech and Hearing Disorders*, 1974, 39*, 445–456. ("Amerind" is a gesture communication system based on American Indian Hand Talk.) https://doi.org/10.1044/jshd.3904.445.

Snell, Martha. Sign language and total communication. In Louise R. Kent, *Language Acquisition Program for the Severely Retarded*. Research Press, 2612 North Mattis Avenue, Champaign, Illinois 61820, 1974. (chapter 16, 147–184)

Stohr, Pamela G. and Van Hook, Karen E. *Have Hands-Will Sign.* Ranier School, P.O. Box 600, Buckley, Washington 98,321, 1973.

Talkington, Larry W. and Hall, Sylvia M. *A Manual Communication System for Deaf Retarded.* Austin State School, P.O. Box 1269, Austin Texas 78,767, 1970.

Topper, Sue T. *Gesture Language for the Severely and Profoundly Mentally Retarded*. Denton State School, P.O. Box 368, Denton Texas 76,202, 1974.

Vail, Jacqueline L. and Spas, Diana L. A manual communication program for non-verbal retardates. NWSEARCH-Title 1, 145 Fisk Avenue, DeKalb, Illinois 60115, 1974.

Wilson, Paula Starks, Goodman, Linda, and Wood, Robin K. *Manual Language for the Child Without Language: A Behavioral Approach for Teaching the Exceptional Child.* Development Team, 79 Elm Street, Hartford, Connecticut 06,115, 1975.

Wilson, Paula Starks; Wood, Robin K.; Goodman, Linda, and Roberts, Terry. *Manual Language Dictionary: Functional Vocabulary for the Retarded, Booklets One, Two, and Three.* Developmental Team, 79 Elm Street, Hartford Connecticut 06,115, 1974. (Order from Earl Robinson, Jr., Occupational Training Center, Mansfield Training School, Box 51, Mansfield Depot, Connecticut 06,251.)

9. Other Related Information

Cairns, R.S. and Jousse, A.T. Touch operated selector controls-TOSC. *Medical Service Journal Canada*, 1966, 22(7), 714–718. https://doi.org/10.1016/0031-9163(66)90716-5.

Deacon, Joseph John. *Tongue Tied*. London: National Society for Mentally Handicapped Children, 1975.

Ehrlich, Michael D. The Votrax Voice Synthesizer as an aid for the blind. 1974 *Proceedings on Engineering Devices, in Rehabilitation*, Boston, Massachusetts, May 1974.

Eulenberg, J.B. Representation of language space in speech prostheses. In *Proceedings of the Fourth Annual Conference on Systems and Devices for the Disabled*, Seattle, June 1977. Sponsored by the Department of Rehabilitative Medicine, University of Washington. Available from: Continuing Medical Education, University of Washington, School of Medicine, E305 SC50, Seattle, WA 98,195.

Gertenrich, Roger L. A simple mouth-held writing device for use with cerebral palsy patients. *Mental Retardation*, August 1966, 13–14.

Goldenberg, E. Paul. A computer technology for children with communication handicaps. Boston, Massachusetts: MIT Logo Lab, 1976.

Home of the Merciful Savior for Crippled Children. Use of System 80 instructional programs with cerebral palsied children. Philadelphia: Home of the Merciful Savior for Crippled Children, 4400 Baltimore Avenue 19,104.

Jacobs, William and Burns, Nancy. Use of the Borg Warner System 80 audio/ visual unit with physically handicapped children using special adaptive headgear. Adaptive Therapeutics Systems, Inc., Madison Connecticut.

Lencione, Ruth M. Language and speech disorders in cerebral palsy. In W. Cruickshank (Ed.), *Cerebral Palsy*. Syracuse: Syracuse University Press, 1974.

Lorenze, E., Sokoloff, M., and Cruz, R. Prognosis for deficiencies in speech accompanying cerebral palsy. *Archives of Physical Medicine and Rehabilitation*, 1962, 43, 621–26.

McDonald, E.T. Identification of children at risk. In Vanderheiden and Grilley (Eds.), *Nonvocal Communication Techniques and Aids for the Severely Physically Handicapped*. Baltimore: University Park Press, 1976.

Moogk-Soulis, C.A. An experimental evaluation of selected communication technical aids. In *Proceedings of the Fourth Annual Conference on Systems and Devices for the Disabled*, Seattle, June 1977. Sponsored by the Department of Rehabilitation Medicine. Available: Continuing Medical Education, University of Washington, School of Medicine, E303 HSB SC50, Seattle WA 98,195.

Muller, Bruce. Review and analysis of the Mancino adaptive headgear with respect to standardized psychological testing. Madison, Connecticut: Adaptive Therapeutics, Inc., 1973.

Nelson, P.J. Speech synthesis for non-verbal children-A progress report. In *Proceedings of the Fourth Annual Conference on Systems and Devices for the Disabled*, Seattle, June 1977. Sponsored by the Department of Rehabilitation Medicine, University of Washington. Available: Continuing Medical Education, University of Washington, School of Medicine, E303 HSB SC50, Seattle WA 98,915.

Newell, A.F. and Nabavi, C.D. VOTEM: The voice operated typewriter employing Morse Code. *Journal of Scientific Instrumentation*, 1969, .2(2), 655–657. https://doi.org/10.1088/0022-3735/2/8/314.

Rahimi, Morteza Amir and Eulenberg, John Bryson. A computer terminal with synthetic speech output. A paper presented at the *National Conference on the Use of On-Line Computers in Psychology*, St. Louis, Missouri, 31 October, 1973.

Rehabilitation International. European conference on integration of the severely disabled into the community. Lisbon, Portugal (Proceedings). September 23–27, 1974. Lisbon: The Portuguese Society of Physical Medicine and Rehabilitation Center for Medical Rehabilitation, Alcortao-Estoril, Portugal ($15.00, U.S.)

Robinson, Alison and Hendley, Marjorie. Some aspects of the effect of stress on the performance of brain-injured children. City of Manchester Education Committee. The Margaret Barclay Residential School for Physically Handicapped Children, Mobberly Hall, Mobberly, Cheshire, England.

Smith, Alma I. Non-verbal communication through touch. Doctoral thesis, Georgia State University, 1970. 85 pp. University Microfilms # 71–3948.

Sontag, E., Smith, J., and Certo, N. (Eds.) Educational programming for the severely and profoundly handicapped. Reston, Virginia: Division on Mental Retardation, 1977. https://doi.org/10.1177/002246697701100103.

Sullivan, Richard A., Frieden, Fred H., and Cordery, Joy. Telephone services for the handicapped. *Rehabilitation Monograph XXXVII*, Institute of Rehabilitation Medicine, New York University Medical Center, 400 East 34th Street, New York, NY 10,016.

Warrick, Anne, et al. Synthesized speech as an aid to communication and learning for the non-verbal. In P. Nelson (Ed.), *Proceedings of Workshop on Communication Aids*. Canadian Medical and Biological Engineering Society, c/p National Research Council, Ottawa, Ontario, Canada KIA 0R8, 1978.

White, Silas D. A modular communication device for paralyzed patients. *Archives of Physical and Medical Rehabilitation*, February 1974, 55, 94–95.

MIX
Papier aus verantwortungsvollen Quellen
Paper from responsible sources
FSC® C105338

If you have any concerns about our products,
you can contact us on
ProductSafety@springernature.com

In case Publisher is established outside the EU,
the EU authorized representative is:
Springer Nature Customer Service Center GmbH
Europaplatz 3, 69115 Heidelberg, Germany

Printed by Libri Plureos GmbH
in Hamburg, Germany